IN AND
OUT OF THE
MAASAI
STEPPE

JOY STEPHENS

Published by BestRed, an imprint of HSRC Press
Private Bag X9182, Cape Town, 8000, South Africa
www.bestred.co.za

First published 2016

ISBN (soft cover) 978-1-928246-12-1

Copy-edited by Inga Norenius
Typeset by Orchard Publishing
Cover design by Riaan Wilmans
Cover photo by Joy Stephens: Maasai Steppe mirage
Title page photo by Joy Stephens: Nyumba ya Mungu lake with Mount Kilimanjaro in the distance

Printed by Creda Communications

Distributed in Africa by Blue Weaver
Tel: +27 (021) 701 4477; Fax Local: (021) 701 7302; Fax International: 0927865242139
www.blueweaver.co.za
Distributed in Europe and the United Kingdom by Eurospan Distribution Services (EDS)
Tel: +44 (0) 17 6760 4972; Fax: +44 (0) 17 6760 1640
www.eurospanbookstore.com
Distributed in North America by River North Editions, from IPG
Call toll-free: (800) 888 4741; Fax: +1 (312) 337 5985
www.ipgbook.com

About the author

Joy Stephens has worked in Africa and Asia as a social researcher and development practitioner. She has travelled widely, and is the author of *Window onto Annapurna*.

Contents

Acknowledgements

I am deeply indebted to the staff of Tanganyika Christian Refugee Service: to Ruth Shija, for the initial invitation to visit the Project; to Boniface, who provided language interpretation and information on Maasai culture; to Mtataiko, for his patience in dealing with my sometimes inconsiderate demands for workshops and extra support for the women's groups.

Frida Tarimo played a pivotal role in the development of the Mama Masai groups, and I am immensely grateful for her moral and practical support to me. I could not have managed my visits during the years 2007 to 2013 without her assistance. She drove me around, and I passed many comfortable nights at her home in Nyumba ya Mungu. My thanks go also to her daughters, Flora and Fortunata, who assisted me with training workshops, internships, and translation services in the latter years. I take my hat off to the family team 'F–F–F' for their amazing spirit and their dedication to the people of the Maasai Steppe.

Many volunteers, Tanzanian and expatriate, have given their time to support Mama Masai through Fair Trade Friends (FTF); it is impossible to name and thank everyone, but I want to mention a few. Montse Pejuan continued to support both organisations for many years. I relied greatly on her advice and organisational skills during the literacy and business skills project from 2010 to 2012, and her readiness to jump on a bus and make the long trek to the Mama Masai groups.

I owe a special debt to my friend Meredith Murnyak for the energy she invested in developing markets for Mama Masai products in Arusha and Moshi. After her sudden death in 2005, it proved impossible to maintain these market links for the western cluster of Mama Masai. Having to abandon Esta and her group at Namalulu remains one of my biggest regrets.

My thanks go to Fay Foster, Gitte Volk Johansson, Bodil Torp and Mark Waite, whose enthusiasm and practical support led to the establishment of FTF; to Dominique Wiehe Gibson who worked tirelessly to market Mama Masai products, and who hosted my visits post-2006;

and to Hilary Tagg and Sona Shah under whose leadership FTF and Mama Masai became Tanzanian NGOs and established a retail shop in Dar es Salaam.

Above all, I wish to thank the Maasai women for their generosity and openness to me and my inquisitive nature. Their warm welcome never cooled; their patience with my ignorance never failed. They dropped other work to attend to my needs, and their kindness and good humour were limitless. My particular thanks go to the families of Kaika and Mboi for their hospitality; also to Esta and her family; to Nyange and to Baba Kicheche (Zakaria) for their patience in explaining Maasai culture; and to all those named in this book, for permission to share their stories. To all the members of Mama Masai, your husbands and children, thank you for your friendship and the journey together. May the Steppe blossom green for you and your children!

This book has been written in two stages. I would like to thank my friends who read the first draft: Cherry Barnes, Ro Cole, Lucia de Vries, Vivien Stone and, in particular, Carol Filby and Omar Sattaur who gave detailed feedback which has guided me in the task of rewriting.

Finally, I wish to thank my family for allowing me to 'escape' to the Maasai Steppe from time to time: my children Jerome and Sharmila for their easy acceptance of strangers and strange situations when they were growing up, and for allowing me to describe them as I do; and my faithful husband Duane for his constant support and encouragement – and his forgiveness for the beatings which I gave 'his' car in the Maasai Steppe.

Joy Stephens, 2016

Author's note

'Mama Masai' is the collective name for the groups of women with whom I worked in the Maasai Steppe, and who are the focus of this book. Their language was never a written language, so inconsistencies are found when trying to capture its pronunciation in letters, and the spelling variations 'Masai' and 'Maasai' are both found in the literature. The word is derived from the language 'Maa' and 'Maa-sai' means 'my people'. Since the accepted spelling has become 'Maasai', this is what I have used throughout the book, the only exception being the women's groups. When they were formally registered their name was spelt Mama Masai, so I have kept this spelling when referring to them.[1]

Where other Maa words have been used, I have chosen the most common spelling and their meaning is explained, together with Swahili words, in a glossary at the back of this book. Most of the names of people in the book are genuine and used with permission, but a few have been changed, either to prevent confusion, or to preserve anonymity because I was unable to contact the person to ask their permission. Readers will find the word 'Bantu' in this book. Similar to 'Maasai', the word means 'people'. I use it as a neutral, non-derogatory term to refer to speakers of the Bantu group of languages whose ancestral origins lie in western Africa, to distinguish them from the Maasai, who speak a Nilotic language and whose origins lie to the north.

The 'Project' referred to in this book was the Simanjiro Rehabilitation Project (1998–2003) implemented by the Tanganyika Christian Refugee Service (TCRS) which at that time was part of the Lutheran World Federation (LWF).

I lived in Tanzania from 1998 to 2006, and the storyline about the Mama Masai groups is broadly chronological. Chapters 1–14 largely concern the years 1999–2003, when the Project was running. Chapters 15–23 cover the years after it closed down but with less of a chronological structure. Some of the material for these chapters is drawn from the years 2004 to 2006 and some from my visits in the period 2007–2013, when I was involved in providing further training and support for the groups. My last visit took place in August 2013.

Prologue

On maps of Tanzania it is marked by a void, a vacant spot south of Mount Kilimanjaro where cartographic symbols disappear. There are no roads, no rivers, no settlements – no geography worthy of note, or so it appears.

Welcome to the Maasai Steppe.

Imagine a vast, vacant lot stretching from far horizon to far horizon, featureless save for a long, low ridge and a solitary summit in the distance. Into this space shake a sprinkling of thorn bushes – you can be generous so long as their thorns are sufficiently vicious to repel goats and antelope.

As you swivel around it appears that this land is uninhabited. Your gaze falls on some distant pastel mountains and you wonder whether these too are a mirage – like the string of lakes ahead that shimmer in the heated sand. You get back into your four-wheel-drive vehicle (for if you are a *mzungu* that is how you travel there), and as you drive on, leaving a billowing cloud of dust in your wake, a red-robed figure comes running out of what appears to be a thicket of thorn brush, but which you belatedly realise is a circle of huts.

The red-robed Maasai leaps directly into your path and flaps his arms frantically. It must be a medical emergency. You slam on the brakes and your vehicle and he are engulfed in a whirlwind of dust.

When it clears, he is smiling. "Welcome," he says.

"Thank you. You have a problem?"

"Thank you. Welcome again. No problem." He holds out his hand and shakes yours three times with the alternating grip of the African bush.

"Thanks. You're sure there's no problem? I'll be going on then."

You rev the engine, but you can't move forward because he is leaning heavily on the open window of the car and has inserted the whole of his head and shoulders inside.

"This is the first vehicle for two weeks," he informs you, wishing to expand the conversation while his eyes rove around the interior. He spots an almost empty bottle of mineral water – essential survival kit for *mzungu* who enter the Maasai Steppe. "Do you want that?"

You shake your head and he tucks the bottle inside his robe.

"Look, I'm sorry, I have to be going. It will be dark soon."

It is then he draws his trump card: "I need a lift."

You have fallen for the trap. You try to think of an excuse. "Where do you need to get to?"

"Where are you going?"

"No – I asked first. Where are *you* going?"

It is a game. For both you and he know that it doesn't matter where you are going. Anywhere will do for him. Any distance near or far, in the comfort of your air-conditioned 4x4. Whatever destination you mention will happen to be just the place he is planning to go to. He had no plans before he saw your car, but since you happened to pass by his stretch of scrub, he will seize the opportunity. He is bound to know someone where you are going.

"I'm not passing back this way for over a week."

He laughs with relief, and arranges his long legs and stick in the front seat with a jangle of sequins and beads. If you don't want to give him a lift, you will have to think of a better excuse than that. A wait of seven days is no deterrent. Time is the one resource the Maasai Steppe has in abundance. But he is big and strong and will come in handy with a spanner – and punctures are a common punishment to cars that venture into the Maasai Steppe.

He is smiling and having fun with the electric window as you rattle over the sandy track heading westwards into the dying sun, which transforms the thorn bushes of the Maasai Steppe into a gallery of exotic art.

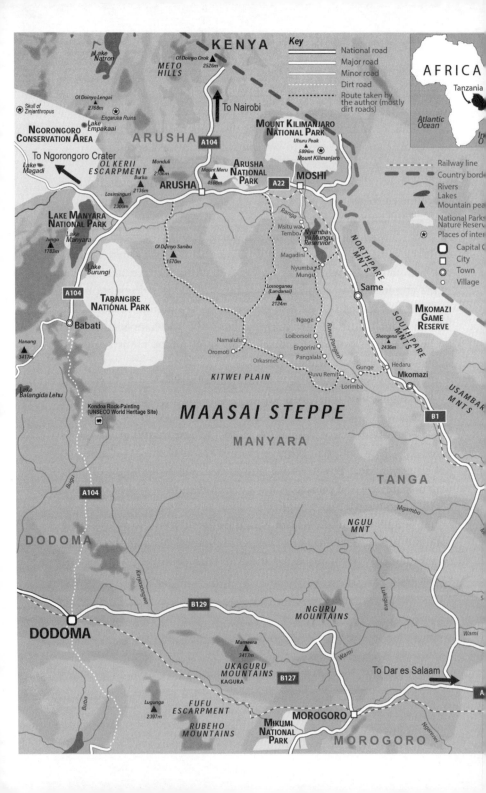

1

Stepping stones in the Steppe

My first visit to the Maasai Steppe took place as the rest of the world was preparing their computers for the new millennium. The embarkation point was the Ruvuma Pub, a video bar under a shady tree in an otherwise unmemorable settlement on the Dar es Salaam–Moshi Highway. Lounging in its white plastic chairs enjoying bottles of Coke and the rhythms of *bongo flava* were a group of Maasai men. As I got out of the car they rose to introduce themselves.

Although he was in Western dress, Oloserian was distinctively Maasai: tall and thin, the darkness of his skin exaggerating the whiteness of his teeth. His charming smile revealed the identifying mark of the Maasai – a gap in the lower incisors where two had been removed. Oloserian explained he would be my guide and interpreter for the trip.

"*Polé*," he said. "Sorry."

"*Polé kwa safari*," said each of the Maasai men in turn, grasping my hand in the three-grip handshake.

"Why are you saying sorry to me?"

"Sorry because you've suffered the journey to come and see us."

"*Suffered?* But travelling's a pleasure!"

They smiled politely and said '*polé*' again, as though they were sorry that I didn't yet understand the pleasures in store when travelling the Maasai Steppe.

After plates of chicken and chips, and a prudent use of the toilet, we set off. All spare seats of the car and its luggage space were suddenly filled with the crimson robes of male Maasai. They were tall, and there were many of them, but with a fluent concertina-folding of their long limbs they managed to close the doors.

Leaving the smooth tarmac highway, our landcruiser bumped down an alleyway opposite the pub. We emerged into an open space crowded with market stalls which the driver negotiated slalom-style, weaving between the stalls in a crazy zigzag. Women scattered in alarm, bright buckets of bananas and tomatoes bobbing on their heads. Beyond the market lay the steep embankment of a railway line. Without the slightest glance to left or right, our driver sent the landcruiser soaring over the tracks.

On the other side lay a bewildering maze of bumpy and sometimes dead-end tracks, the consequence of drivers striving to avoid a rainy season gully that was inexorably devouring the route to Simanjiro District. On each of my subsequent trips the gully had grown new forks swallowing more land and forcing drivers to make bigger and bigger detours in an effort to find stable ground for their wheels.

After ten kilometres we reached the defining feature of the eastern frontier to the Maasai Steppe. It is marked by a rather lonely road sign indicating humps, offering travellers reassurance that they are, indeed, still on a road. The humps signify a bridge that spans a miniature gorge at a place called Gunge. At this point the Ruvu is a small river, but in such a dry land flowing water of any kind is an anomaly. On that first trip I had yet to realise its true significance. In the jolt of an eyelid we had crossed the small gushing stream with its eyeliner strip of green, and had entered the Maasai Steppe. For the next two hours we must have followed its course, possibly never more than a few hundred metres from it, and yet I never realised. The river stole through that parched land like a foreign spy, leaving no incriminating evidence of its passage.

As the Usumbara mountains at our backs faded into bluish haze and we headed westwards into their rain-shadow, the people, the baobab trees, the vegetation and soil became more and more sparse, until there were only the dry sandy tracks and silent thorn trees of the Maasai Steppe.

Despite its barrenness and fragility, the Steppe was not uninhabited. Dust clouds traced the movement of distant cattle herds. The Maasai herders were impossible to miss. Striding on long skinny legs, a staff in their hand or carelessly thrown across their shoulders, crimson shawls flapping in the post-meridian wind, they floated like sailboats across the shimmering mirage-lakes of the savannah. Where the sun and drought had bleached all natural colour from the land, one could understand their compulsion to wear such a flamboyant colour.

Ever since explorers and missionaries first set foot in East Africa, Maasai have cast a powerful attraction on Europeans. 'They are dreaded as warriors, laying all to waste with fire and sword, so that the weaker tribes do not venture to resist them in the open field, but seek only to save themselves by the quickest possible flight,' wrote Krapf, a missionary-explorer, in 1860.[1]

I was sitting squashed against them. Flexing my elbows, I tried to make a little more space for myself. My scar-faced neighbour glanced down and spotted me under his armpit. He broke into a smile, and when I smiled back, he relaxed into a full-body laugh. Reaching over, he clasped my white hand firmly in his and held it there for several minutes.

British colonials jokingly invented a medical condition to account for attraction to the Maasai. Some greatly disliked the Maasai saying they were stubborn, aloof, arrogant, whereas others saw them as magnificent, dignified, courteous, and became their champions. The former teased the latter about being infected with a blindness, or suffering from 'Maasai-itis'.[2] I could feel the infection attacking me. There was no denying that I found something compelling in their distinctiveness, in their blatant disregard for the conventions of modern-day life.

My first encounter with the Maasai did not hold pleasant memories. I was 18 at the time, on a volunteer gap year at a school in Uganda. During my holidays, I travelled to Tanzania to climb Mount

Kilimanjaro. From the windows of the mini-bus I was intrigued to catch my first glimpses of Maasai driving their cattle in a cloud of dust. They were hard to miss in their fiery robes, and I was fortunate to be in the front passenger seat. The road between Nairobi and Arusha is straight and flat with few settlements, and the mini-bus was flying at full speed when I spotted some Maasai with a herd of goats crossing the road in the distance.

The driver had more than enough time to apply the brakes, but instead he accelerated. We sliced through the goats at full speed. By that time my eyes were closed, but I felt a series of bumps and jolts and heard the shouts and bleats. When I opened them again, we were speeding along an empty road as if nothing had happened. The driver laughed at my exclamations of horror as I glanced back and saw carcasses strewn in our wake. Nobody else on the bus uttered a murmur. It had been deliberate slaughter.

At the time, I could not comprehend the driver's behaviour, but I promised myself that I would return to find out more about the Maasai. There had been a long delay as my life went in a different direction – to the mountains of Nepal as it happened – but finally, nearly thirty years later, I was back in East Africa, and about to fulfil my long-held dream to visit a Maasai settlement.

This opportunity had come about through a drought rehabilitation project. During a prolonged drought in the late 1990s, the Steppe had depended on emergency food distribution. With the return of the rains, the project wanted to rehabilitate the environment and set up measures to mitigate the effects of any future droughts. One of these was the establishment of income-generation groups for women. When the Project learnt that I had worked with such groups in Nepal, they invited me to visit and advise the Maasai women on how best to set about earning money. Although I was doubtful that my experience with women's groups in Asia could be transferred to such a different context, I did not allow my doubts to forestall the opportunity of a visit.

The Maasai men talked over my head, now and then breaking off their conversation to shout directions at the driver. Left in peace, I was content to study the landscape. We forked right near a solitary shop and a primary school under construction. This minor track was in slightly better condition; traffic was light and left only hoof-marks. The drought had ended and there were herds of zebra and impala grazing on new grass as well as troops of baboon. A dik-dik darted into the scrub as we sped past. In a thicket further on we passed some gerenuks stretching their giraffe-like necks to reach leaves high on the branches. I had never seen one before. They are rare in game parks, but in the arid Steppe they are at home.

But I was most struck by the expansiveness and emptiness of the Steppe. Our vehicle shrank to a tiny dot in that vast space. When we stopped for a break, the peace of the landscape was a physical presence. The Maasai fell silent. They stretched their long bodies and leant on their sticks, crooking one foot against the other leg. The distant horizon drew our focus away from ourselves and one another. I felt suddenly unencumbered.

In places the trail took a respite, leaving the driver to navigate his own route across vast pans of flaking dried mud, devoid of vegetation – long enough and flat enough to land a jumbo jet, although one could think of nothing more incongruous.

"There's sulphur in the soil. It's toxic. Nothing grows, not even grass," explained Oloserian. The speedometer clocked 130 kilometres per hour and our dust trail was evidence of the havoc we were wreaking on the fragile environment.

Oloserian was a livestock specialist seconded to the Project from his normal government post. Ironically, his main task was to convince the Maasai to keep fewer animals, to establish other sources of income. If the Maasai continued to depend solely on their herds, they would remain extremely vulnerable to drought and famine, he explained. Throughout the 1990s droughts in the Maasai Steppe had increased in frequency and severity. While nobody could prevent the droughts from occurring, or predict when they would occur, there were steps that could be taken to diminish the likelihood that famine would follow in their wake.

The Project's approach was to empower communities to do things for themselves, and this was the logic behind the women's groups. In the past, development aid was largely about 'gifts' – providing a new school, a clinic, a drinking water system. But experience had shown that gifts tended to deteriorate quickly and left behind few signs of progress. The organisation for whom Oloserian worked wanted to create a sustainable change process by providing communities with skills and tools to manage their own development initiatives. The way I understood it, the approach offered people an embarkation point rather than the endpoint. Like the Maasai and the passing car, it was the journey that counted, not the destination.

In the middle of nowhere the driver pulled up in a storm of dust and the Maasai men got out. There was prolonged handshaking, and then they turned their backs on the car and strode off carelessly to nowhere.

I took a deep breath and spread myself over the back seat as we rattled on. Watching the thorn trees and dust clouds float in hypnotic drifts past the window, I prepared myself for the encounter which lay ahead. What sort of a reception might I receive from the Maasai women and their groups? Was there any advice or information that I could offer which they did not already know?

At that time, I was as ignorant as most tourists. My knowledge of the Maasai was based on TV documentaries and coffee-table books. These suggested that they wore many beads but few clothes, lived on a diet of cow's milk and blood, practised circumcision, and hunted lions armed with only spears and shields. I expected that my visit would engender some shyness and inhibitions so I prepared myself to be sensitive to cultural taboos; warned myself that it would take time to be accepted by them, to be invited into their homes.

After another hour we arrived at a small settlement. There were scattered huts, one or two tin roofs, a primary school, a small shop, and the village office with an antenna and a solar panel on its roof. Passing straight through the village, we arrived at a large but dishevelled cluster of huts enclosed by a barricade of cut thorn brush – a *boma* in Swahili, or *engang* in the Maa language of the Maasai. The driver drove through its narrow entry point and parked the car under a thorn tree between the inner and outer thorn walls. These were half decomposed and encircled some equally decrepit-looking huts, though one of them sported a tin roof, suggesting a person of rank and wealth.

The *engang* had the air of an abandoned film set, lifeless save for a few small children and goats. Some Maasai shawls hanging from the thorny enclosure suggested that people had recently been here. Goats wandered over and sniffed our car from front to back, licking the tyres and settling in the shade beneath it. Where were the women we were supposed to be meeting with? Oloserian went off to inquire.

A few minutes later he came striding back. "The women say *polé* – they are in too much of a tizzy to hold a meeting right now. But they request your presence. They say your presence will help to calm them down."

"*What?* They want *me* to calm them down?!"

"That's what they said. Go ahead. You'll find them inside that *enkaji* over there." He pointed to one of the huts.

I got out of the car. "Hold on. Tell me what's happened first."

But Oloserian merely pointed his finger. "Go over there, and go inside. Then you'll understand." He led me to one of the huts. At the entrance I signalled for him to lead the way. If I was to face a Maasai brouhaha I needed an interpreter at my side.

Oloserian shook his head. "You must enter alone," he insisted.

It sounded more and more suspicious. "But I hardly speak Swahili – and not a single word of Maa!"

"They are asking for *you* – 'the *mzungu* woman will know what to do'; those are their words."

He gave me an encouraging push along the entrance corridor, which was more like a tunnel. I put out my hands as I stumbled against the threshold step.

I could see nothing save tongues of fire encircling a blackened cauldron which a disembodied arm was stirring. A torrent

7

of excited voices assaulted my ears. Everybody seemed to be saying *"oroiloroiloroiloroiloroilo ..."*

As I hesitated on the threshold, hands pulled me over to sit on what felt like a low wooden fence. I sensed myself surrounded by a shadowy crowd. They addressed me in fast flowing stanzas, assuming I could understand. Hands stretched out to shake mine, to finger my hair and my unfamiliar white skin. As they touched me I could hear them sucking air in through the gap of their missing lower teeth, with a loud hissing sound. How did I measure up? Did my skin feel different to theirs? I smiled tentatively, and sets of perfectly white teeth materialised from the darkness and smiled back at me.

As my eyes adjusted I became aware that a dozen women were examining me with frank curiosity. They were shoulder to shoulder against the mud and wattle walls of the small womb-like room, some sitting on upturned buckets or low stools, and some resting on a raised platform. They had smooth, shaved heads. But my eyes were drawn to the beads which dazzled in the firelight and seemed to pour from their ear lobes like rivulets of milk.

A mug of tea was thrust into my hands. Far from being in a tizzy, the women were in party spirits, laughing and chattering. Except for one, who was lying on a low platform. She was moaning softly as her back and legs were massaged by two attendants. All of a sudden it dawned on me that I had intruded on a labour party. One which had nothing to do with politics. It was a female-only affair, hosted by the mother-in-law, and every neighbour woman had come to offer encouragement and support.

It was surprising how much we managed to communicate in sign language and single words. Since their Swahili language was as limited as my own, I had no inhibitions in using it. We exchanged the number and sex and ages of our children. When I indicated that I had only one son and one daughter, their faces showed pity and they gestured that *Engai* (God) would surely bless me with more in the future.

Cautiously I pulled out my camera, unsure whether photos were permitted. I had heard that Maasai are camera-shy, even aggressive when tourists try to take their photos, and this was the most intimate of gatherings. I waved the camera and lifted my eyebrows. Hands went up in defence. Quickly I stuffed the camera back into its bag. But my neighbour seized it from me. It transpired that they were happy to oblige, but – like women the world over – they wished to look their best for the photo. I waited while they adjusted their robes and ornaments. The hostess poured out a new round of tea and the women lifted their chipped enamel tea-mugs in a toast to my camera.

Like all Maasai births, this one was taking place in the home. There was no choice in the matter for health facilities are few in the Steppe. One woman acted as the midwife. Her qualifications were nine babies of her own, and she was versed in the herbal treatments passed down within the Maasai community. Later I learnt from Oloserian that she had also attended Project training on safe birth practices. This was a first-time delivery. Higher risk for mother and baby. Herbs and root extracts had been put into the tea – certain ones to bring on the contractions, and others after delivery to control bleeding. But nothing for pain, they stressed. Though they are familiar with narcotic plants, they prefer to endure with the stoicism for which they are famed.

After a couple of hours there were no clear signs that the baby's arrival was imminent. It could be many hours, and Oloserian was waiting patiently. He wanted to show me a spot by the river where they were growing onions with irrigation. Besides advising the women's groups I was delegated to interview beneficiaries and write an article about the work of the Project. Regretfully, I withdrew from the scene.

The onion-growers turned out to be non-Maasai farmers who were slowly encroaching into the more fertile parts of the Steppe. I praised the onions effusively, hoping to escape quickly and get back to the delivery. It was a mistake. The onion-grower was thrilled; he insisted that we went to his home so that his wife and children could meet me.

By the time I could escape and return to the birthing chamber, a small baby was feeding serenely at the new mother's breast.

We finally held our meeting. It was brief, as the women had chores to do and we had a journey to the next group. But what I had witnessed had been much more illuminating than a formal meeting. It had overturned my preconceptions. I had been wrong-footed by their warmth, their openness, their lack of formalities, their ability to jump the cultural divide and connect. It had also shown me that the bond among women is very strong, stronger in this case than the bonds of language, culture and nationality. Though I was a complete stranger, and a *mzungu* foreigner, my presence had been allowed at this intimate event, whereas men were not permitted. It encouraged me to think that establishing women-only groups was a good strategy which might fit well with their culture.

We said farewell and drove on to Loiborsoit, where we were due to hold a meeting with a second group. The night was a moonless black, and the driver struggled to remain on the track, driving slowly because of hidden ruts. By the time we arrived it was very late. There were no lights and we assumed that everyone had gone home to sleep. But as we got out, we were suddenly surrounded by excited Maa chatter – gibberish to my uncomprehending ears. The women we had come to meet were still there; they had been patiently waiting since midday – the time they were given for the meeting. I was amazed and humbled by their genuine pleasure at our extremely late arrival. It was not that they didn't have other work to do, cows to milk, food to cook, children to feed, but they had been told to wait for the meeting by those people who moved around in their 4x4s, and so they had waited.

Someone produced a hurricane lamp and a young woman called Anna spoke quietly and earnestly about their group plans. As she made each of her points, the baby asleep on her back nodded its head against her shoulder blades.

"For a very long time we've dreamed of doing something for ourselves, but we didn't know how to get started," she explained. "Then the Project gave us this 'stepping stone', they showed us how to start our own group and gave us a loan. Now we're ready to start some business activities. We're serious. We're determined to advance ourselves."

An older woman intervened: "You must understand that as women we've nothing we can call our own. All the animals belong to men. We don't get any money from them. If we want to give a gift to a friend, or buy a bar of soap for ourselves or an orange for our children, we have to beg the money from our husbands. Usually they refuse."

"And what do they think of this new plan?"

"The elders have given their approval."

It was past ten o'clock and though everybody was tired nobody wanted to break up the meeting. They talked on – about their desire to have their own source of money; how they would use this to send their children to school. In the past, they had never felt that they could do anything to change their circumstances, but now they had caught a glimpse of a possibility. They were not yet sure what they would do, or how they would do it, but they were emphatic that they were going to do something. Despite my fatigue I felt re-energised seeing their enthusiasm and commitment. They were ready to embark on a journey.

"What is development? It's taking a step forward, isn't it?" went on Anna, echoing my own thoughts. "And women can do that just as well as men. We're naming our group *Matonyok,* which means 'effort'. Development will only happen by our own effort."

2

Encounter with beads

Red shawls, purple robes and royal blue . . . white beads and lustrous dusky skin ... shaved heads and long braids ... chalk-white and ochre-red faces ... necks engulfed in beads, ear lobes drooping and looping with paraphernalia ... goats and babies bleating ... calabash and knob-kerries ... wafts of smoke and roasting meat. My first visit happened to coincide with a circumcision ceremony.

I was escorted to the enclosure by the village leader and introduced to the Maasai elders who gave me carte blanche to take as many photos as I wanted – quite contrary to what I had been told about their camera shyness or demands for payment. The fact that they offered me this freedom before I had even requested permission, intimated that they were well aware of foreigners' addiction to photography. The slightly amused look on the faces of the elders as I double-checked to make sure I had understood, seemed to say "It's our pleasure to humour you; we know about *mzungu* and their customs."

Thanking them profusely, I stationed myself in a corner to survey the scene. The opportunity was so mesmerising that I didn't know where to start until Oloserian reminded me that we could not stay all day. There were other communities on our agenda and distances to travel before the end of the day. Reluctantly I promised him that we would leave on time, and returned to my favourite activity – people watching.

Women were gathered in clusters and they, too, were engrossed in this activity. As outbursts of singing and dancing announced the arrival of new guests, they craned their necks to see who it was. From our different cultural perspectives we assessed the décor and dancing of each new troupe. The young women were natural models. Tall, slim and graceful; heads held high; their bodies moved with an unconscious grace and suppleness, their dark skin the perfect setting for the hundreds of pearly-white beads they wore. Even the women's shaved scalps, which I found unappealing at first, began to grow on me. It allowed their skin to flow from their bare shoulders up their necks and over their heads in a single, smooth, graceful line.

Cascades of beads and sequined chains poured from every part of their ear lobes. Around each slender neck were two, three, or four bands of beads like the rings of Saturn. Chokers of cowrie shells and beads encircled throats; coils of brass and copper wire snaked their way up legs and arms. Some sported a beaded crown with a flap over their brow from which a cobweb affair of chains, beads and sequins dangled across their faces like a mask. Where bare skin was visible it gleamed with a lotion of animal fat and red ochre to which they added elaborate patterns of dots and dashes in white paste. Earrings were so heavy and numerous, some of a curious branching design, that their lower lobes stretched in gaping loops, or their upper lobes folded over the lower with the weight. Several women had lost portions of their ear lobes to necrosis, brought on by the kilos they carried.

The young men – known as warriors or *morani* – were just as adorned as the women. Leggings of beads wrapped their ankles and shins; gauntlets of them guarded their wrists. Slung across one shoulder, sequined necklaces dangled to their hips. Hair was parted in a line from ear to ear; the front forelock was gathered into a silver clasp on their forehead, while at the back it hung to their waist in hundreds of fine braids, artificial hair woven into the real and gathered into bullet-shaped silver clasps. Everywhere there were sequins. The *morani* strutted and posed, conscious of how fine they looked. If I had not already seen photographs I might have been surprised to see men so bejewelled. But I liked it. Here were Maasai warriors, strong and brave enough to kill lions with a thrust of their spears, in their jewellery and make-up. How drab other men seemed in comparison; how restricting our gendered conventions of dress. I like to imagine how business and politics could be livened up if men were to abandon grey suits and ties.

Even the elders looked splendid. Their scarecrow-thin frames were buried beneath layers of scarlet *orlokaraha* wraps. Some wore earrings. One grandfather had a film canister pushed through his ear lobe, another a roll of silver foil; others had a gaping hole where once the decorations had been. Content to watch the younger generation celebrating, they leaned against a tree or on their staffs.

But one vital component of the occasion was missing. "Where are the boys to be circumcised?" I asked Oloserian, as he came over to remind me it was time to leave.

"Inside the hut – the one marked with the green boughs. They've already been cut. Now we celebrate – while they suffer. Believe me, they don't feel like dancing right now!"

The dazzling array of beadwork reminded me of my earlier discussions with the women. Some groups had mentioned goat-rearing or growing maize, others a tree nursery or opening a small shop, as ways to generate income, but the one activity everyone was passionate about doing was beadwork.

"Beadwork is a skill every woman has," explained Mama Kicheche, the grandmother of the new baby. "We've never farmed; we don't know how to cultivate maize or cassava. We might fail. We've never been shopkeepers; we can't even read the numbers on money notes. But beadwork we know; we're sure we can do it."

I could appreciate their doubts about trying totally new activities. There *were* risks in farming, not least the vagaries of the rainfall. For an environmentally fragile area, vulnerable to drought, beads represented the greenest option, one they could depend upon irrespective of the weather. There was just one problem in turning their skills into an income-earning activity.

"Who buys your beadwork? Do you sell any at the moment?" I asked.

"The *morani* buy a few."

"And what about other Tanzanians? Do you ever trade your ornaments outside your locality?"

Their beads jingled as they gave a negative reply.

"So where are you thinking to sell them? Who will buy them?"

There was a pause before one of them ventured: "We thought you would be able to tell us that. *Mzungu* like you – maybe they will buy?"

It was the reason that they had invited me. They might be living in a remote spot, but as the photography incident had shown, they were not unaware of foreigners' fascination for all things Maasai.

I hesitated before replying. It was not that I wished to dampen their enthusiasm, but I had some inkling of the challenges involved in producing handicrafts geared to foreign tastes and standards. I didn't want to raise their expectations and then disappoint. "It's best to start with activities that have a local market," I said.

Reluctantly they agreed, while I promised to investigate the market for beadwork. In case I should forget, they sealed the deal by slipping a beaded bracelet over my wrist.

On my return to steamy Dar es Salaam, I felt as though the Maasai had followed me. Wherever I turned I was confronted by their bead-adorned images. They stared – in that frank, unflinching gaze of theirs – from the pages of guidebooks, from picture frames in restaurants and from advertisements on my TV. No safari company, it seemed, could hope to be successful if they did not showcase the Maasai in their promotional literature. Even in Arab Zanzibar their images followed me, and real-life Maasai spread their beaded products at my feet as I trod the winding alleyways of Stone Town.

When I embarked on my research, I was surprised to discover that the Maasai are relatively new immigrants to the country, the bulk of their migration into Tanganyika[1] taking place not long before the first European explorers arrived – in the late eighteenth and early nineteenth

centuries. As for the phantasmagoria of beads at the circumcision ceremony, those glass beads were first brought to East Africa from Europe
in the nineteenth century, and spread through Arab trading caravans.
Before that time, accounts of the early explorers suggest that the main
decoration of Maasai women was coils of brass and copper, and ornaments made of small chains and metal beads.

The origins of the Maasai people are hazy and the source of some
debate. There are few written records. The name 'Maasai' occurs in
the Bible,[2] and some have suggested that they might be one of the lost
tribes of Israel,[3] though few support this theory. In the fifth century
BCE the Greek historian Herodotus wrote: 'The Macae, a people who
wear their hair in the form of a crest, shaving it close on either side
of the head, and letting it grow long in the middle: in war they carry
ostrich skins for shields.'[4]

Linguistic evidence is more reliable. My brief visit had shown me
that their Maa language sounds very different to Swahili and the Bantu
group of languages. It marks the southern limit of the Nilo-Saharan
group of languages, and with their lean physical features and pastoral traditions, it places the Maasai with the Nilotic or Nilo-Hamitic
people, suggesting an origin from somewhere in the Nile Valley of
Sudan.

Their own myths tell of a deep crater or valley at Endikir-e-kerio
(the scarp of Kerio) and a severe drought. Half the people and their
livestock are said to have escaped out of the crater over a bridge built
for this purpose. Then the bridge collapsed and the remaining people
were trapped and left behind. When later they were able to scramble
out of the ravine, this group travelled eastwards into the highland
areas of Somalia. Those who escaped earlier, via the bridge, travelled
southwards into northern Kenya, and became the present-day Maasai
and the closely related tribes of the Samburu and the Turkana. In the
myth they are said to have crossed 'the Brown Plains' leading some to
speculate that this refers to the Sahara Desert.

Drought and desertification possibly triggered their initial southerly migrations, but political events have played a role in subsequent

movements. For some time the south-travelling tribe settled in the area around Lake Turkana bordering Kenya, Ethiopia and Sudan. From here a further migration began in the eighteenth and nineteenth centuries, breaking them up into separate groups: the Samburu and the Turkana, who remained in Kenya, and the present-day Maasai who continued in a southerly direction, some of them crossing into Tanganyika and occupying the fertile highlands around Mount Kilimanjaro, Meru and the Ngorongoro Crater highlands. By the time Europeans arrived in the late nineteenth century, the Maasai occupied an area which stretched from Lake Turkana in northern Kenya, down through the Rift Valley and the Maasai Steppe to Dodoma in central Tanganyika.

Within twenty-five years of colonial rule, their territory had shrunk to one quarter of its former extent. Since the country gained independence, the trend of land appropriation has continued. Some say the days of the Maasai are numbered.

3

Dawn to dusk

Dawn. A soft red blush streaks the sky and touches the remnant pyra-mids of a long-extinct volcano on the horizon. There may be a dewfall, dampening the dust and stretching a thread of crystals on the webs which spiders weave from thorn to thorn.

In the engang *cattle are lowing, goats bleating, donkeys braying. Weaver birds, the brazen sparrows of the savannah, chirp their greet-ings from colonies in the sitting tree. The only sound one doesn't hear is a cock crowing. Wrapped in thick red shawls and silhouetted against the lightening sky, men break a hole in the thorn barricade and enter the inner corral. They wander across its soft dome of sun-dried cow dung and take the attendance roll, checking that each cow is alive and well. The inspection is thorough. This is their livelihood, larder and savings account.*

Women emerge from the huts holding beaded, bottle-shaped gourds. They ease open the wooden wedge bars on thatch-roofed pens and warm, wet muzzles reach out to greet them. As the calves are released they buck and dance in freedom and gallop away on tottering legs to search for their personal udder. Women commence the task of milking. While a calf guzzles at one teat, the women's hands squirt a stream of milk into the narrow neck of calabashes jammed between their knees. In an open pen on the far side of the corral, children play a game of tag with the sheep and goats. When at last one child corners a nanny-goat, holding it captive by its horns or straddling its shoulders, another empties the contents of its udder into an enamel mug.

As the sun rises, thorn trees stretch out their first faint shadows. Mouths are dry and thirsty from the night's sleep, but there will be no tea to drink until milking and water collection is finished. Saddle bags of stiff crumpled leather are strapped onto donkeys and loaded with jerrycans. Somebody pulls aside the thorn branches which secure the outer corral and the donkey train departs to fetch water. Tracks in the sandy paths leading to the river reveal who else felt thirsty in the night. Invariably, there are prints of savannah hares and guinea fowl; occasionally, the hoofprints of dik-dik, impala, zebra, or even buffalo, and rarely – very rarely –the paw-marks of lion or leopard. In the light scrub around the engang, birdsong breaks up the silence. Hornbills flap from treetop to treetop; families of tiny turquoise cordon-bleu peck in the dust, and the go-away bird warns intruders to 'gerwhay! gerwhay!' For a place so dry and barren there is an astonishing variety of birds.

Within the inner enclosure men wrestle a sick cow to the ground and inject her with medicine. Milking over, women lean their full gourds against the walls of their enkaji. Each wife has her own hut where she lives with her children, spaced in a circle between the inner and outer barricades. In a young family there may be only two or three huts, but others have a dozen or more. When the donkeys return, she lights the fire and brews a pan of tea, rich with sugar and milk. If there is food in the house, she may cook a morning meal, but in times of scarcity two big mugs of milky tea suffice to see people through the day, while children scrape the pans from the night before.

Flies wake up and cluster round the eyes and mouths of babies. While children fortunate to attend school prepare to leave, a clanging of bells announces that cattle are going out to graze. One or two morani go with them, armed with sticks or knives. A few carry spears, but in this part of the Steppe, wild animals are not many. Boys follow behind them with the flock of sheep and goats.

Women, young children and young calves remain in the engang. The male elders may stay home, or they might travel to neighbouring *settlements to trade animals, or walk to the nearest road to buy supplies. In the engang there is work to do but also time for leisure in the heat of the day. After feeding their babies and boiling excess milk, the women gather firewood, repair their huts, spread what grain they have on leather hides to dry in the sun, or stake out new skins of leather to stretch and dry. Chores done, they retire to the shade to sew new robes and fashion leather or bead ornaments.*

As the morning moves on the heat builds, and the first dust-devils scurry across the plain. When conditions are right, these grow into skyscrapers of dust, spiralling like mini tornadoes. There are times when the plains are full of them, racing after one another like a caravan of bonfires.

The boys or young men lead the cattle into the dense scrub of the escarpment, or to the river plains if rain has fallen recently. The cattle nibble at green shoots barely poking through the over-grazed stalks and stubble; goats balance their forelegs on branches to nibble at thorn-tree leaves. The sky blazes blue. Thunder clouds appear in the distance, but rain does not fall.

Life slows almost to a halt. The birds have vanished, though insects remain alert and noisy. The herds wander up dry ravines where mica chips dazzle the eye. Even the goats search out a spot of shade in which to rest. In the engang, flies reign supreme. As the babies and toddlers nod off to sleep, the women cover their faces with a cloth to keep the flies away.

When children return from school, more tea is brewed. The sun begins to lose height; the cattle leave their browsing and head to the river for a drink. The toddlers wake up and play games around the compound. They run barefoot across the thorn-speckled sand; their tender young feet are already scarred with festering wounds. The cattle return and the milking ritual commences afresh. Fires are lit in every hut and maize meal is cooked. Sometimes a goat is slaughtered, or there may be strips of dried beef hanging from a nail.

When everyone has returned for the night, thorn brush is pulled across the gaps in the enclosures and piled high. In the indigo sky stars appear one by one, faint at first, but strengthening and multiplying as the light fades until the sky resembles a pointillist canvas, crowned with the broad arch of the Milky Way.

It is then, when all the chores are over and the cattle dozing safely inside the inner fold, that the songs of young voices float across the night air. The singing is perfect in pitch and harmony, weaving a sublime counterpoint to the night sky.

4

Koko!

The tin roof of the training room vibrated with the rolling rippling syllables of Maa chatter. Maasai women are noisy; they love to talk! Maa language has a way of rolling off the tongue, and once in motion, it is hard to put the brakes on it, even to reduce its speed or volume. The women were revelling in the novel experience; not only did they have a holiday from their chores, but the added pleasure of beadwork.

"Welcome! Can you hear me? Are you listening?" I shouted.

Deaf to my pleas, they crowded around the long table, eyes drawn to packs of beads which I had spread in the middle. Arms reached out. Red, yellow, white, blue, turquoise ... hands touched each in turn, resting a moment as they imagined what they might make, as though they could divine the ornaments they would create, through the plastic wrap. Some skeins were already unpacked and they fingered them excitedly, letting the strings of beads slide through their half-closed palms like hundreds of delicate rosaries.

I shouted again through the Maasai hubbub, with no greater success. These were women who had never sat on a school bench, who had no prior experience of a training workshop, and knew nothing of acceptable behaviour in a learning environment. They were refreshingly uninhibited. The idea that they should be silent and listen to what the trainer was saying never occurred to them. But then, my words were in a language they did not understand.

Oloserian interpreted for me, and I soon noticed that he always started his translation with the word *etejo*, which he exclaimed several times, until they fell silent. Guessing that it must mean 'Please listen', I thought I could master this phrase myself. But Oloserian explained that the translation was 'She says'.

"She says!" Oloserian shouted above the uproar every few minutes, converting me into a soothsayer. These are not just anybody's words; these are *her* words. "*Etejo!!* ... " Oloserian hollered once more above the tidal flow of Maa camaraderie. She says that you should ... "cut the leather in a straight line ... measure before you cut ... if you don't know how to count, ask someone to teach you ... hide the finishing of your beadwork on the wrong side of the leather ... don't use ballpoint pen on the good side ... don't allow children to play with the knives!"

It was like shouting in the wilderness. His words went in through one beaded earhole and out the other. But the noise in the training hall was so much more gratifying than a roomful of blank faces. These women were embarking on a journey. They were excited.

The workshop was the result of a call from Oloserian, about a year after my initial visit. In between, I had heard nothing of the groups and feared they had failed to get off the ground. But Oloserian told me the women had had a moderately successful first year. Some had cultivated maize and managed to get a harvest; one group had set up a small shop; another had made money buying and selling maize.

"They beg you to visit again. They say they are ready for beadwork. They want you to give them training."

"But they know everything there is to know about beadwork!"

"But you understand the things which *mzungu* like to buy."

My research had been discouraging; the market was swamped with Maasai beadwork, some of it made by genuine Maasai and some by counterfeiters. It would be hard to compete. They needed a market niche. During my earlier visit, I had noticed that the Maasai sewed beads on leather artefacts, and Oloserian had pointed out a leather tanning workshop at Loiborsoit. Nowhere in the market had I seen any beaded leather products, and I thought that small beaded leather bags might be the market niche. The leather tannery was closed on the day of our visit, but Oloserian promised to send me some samples. When these arrived, I prepared some templates. The purpose of the workshop was for the women to learn how to make bags, and for me to understand how they did their beadwork on leather.

In the workshop there was much to digest – new concepts and foreign tools. Measurement was a new concept for most had never been to school or learnt to count above ten. Scissors were a novelty, as were needles, utility knives, wire-cutters and tape measures. Even sitting on a chair and working at a table was a strange experience – one they found rather uncomfortable.

Maasai women can do beadwork in any position, but their preference is on the ground in the L pose: legs and back straight, toes and head pointing to the sky. Beadwork, Maasai-style, involves many parts of the body, and this pose allows them to utilise their toes to control the long coils of wire required to bead their 'rings of Saturn' *esosi*. For threading their 'needles' they use their thighs. Their needles are a stiff grass or some hessian fibres unpicked from a hessian sack, which are rubbed together against a bare thigh until the fibres of the one entangle with the other. Loose ends of nylon thread are clamped by burning with a match. Teeth act as wire-cutters, but for piercing holes in the leather each woman had her own awl, fashioned from a bicycle spoke.

For cutting the leather I provided a wooden board and a metal ruler, but the women regarded these with disdain. They showed me how to cut leather the way they cut their meat – in the style of a kebab take-away. In the *engang* it was common to see one person holding up the barbecued hind-quarters of a cow while another sawed strips from it with a knife. It was futile to beg them to keep the knives away from children's hands; I even spotted one woman deliberately handing her toddler a knife to play with.

There were twelve official participants, and almost as many gate-crashers. The latter were members of the leather-tanning cooperative, or those hired to cook our food. While the leather was soaking or the food simmering on a bushfire, they smuggled their way into the workshop. Without my friend Montse at my side I would not have coped. She not only spoke fluent Swahili but was adept at organising chaos into calm. I was thankful she had accepted my last-minute invitation. But the women were so open and friendly, so natural, so utterly themselves, willing to laugh at their own mistakes as well as mine, that I felt an instant liking for them. In age they ranged from teenagers to Sainoi, in her seventies. Many had both a Maasai name and a Christian name. Some preferred to be called by one and some by the other. There was Mariumu, Magdalena, Paulina, Anna and Esta. Others were known as the mother of such and such child, like Mama Nyeyesu and Mama Kicheche. For the remainder my tongue had to negotiate Nailole, Namunyak, Naisujiak and Naitapuaki.

Learning their names was not easy. There were few differences in dress or hairstyle to help. All dressed identically, in blue serge cloths onto which they had appliquéd zigzag patterns in white. This cloth is attached at one shoulder with a knot or a safety pin, and caught around the waist with a leather belt. When going into the outside world, they add an outer shawl of thin print material, also knotted at one shoulder, predominantly red or purple in colour. Under their wraps they wear nothing. Underwear is unknown; they are free to breast-feed or take a pee in the bush.

All had branded circles on their cheeks and were missing their two lower front teeth. Every woman had the same hairstyle: shaved bald.

"Why do you shave your hair?" The question sounded rude, but I couldn't help my curiosity.

"To look beautiful!" they answered, adding that they feel ugly if even a millimetre of hair begins to show.

"So what do you think of hair like mine?"

"It looks nice on you, but it would look bad on us," they answered. Such diplomacy!

"And your front teeth – why do you remove them?" I went on boldly since they didn't seem offended by my questions. "Is that also a beauty treatment?"

"We pull them out in case we contract lockjaw. So we can be fed milk through a straw."

My best guide to a woman's identity were her ears and earrings. Mama Baraka's ears stuck out like aeroplane flaps and the upper lobes lolled over the lower. Naserian had portions of ear missing, while Sainoi's lobes were so elongated by beads that they drooped to her shoulders. Sainoi was one of the gatecrashers. She was supposed to be processing more leather, but when she had a spare moment, she slipped into the training room and started sewing. At the end of the day she begged me for beads and leather and returned the next day with a bag, beautifully crafted.

"Ask her how many wives her husband has," Oloserian prodded me.

"We're twelve," answered Sainoi, flashing a toothy smile.

I tried to hide my amazement. "And – are you happy?"

"Very happy, although I'm old. I've many children and grandchildren. I love doing leatherwork. I thank God because I love everything I do."

Among the participants was Anna, the woman who had spoken so fervently about their efforts and determination, and Mama Kicheche, the grandmother of the baby whose birth I had witnessed. As the training progressed, the personalities and traits of each woman became more distinct. Some worked fast but sloppily; others slowly and meticulously. Then there was the Queen of Sheba. Montse gave this nickname to a striking young woman whose dark skin was accentuated by a glittering array of white beads. The Queen of Sheba spent most of the workshop yawning or lying down and I wondered why she had bothered to come.

In contrast, Esta was a participant every trainer loves to have. She listened with rapt attention, asked questions, and helped explain to those who didn't understand. Esta was also a gatecrasher, in a sense. Through a distant relative she had heard that the Project was establishing women's groups. She had gone to their office and pestered them to help her start a group in her village. When told that they could not provide a start-up loan as it was not on the budget that year, she went ahead and formed a group independently. Pooling their own money they bought some beads and began making products to sell. Impressed by her determination, Oloserian had added her name to the training list.

She was the only participant who had been to school. Just five years, but those five years might have been five centuries, the difference they made. Esta was articulate, confident and enthusiastic. Thanks to her schooling she was fluent in Swahili, the national language, and as my Swahili improved we were able to communicate without an interpreter. But the biggest bonus deriving from Esta's education was something more intangible. It was an awareness of the world outside, and a curiosity and confidence to engage with it.

Like other women on the training course, Esta came with attachments. Hers was a toddler called Jaki. After days of Jaki's screaming I assumed that she was sick and offered to drive Esta to the nearest health post. But Esta insisted that Jaki was not sick. Jacopo, the guard, happened to overhear and burst into laughter.

"That child," he corrected me, clearly speaking from the depths of personal experience. "That one not sick. That child *mkali*." Fierce, like the wild animals.

Understanding leapt across the cultural divide. Jaki was one of those – a strong-willed child. Esta was able to ignore Jaki. I watched her sew a straight line of beads onto a leather strip as Jaki, strapped to her back, threw one tantrum after another. I resorted to bribing her with biscuits. If Jaki was the price I had to pay for having Esta in the training, I was happy to pay.

As for myself, the women gave me two nicknames: Joisie was their pronunciation of my name, but more commonly, they called me *Koko*. It meant grandmother. It was intended as a mark of respect, but transposed into my culture, sent me into a state of shock. I had no idea I looked that old. I felt young – my children were just entering their teens! But it was useless; I couldn't fight it. "*Koko!* Come here!" I would hear them calling from all corners of the room – "*Koko*, I need help ... *Koko*, my needle's broken ... *Koko*, I've a problem ..."

It was the first word of their language I learnt by heart. The greetings were more challenging, varying with respect to status or gender, but I eventually mastered them – wrongly as it later turned out. Beyond these, every word seemed to begin with the prefix 'eng'. *Engai* was God; *engang* – their homesteads; *enkaji* – their huts; *engerai* – a child; *engitok* – woman; *engiteng* – cow and *engare* – water. Later I was to understand the significance of this prefix.

At the end of the first day there was a heap of litter on the training-room floor. Tidiness did not appear to be a feminine virtue of the Maasai. I was exhausted but also elated. Our relationship was refreshingly relaxed; I felt as if we had known each other for a much longer time. As I watched them breast-feeding their babies, laughing together and helping one another, I had a strong sense of déjà vu. It was as if the spirits of the women I had worked with in Nepal had reincarnated themselves. The differences were superficial; the commonalities suggesting a womanhood which transcends cultural differences.

The workshop was being held at a training centre in Loiborsoit, the place where I had witnessed a circumcision ceremony on my first visit. The name Loiborsoit means 'shiny rocks' – a reference to the crystals in a rocky outcrop on the edge of the village.

The centre had been built by another organisation, and apart from a primary school, was the only permanent building, at that time, within a fifty kilometre radius. It was wonderful to have this facility in such an undeveloped locality, and the Project used the centre for all manner of short training courses. It provided shelter from the noonday sun, the rain, the wind and the dust, all of which could sweep across the plains. Its large compound was enclosed by a wire fence. The fence provided a psychological boundary, rather than a physical one, since there was no gate, simply an open space through which I drove my car. The interior of the compound did not differ in essentials from the exterior, but had more sand and fewer thorn bushes than outside. One or two acacia trees had been kept for their shade.

On my arrival I was introduced to Baba John and Jacopo, the day guard and night watchman respectively. Jacopo was a powerfully built Maasai who could have felled me with his little finger. He gave me a tour of the premises. It consisted of a large training room, an office and two guestrooms. Each had two beds with sunken sponge mattresses and frames for mosquito nets.

Although relatively new, the centre already had that down-at-heel feel. Some of the glass window panes were broken; the solar panel and battery system providing lighting were failing, and the solar water pump had never been installed.

In a commanding position in the centre of the compound was a row of latrines and shower cubicles. Their doors no longer closed properly and the showers had taps but no water, but these were minor problems. Every few days some mangy donkeys ambled into the compound and lowered their heads next to a cement tank. In their crumpled saddlebags were barrels of water, carried from the river. In addition to the ground-level tank there was a brick water tower with a water drum on top. The original concept, I believe, was to pump water from the ground tank to the tower, using solar energy, and from there pipes would supply it to the shower rooms, using the force of gravity. As far as I could see, the water tower connected only to fantasy. But a bucket of water was heaven in the Maasai Steppe at the end of a hot dusty day.

To take a shower one first had to fill the bucket. If Baba John or Jacopo were not around I learnt how to scramble onto the roof of the tank and lower the bucket using a forked stick. It was not as easy as it looked. One needed the skill of a puppeteer to swing the bucket around and direct water into it without losing it. More often than not, I had to fish for the lost bucket, but motivation is the key to new skills. The thought of that bucket of water at day's end would give a small lift to my flagging spirits when the sun was at its zenith.

It was at the end of the first day that I learnt we were sharing the training centre with a number of non-paying guests. As the sun sank and an inky-blackness spread across the sky, from invisible holes in the eaves those uninvited guests took to the air – first one, then another, until a steady stream of shadows flitted and merged into the darkness.

In our bedroom I found my friend Montse contemplating the sagging ceiling over her bed, which had a large, dark stain.

"It's you-know-what," she said. "Bat poo."

"Guano," I corrected her. "David Attenborough loves the stuff. He wades in it."

"I don't care if he swims in it. I just don't want it dropping on me. Let's shift the beds."

We shifted the beds and opened the shutters. Montse had come with a Tanzanian woman's essential travel kit: a number of pieces of colourful *kanga* cloth. These have multiple uses. They can be wrapped around the top of jeans to provide a façade of appropriate rural dress; they can be used as shawls, as towels, as sheets or pillow covers. In this instance we used them as curtains and opened the metal shutters, which allowed a faint breeze to dilute the smell of the guests in the roof.

5

Income generation?

One morning during the training, Sainoi entered the meeting room and I stopped in my tracks. This elderly woman was semi-topless and bedecked with beads as usual, but wearing the interesting accessories of gumboots, plastic apron and rubber gloves. She had come to collect me for a tour of the leather-tanning workshop.

The tannery stood in a corner of the training compound and was a classic example of appropriate technology. It had a roof but no walls. There was a heavy-duty workbench, two cement troughs and six plastic buckets for soaking skins, a scrub board for scraping and large wooden boards for stretching and drying the leather.

"When I was young we used to wear leather wraps, not cloth," Sainoi recalled as she showed me around. "They were made from very thin sheepskins. I tanned and sewed my own leather. It took four skins to make one garment. Then I sewed on beads. It took a month to finish one wrap, but I loved the work. Whenever I was free from herding chores, I used to sit in the *engang* beading my skins."

"Why did you stop wearing them? Were they too heavy?"

"Not at all! They were light – very comfortable to wear. The leather was soft and thin, very pliable. I preferred them – and they cost us nothing to make. These cloth garments are more trouble – we have to wash them with water and soap. Our skins never needed washing – we simply smeared more oil on them. And they didn't wear out nearly as quickly as cloth."

"So why did you stop wearing them?"

"The government ordered us to stop."

"Do you mean the *mzungu* government, long ago?"

"No. It was after Freedom."

"Nyerere?"

"Yes. Nyerere. For a while we continued to wear the leather skins underneath our cloth shawls, but finally we abandoned the leather. Nowadays women wear them on special occasions – for instance, when they get married. But few remember how to make that leather."

Questioning Sainoi further I learnt that every Maasai woman knows how to prepare the large cow hides that form the 'mattresses' on which they sleep and the leather saddlebags for their donkeys, but this leather is crude and stiff – and rather smelly. The tannery used a natural but refined process to produce leather of better quality.

The shortage of leather for the training was causing me headaches. On my arrival I had been dismayed to learn that the tanning workshop had not been in operation for more than a year.

"Those samples you sent me were good. Where did they come from?" I asked Oloserian.

"From old stock. I didn't send you their recent leather because the quality is poor," he replied.

I choked back the question 'why didn't you tell me there were problems?', knowing the answer would simply be 'you didn't ask'. The error was my own; I had assumed the samples he had sent me were typical of their current production quality. We inspected the leather in their storehouse, but I found only a few skins of useable quality; the rest were stiff and covered with a rash of white spots.

"When will the new skins be ready?"

There was a hasty exchange in Maa. The answer was, "*Bado*." This is a frequently used word in Swahili. It means 'not yet' and is usually offered in an optimistic tone, suggesting that what you desire has not yet come to pass but will do so very soon.

"Will the new skins be ready before the end of the week so that we can use them in the training?" There was another exchange in rapid Maa, and from their faces I could guess the answer.

"They began yesterday," said Oloserian. "The process takes fifteen days."

A sigh of annoyance escaped my lips.

The tanning workshop had been established by a local Maasai organisation with the similar goal of empowering women through boosting their income-earning capacity. The cooperative had produced several scores of hides before stopping because of a deterioration in the quality. Nobody was able to give a reason, so Oloserian had called a meeting of the group to discuss the problem. A dozen men and women were present.

"If it's a women's group, what are the men doing here?" I whispered to Oloserian.

"They are merely advisors in case the women need help," he explained.

"Women can't manage all the tasks," added Jacopo. "Some tasks require strength. Stripping the skins and stretching them. Water has to be carried."

The skins first went through a series of soaks; they were then scraped clean and returned for further soaks in solutions containing lime, unripe papayas and mimosa. When ready, they were taken out, animal fat and soap applied to their inner side and vegetable oil to their outer. Finally, they were stretched on a wooden frame and left to dry.

As they described the tanning process, we walked around the workshop, hoping that we could pinpoint where the errors were occurring. According to the men, the problem was the women! They were not turning up on time according to the work rota. As a result, Baba John often did the tasks for them. Being the day-guard for the centre, he was always around and had some spare time. He explained that the duration of certain soaks was measured in hours, not days; if they soaked too long the skins were ruined. I could see this might present problems. Women told the time of day by the sun and the shadows, and the time of night by the movement of the stars.

A further complication was the distance they had to travel. The group had been constituted to include those of the older generation who could remember leatherwork from the past, and their *engang* were scattered over a wide area. Sainoi's *engang*, for example, lay fifteen kilometres from the centre. It was hard to imagine her walking that distance simply to shift skins from one bucket to the next at the correct time.

We moved on to discussing their expenditure and income. It was then I realised the problem was not simply technical. The group had tanned eighty skins, of which sixty had been sold, according to the man who kept their records. It was very encouraging. To find out their profit, I helped them to calculate their expenses – the cost of the mimosa, the oil, the soap – and their labour.

"Do you pay yourselves an hourly or daily rate, or do you share out the profits at the end?"

"We don't pay ourselves a wage," replied Namunyak, their leader.

"So you simply share out profits after the sales? How much income has each member received so far?"

Some women stared at the ground; others hid their faces in their shawls to muffle their laughter. Namunyak explained that the income was in their account; it had not been shared out yet. She had no idea how much was there as the men kept the books.

After consulting the books, the men said there was a paltry fifty thousand shillings in the account. There should have been about eight times that amount. "What's happened to the rest of the sales income?"

The women's faces remained blank. "Some of the skins were sold on credit," said the record-keeper.

"Didn't you send forty skins to your friend in Arusha?" queried another man.

The women and I looked on with bemused faces as the men became entangled in a web of who had done what, who had touched the money. It struck me that the main cause behind the decline in leather quality was the loss of the women's motivation. For why should the women bother to walk all that distance and carry out the tasks correctly if they were not getting any income? The only surprising fact was that they had produced eighty hides before going on strike.

Concerned by the women's lack of numeracy and financial capacity, I invented a trading game which we played during the workshop. Its purpose was to help them understand how to find the optimum price for maximum income. Half the women were traders and the other half buyers; the commodities were tiny bags of peanuts, and the money was cardboard notes. Some of the traders were told to sell their bags at a high price, others at a low price, while others were given free rein. The buyers were all told they had to buy three bags at the lowest price they could find.

The women threw themselves into the spirit of the game. Fierce bargaining ensued, with much rolling of Maa syllables as they rushed around the training room. At the end the traders counted up the cardboard money they had earned and we went around the room to see who had earned the most. As I had hoped, those who had priced in the middle – neither too high nor too low – had come out ahead. All was as I had anticipated until we got to Mama Nyeyesu's turn.

"How much money did you earn?" asked Esta impatiently.

Mama Nyeyesu held up two brass coins stamped with President Nyerere's head.

"Mama Nyeyesu! *Koko* doesn't mean that sort of money – she wants the cardboard money."

Among the participants, Mama Nyeyesu had the most destitute appearance. "This *is* the money I earned. You told me to sell them to the highest bidder," she insisted.

"Yes, but where's the cardboard money?"

"I don't have any."

"What did you do with the peanuts then?"

"I sold them, like I said." She walked over to the window and called out. Into the training room walked three Maasai warriors munching on peanuts.

"Yes – *she* sold us these peanuts," they confirmed. "*We* paid with those coins. They're good peanuts, not like the ones you get here."

Mama Nyeyesu had trumped us all with her trading skills! The game was such a hit that we played it again the next day, and they wanted to play it a third time, but by then, alas, not a single peanut remained uneaten. Instead, we ended the workshop with a contest to choose a name for their network of groups. Various ideas were proposed, but the final choice was unanimous. Viva MAMA MASAI!

6

•○◯◯●●◯●◯◯◯●●◯◯◯◯●●◯◯◯◯◯●●●●●◯◯◯◯●●◯◯○

Afternoon

*Quiescent, under the towering spotlight of the noon sun, the land
swoons. Life retreats. Even rocks appear to fragment and dissipate into
waves of heat that shimmer from their surface.*

*To a passenger looking from an aeroplane window, the land below
seems flat and interminably dull, a monochrome khaki. The only
feature which stands out is a crop of brown circles – like horseshoes,
but round not ovoid – which appear to have been randomly stamped
on the landscape.*

*Unseen by the passenger, a young woman emerges from one of
these, balancing a blue bucket on her head. On her back she carries a
baby, in one hand a rolled-up cowhide and a toddler trailing from the
other. Hearing the discordant note above the insect chorus, she glances
up and spots the vapour trail cleaving through the flawless blue. It is
the regular mid-week flight, she notes. Some days it passes a little to
the east, or to the west, but always around this heavy time of day.*

*She walks quickly, barefoot, across the baking sand, and wonders
how it feels to fly. She imagines her body becoming very light, weight-
less and floating upwards, and guesses it must feel something like the
way it did when she used to dance with the* morani. *Her feet would
leave the ground for several seconds at a time. A surge of electricity
tingles through her body. She hasn't danced since she had her last baby.
She pauses and gives an upward thrust of her hips, as though to launch*

herself into flight, but instead hitches the baby further up her back and tightens the cloth that holds her in place.

Under a spreading acacia she unrolls her cowhide and joins a group of women sitting in its dappled shade. From her bucket she pulls out strings of beads and a complex web of wires which she rests on the bulging shelf of her belly. Turning the bucket upside down she places on it a beaker of loose beads.

"Who have you been making love to – an elephant?" asks an old woman. "Already this size and you say it's not due for another four moons?"

"It's big because it's a boy. I'm sure of it." The young woman drops her head to hide the smile that plays on her lips. Taking a thread of pearly white beads, she slides a dozen from it. In the crack of dark skin between her thumb and forefinger they glisten like droplets of milk.

"Take my advice – stop drinking milk and eating meat, or it'll grow too big to get out!" continues her neighbour.

She acknowledges this comment with a slight movement of her head, keeping her shoulders motionless in case her baby stirs. The skin on her back and shoulders is a smooth, dark coffee, and her baby's face, pressed against her flesh, appears as its pale creamy froth.

In one quick motion of her hand she sends beads dropping down her length of wire, coil after coil after coil, until they reach the inner web. From another string she draws off more beads – blue, turquoise and yellow. The one with a chipped edge she rejects with a quick flip of the wire. Another is tossed for being too slender and a fatter bead selected in its place. Each must be a perfect match so that the patterns will flare from the centre. Satisfied, she drops them down the coils and weaves them into place with a spoke of wire. She holds the piece of beadwork at arm's length and scrutinises it with a critical eye. It is not quite perfect. With a kneading motion she presses the coils of beads until they obtain a better, flatter shape.

"Is it good?" she asks her neighbour. "Will it sell?"

"Who are we to say what mzungu *will buy?"*

38

It doesn't matter, she tells herself. She knows her work is good, the beads look beautiful. If she earns money she will buy some birthing cloths for the new baby. It's going to be a boy, she is sure. Her first two are girls, and she wants a boy. A son would improve her status and bring favours from her husband. Happy in her thoughts she begins to hum the melody of a song and others join in, adding words and harmonies.

The notes drift past the children who are playing in the sand. In it lies the detritus of life: thorns, leaves, balls of goat dung, scraps of plastic, threads of cloth, seeds, beads, berries, tiny crystals of quartz, snailshells and chips of birds' eggs. A dung beetle rolls a dung ball; each time it nears its destination the children remove the dung ball. Confused, the beetle runs hither and thither, searching for its trophy.

On her back the baby stirs and begins to whimper. Hurriedly she clamps beads into place and offers it her breast. Cradling the baby in one arm she begins another row. With startled eyes the baby twists its head around and gazes at the beads dropping down the wire. Its free fist jabs at the beadwork. She murmurs to her baby and presses its head back against her breast. It sucks extra quickly before relaxing into a steady rhythm.

A breeze graces the warm air, shaking loose a shower of curled seed-pods from the acacia tree. Goats race over to gobble them up.

As the flies and the heat are making the young ones fretful, a fight breaks out over a stick. Smeary and teary-faced toddlers retreat to their mothers' laps. She offers her child a calabash of milk. The girl throws it down and grabs for her mother's free breast. A goat kid leaps forward to nuzzle the fallen calabash and its hooves just clip the beaker of beads on the upturned bucket.

Thousands of tiny seed-beads shoot into the air and plant themselves in the sand.

There are no recriminations, no gestures of irritation.

"A goat is born for jumping," says an older woman. She lays her beadwork aside and begins to retrieve the beads with a length of wire, one by one.

7

Money doesn't grow on thorn bushes

It didn't feel like Christmas as my friend and I arranged the Maasai leather bags and beaded products on our stall under the shade of a frangipani tree. Beyond the high-security gates of the compound lay the palm trees and shimmering waters of Oyster Bay, dotted with the lateen-rigged sails of small *ngalawa* fishing boats. So different to the arid landscape from where the products came. Yet Tanzania encompassed both, and the hunter-fishermen of the coast were held in no higher regard than the pastoralist Maasai.

It was a Saturday, and Oyster Bay was crowded with locals escaping the December heat of Dar es Salaam city. Among the crowds on Coco Beach, some stood out more than others. Certain tall, red-robed men with long braids. They were a long way from home, but in this suburb where the international community and wealthy business people lived, it was a common sight to see Maasai men striding the tree-lined avenues, blending with the extravaganza of tropical flowers spilling from well-watered gardens. They moved with the same fluid stride in which they herded cattle over miles of savannah scrub. I liked the fact that they were not ashamed to wear their tribal dress in the city, their only concession to the urban terrain being strikingly white plastic sandals in lieu of bush ones made of leather or recycled tyres.

What brought them to the city? Why were they not herding cattle? They were all of *morani* age – the warriors – those whose duty is to wander with the cattle, seeking out the best grazing, sleeping rough, guarding the herds against wild animals. Talking to me, they described how their traditional grazing lands have shrunk year on year. Cultivators had moved in and occupied the better-watered parts of the Steppe. Sometimes the Maasai had tried to contest the invasion, but sometimes they had allowed outsiders to farm the land. In the past, there had seemed sufficient for both, and the Maasai are content with very little. But now there was a more powerful threat. The rains were becoming less frequent and less predictable.

The Maasai have been forced to wander even further from their homeland in their search for alternative or supplementary sources of income. Arriving in the city, they soon found a way to make money from their famed fighting skills. Which is why, in the lush green suburbs of Dar es Salaam, you can see Maasai warriors guarding the compounds of the rich against urban predators.

"Is it easy to find work in Dar es Salaam?" I asked a group who worked in my neighbourhood.

"It's not hard; it doesn't take long."

"But there's so much unemployment. Isn't there a lot of competition?"

"That's true. But many people prefer to hire Maasai as night-guards."

"Why's that?"

My informant paused momentarily before answering in a matter-of-fact tone: "Because they know we don't hesitate to kill."

"You mean – you *kill* burglars?" I studied the beads and sequins dangling from their wrists, as they brandished their spears, and the gleam of their ochre make-up as they tossed their long hair braids. They were deadly serious.

While they might have problems with the law, this reputation did wonders for their employment prospects. In fact, the advantages of being Maasai were such that prospective night-guards who were not Maasai were dressing up in red robes and claiming to be Maasai simply to land a job.

"And what do you do with the money you earn?"

"It covers our rent and food. We save a little."

"What are you saving for?"

"To buy cattle," they responded, as though it was obvious, as though there could be no other possible answer.

It was fascinating and baffling, this dual life they lived. How they could engage and profit from the urban lifestyle and yet remain essentially unchanged by it.

"You're sure you don't want to stay here? Settle in the city?"

They laughed. "It's okay for a few years, but then we'll go home."

"And when you're back home, what then?"

"Get married. Have children. Become an elder."

During the training workshop, I had scribbled two goals for Mama Masai in my notebook. The first, to generate income; and the second, to be sustainable.

Summarised in this way, the destination seemed clear and achievable – not overly ambitious. It was just a question of finding the best route. The first goal depended largely on finding customers who would buy their products, and this of course was where the women particularly needed my help. By now the women were producing beaded leather purses and shoulder bags which I thought were attractive and of saleable quality. It was time to dip a toe in the water and test the market. The Christmas craft fair at the American Club that year presented the opportunity.

In Africa, people with money live in towns and cities; they are not found in the savannah among the thorn trees. Occasionally, tourists from other countries visit places like Ngorongoro Crater or Serengeti. Maasai women who happen to live along the game-park routes have the advantage that the market travels to them. They can set up small stalls or barter through the windows when the safari buses pull up to take their photos. This direct contact with the customer enables them to learn what sells and what does not. They quickly discover that *mzungu* are fussy about quality; they do not like broken fastenings or sharp points.

But the Maasai Steppe did not feature on tourists' itineraries. This meant the women's products would have to do the travelling. After a few months I asked Oloserian to tour the groups and send me any products that looked good quality. When the box arrived, I tore it open. Some bags were crooked, evidence that 'kebab' cutting was still in vogue; and one or two had their makers' initials scrawled in ball-point on the good side of the leather. But on the whole the standard was not bad.

At the American Club there was a steady stream of customers throughout the day and our sales were going well. Around midday, when there was a break in the swell, I toured the grounds to check on our competition and compare prices. Most stalls were selling art and craft items made by individual Tanzanians. My friend, who worked with refugees, was selling a range of Burundian baskets with tall pointy lids. I was reassured to see that nobody else was selling beaded leather bags. For the time being we had cornered the market.

As the sun coloured the sky behind the coconut palms, the crowds on Coco Beach became even more densely packed. A traffic jam built up on the bay road as families of Indians bought *mishkaki* kebabs and roasted cassava slices through the windows of their cars. "*Madafu! Madafu!*" they shouted out to attract the vendors whose cycles were festooned with green coconuts. Weaving between the traffic, small boys touted trays of boiled eggs, sweets and cigarettes.

It was the fate of the urban poor to scrabble a living in this way. It was termed the 'informal sector' in development seminars, as opposed to the public or private sectors, from which the fortunate ones received pay cheques. But the locals had a more colourful term: "I work in the 'hot sun' sector," they would tell me, a wry smile on their faces.

They found inventive ways to earn a survival ration, in the eclectic mix of merchandise they traded at the traffic lights. You never knew – the next carload to stop at the red lights might be just the people who are urgently in need of … a vacuum cleaner! A tailored suit? A framed tapestry depicting Mecca! A pair of hypo-allergenic pillows? An iron-ing board! This cute puppy? A bouquet of plastic flowers! A carved ebony table? A standing fan! A natural therapy formula to lighten your skin? A pair of love-birds (cage comes free)! A Princess Diana glitter T-shirt?

"Sir – you prefer a football shirt? Just name your team and I have the right colours in my bag on the pavement, just give me those shillingi notes in your pocket and I will run the change to the next junction!"

"Madam – you definitely need this toolkit, this car jack. No, you do not already have one! Search your car and see they are missing – removed from your car while parked too long in city-centre car park. Note slight dent on rear door lock."

Petty trading was the most common option open to the poor, but others were more creative. There was the man who dug potholes and filled them in so that he could collect payment from passing cars; and the man who threw nails on the road so he could earn a few shillings by helping to change the punctured tyre; and the men who guarded your car or washed it while you did your shopping. Given the huge numbers without formal employment, with no other means of being productive, with no social welfare support for their dependants, the numbers who resorted to petty crime were very few. It was hard not to be moved by the desperate struggles of those at the very bottom of the economic ladder to stay alive, by the strenuous efforts of those one rung above to keep their children out of street-work and in school, and by the striving of those yet one rung further up to scrape together sufficient savings to buy a small parcel of land that they could call their own, a tiny plot of security for their old age. And so it went on. It was not only the Maasai who lived a hand-to-mouth existence.

The sun had dipped below the horizon and it was time to pack up the few remaining items. I counted the cash in the box. It was a modest amount, but nearly every item had been sold, including some from the box of 'rejects' under the table. It was an encouraging start towards the first goal.

8

The quest for water and land

Sequins glint through the rich murkiness of sunlit dust clouds. Warriors are shouting, running, leaping, brandishing their staves and bringing them down with a crackle like gunfire. Blinded by dust, I follow the action through the cacophony of bells, bleats, brays, bellows, whistles, yells – and the zing and thwack of sticks meeting flesh.

A battle was raging, and the enemy was drought. The wells and waterholes of the Steppe had dried up; the wild animals had migrated westwards to the dwindling swamps of Tarangire National Park, or eastwards to the Ruvu River. All who remained on the plateau – the sheep, goats, donkeys, cattle and humans – have been drawn like a magnet to this spot.

Thousands of animals have congregated in the thornbrush corridor leading to the springs at the foot of Landenai mountain. On the plains below more herds await their turn. Like the spokes of a wheel, queues of animals stretch to the horizon in every direction.

The animals have not drunk in three days. Some have walked over twenty kilometres. Through the day they have waited their turn in the dessicating sun. As they approach the grove of trees, they sniff the water in the dust, sense the coolness of moisture in the air, and they want it. Crazy with thirst, the cattle stampede, throwing their heads to the cloudless sky and bellowing as they storm to drink.

With my camera I try to detach a severed moment of the energy and emotions in the scene, and unwittingly capture solid particles as well as images of dust in its lens. A figure emerges from the turmoil and shouts at me. Tempers are frayed. Fear is as thick as the dust in the air.

Water is the most vital mineral on earth, yet it is never traded on Wall Street. In affluent countries we place little value on it, scarcely thinking about where it comes from or how long it may last. How carelessly we leave the taps running.

In the Steppe, water dictates where one lives, the pattern of life and the social order. It governs the timetable of the day, the seasonal migrations, the timing of initiation to adulthood or eldership. It may even dictate when one dies.

The solitary mountain of Landenai is the highest point in the Steppe. At over two thousand metres, it is high enough and cool enough to capture condensation from the passing warm air. On its slopes a rich diversity of plants and trees flourish, each named and known by the Maasai, providing a compendium of herbal remedies for the treatment of themselves and their animals. Once a year the elders ordain a day when they climb the mountain to gather its medicinal resources. Conservation of the natural environment, both the wild animals and the plants and trees, has a long tradition in Maasai society.

The Project was in the middle of constructing a large water scheme based on the multiple springs at the foot of Landenai and distributing it to various points on the plains. But even a water project could not produce a miracle. It could not produce water from dry rocks. It could only conserve what was there and distribute it without loss.

Times of drought were the only occasion when the Maasai objected to being photographed. It was understandable. The men's pride and the well-being of their families rested on the health and strength of their cattle. They were visibly tense; fearful that this year the rains might not come in time … their herds might die … famine might follow …

'There is no such thing as skill during a drought, only God prevails,' says a Maasai proverb.

To the Maasai, cattle are a symbol of God's love and presence. Specifically, God's love for them, the Maasai people. Each generation of children listens to stories around the fireplace and learns the legend that *Engai* created three groups of peoples: hunter-gatherers (the Dorobo group), cultivators (the Bantu group) and herders (the Maasai group). To the first group *Engai* gave the wild animals and honey bees; to the second group seeds and grain; and to the Maasai all the cattle in the world. In those days the earth and sky were one. *Engai* let the cattle descend to earth along a rope made of bark. Then the hunter-gatherer people severed the rope, and earth and sky became separate domains.

Viewed through this myth it is easier to appreciate the strong bond which the Maasai have with their cattle. God appointed the Maasai to be their guardians. They are like heavenly beasts, a touchpoint with *Engai* on an earth which has been severed from the sky. Each and every cow is named. Each of them is counted out of the *engang*, and counted in again. It is said that an experienced herder does not need to count; simply by sweeping his eye over the herd, he will know which cow is missing. For centuries cattle have provided the Maasai with their food and drink, their clothes and bedding; have functioned as their savings account, insurance policy and old-age pension

But tales of drought, famine and disease are also part of their history and oral tradition, a body of wisdom handed down to each new generation of boys as they prepare for manhood and the responsibility of caring for the herds.

In the 1880s the bovine plague arrived on the shores of Africa. Within a few years it had spread destruction from the Horn of Africa to the Cape. Rinderpest or 'steppe murrain' is a highly infectious viral disease that rapidly destroys entire populations of animals. In Asia it was endemic, but animals there had largely acquired immunity. The evidence points to colonials as the culprits in bringing it to Africa. It is known that Italians imported significant quantities of Asian cattle into Abyssinia in the 1880s and rinderpest appeared shortly thereafter. In Tanganyika (then German East Africa) a subsequent outbreak was traced to a German major who had imported cattle from Bombay for an expedition to the interior.

During a period of ten years, rinderpest, along with East Coast fever, ravaged the continent. Tanganyika was among the countries worst affected. A German lieutenant present at the time estimated that ninety per cent of cattle and fifty per cent of wild animals died during this pandemic. Others calculate that up to ninety-five per cent of ungulates (cattle, giraffe, buffalo, wildebeest, eland, kudu and other antelopes) in East Africa succumbed.

For the Maasai, the loss of their herds was catastrophic. The famine which followed has been graphically described by the Austrian explorer, Oscar Baumann, who travelled through Tanganyika at that time. He describes a Maasai settlement in Ngorongoro Crater:

> There were women wasted to skeletons from whose eyes the madness of starvation glared ... children looking more like frogs than human beings ... warriors scarcely able to crawl on all fours, and apathetic languishing elders. Swarms of vultures followed them from high, awaiting their certain victims.[1]

He also records how Maasai parents would offer him their children in exchange for food. When Baumann refused, the adults abandoned their children in his camp. 'Soon our caravan was swarming with Maasai children and it was touching to see how the porters cared for the little urchins.' One traveller described the corpses of humans and animals lying so thick on the ground that 'vultures have forgotton to fly'. Another declared: 'Never before in the memory of man, or by the voice of tradition, have the cattle died in such numbers; never before has the wild game suffered.'[2]

It is estimated that two-thirds of the Maasai people died.[3]

The plague-induced famine was accompanied by epidemics, and an explosion of the tsetse fly and sand fly (carried there in ships' ballast), which both bore diseases affecting humans. The Europeans were also responsible for importing smallpox to Africa, and its spread was facilitated by the colonial-driven growth in caravan traffic. It spread rapidly from the coastal ports up the newly forged caravan routes such as that which followed the Ruvu-Pangani river to Arusha. By the mid 1890s German doctors noted that every second African had a pock-marked face. Oral accounts of this time are still preserved in the families whom I got to know. Sainoi's husband, the one who had twelve wives, was eighty-five years old, and could recall as a boy hearing stories from his elders who had lived through the great bovine plague and the ensuing famine.

The ramifications of the plague were immense for Africa. Some believe that it caused a levelling of African society to uniform impoverishment, and that its legacy of poverty is still being felt today. Cultivators as well as pastoralists were affected. It facilitated the colonisation of Kenya's great tracts of empty land – land which had been the home of the Maasai. The plague is blamed not only for breaking the social and economic backbone of many of the most prosperous and advanced communities in Tanganyika, but also for initiating the breakdown of a long-established ecological balance.[4]

Such is the hidden legacy of colonialism.

I was forced to slow down as I approached Orkasmet, the district capital of Simanjiro. Thousands of cattle, sheep and goats were on the move. Herds of them were parked under trees at regular intervals and on the dusty trails which radiated from the local wells. Entering the town, I found it taken over by animals, its dusty streets dampened by fresh cow dung. Herds were parked on every corner, and the vacant lot outside the district offices was pungent with the unfolding disaster.

I stayed in a small guest house on the edge of town and hardly got any sleep for the constant ringing of bells, as cattle herds passaged to and from the wells throughout the night.

The Maasai are masters of conservation. They are known to walk their herds at night to reduce dehydration. Some selectively breed their cattle to produce lighter coat colour which is more resistant to heat and drought. As the smaller waterholes dry up, the population around the permanent sources swells, and a complex system of water rationing and rotation swings into effect, governed by the clan elders. The common system is a three-day rotation for herds and humans alike.

Orkasmet lies on a rocky plateau and its name means 'the place of the wells'. The wells are man-made but have existed as long as anyone can remember; the settlement developed more recently and only because of the year-round water source. A traditional Maasai well is a sight worth seeing as it is impossible to do it justice through photographs or description. It is something of a cross between a well and a waterhole, and bears no resemblance to the Western nursery rhyme image which the word conjures up.

From a distance it is hidden. As we approached in the early morning, pushing our way past the traffic jam of animals awaiting their drinking hour, nothing was visible save a low rise where women with water containers and donkeys were congregating. My guide led me to a hidden entrance. We descended steeply in a kind of tunnel slippery with fresh cow dung. Its sides were high and narrow, and although there was no roof, the sky was concealed by a cover of thorn bushes which grew overhead. After a short distance we emerged onto a small narrow balcony. A row of cattle were sucking water out of two long water troughs. At the far end a tall *moran* emptied a bucket of water into the trough. Pushing past the line of cattle on the narrow ledge, we reached the edge and peered over. For the first time I caught a glimpse of the well and an understanding of its structure.

The balcony on which I was standing looked across a large, deep crater punctuated by a complex of holes within it, some visible, some hidden, and a complex of ramps and steps and balconies which dropped deeper and deeper. The perimeter rim of the well at Orkasmet is about a kilometer in circumference, but the crater narrows sharply with depth. Below me a chain of *morani* perched on a series of ladder-like steps were hoisting buckets of water out of the depths up to the water troughs. Like Dante's inferno, there are a series of levels leading down into the bowels of the earth. On certain levels, goats and sheep were drinking; on other levels women were washing clothes or filling their jerrycans; still further down, a row of spears leaned against the crater wall where a group of *morani* had stripped to have a wash. At the lowest level of all, the chain of *morani* with their buckets ended in a small murky pool. A bucket reached the lowest man; he dipped it in the water, heaved it up onto his head and passed it up to the next man, who in turn heaved it up to his shoulders and passed it on up the line. As we retraced our steps back up, there was a warning shout that more cattle were ready to descend. We hurried out. The narrow tunnel ramp is not the place to be in a cattle stampede. Reaching the top, we walked clockwise around the embankment to the next entrance and descended. This one belonged to a different clan. In fact, the well is a series of wells contained within a single crater, for each clan has their own access ramp and watering points for their cattle and each clan's cattle know their own individual approach ramp carved out of the sandy rock. Altogether, scattered around the perimeter there were perhaps eight to ten different clan entrances, each one leading to a series of descending waterholes, so that the whole site resembled an enormous rabbits' warren. It has acquired these dimensions over the years as the Maasai have dug ever deeper and wider in search of the dwindling water. Some families will be regular 'members' of the well, investing in its construction and upkeep. Those who contribute get priority rights. But ultimately, no stranger of a member clan is refused water. It is a point of honour.

It seemed impossible that this small source of water could be sufficient for all the herds that I had seen waiting in the town. I talked to a group of Maasai men to find out how they were coping.

Every one of them agreed that the droughts were becoming more frequent. "In the past, there might be a drought every eight to ten years. Now it's every two to three years," said one elder with looping ear lobes. "How long will this well last? The others are already closed down. What shall we do if this one fails?"

"Drought is not new to us," said another. "We know about drought; we know how to cope. But these days the droughts last longer. We used to save moist grass areas for times of emergency. But since commercial farms were established, these are closed to us."

"How do you cope now?"

"We must travel further and longer."

"We go to Ol Doinyo Lengai mountain and pray for rain," said the elder.

There are many voices critical of the Maasai's love affair with cattle. Some say that they have brought the droughts upon themselves: that they keep too many cattle; that it is their overgrazing which has decreased the ground cover and lowered the water table. But over-grazing by the Maasai cannot account for the melting snowline on the peak of Mount Kilimanjaro which overlooks the Steppe.

Nevertheless, the perilous situation of the Maasai today *is* largely a man-made problem, not a natural one. The early European explorers may have come to Africa for the sake of adventure, or with a genuine thirst for knowledge (although Ptolemy had already recorded snow mountains near the equator, and the Arabs knew that Lake 'Victoria' was the source of the Nile), but those financing their expeditions had their eyes on other things.

Joseph Thomson's book *Through Masai Land* records his exploits in being the first white person to successfully pass through Maasai territory in 1883. It gained a huge readership in Britain at the time, and triggered long-lasting repercussions. Rider Haggard's novel, *King Solomon's Mines*, is said to be based on Thomson's exploits and writings. In a note to the preface of the 1887 edition of his book, Thomson adds that great political changes had taken place in East Africa since his first edition had been published:

Then (1885) Masai Land was for the first time made known to the world; now it has come within the 'sphere of British influence' – a delicate way, I suppose, of saying that it now practically forms a part of our Imperial possessions ... It only remains for the commercial world, seeking new fields and new outlets for its trade, to open its eyes to the extreme fertility of the soil.[5]

German explorers were also in the region. Dr Fischer's expedition into Maasailand followed the course of the Ruvu-Pangani river inland – the route that I followed every time I visited the Mama Masai groups, although he probably travelled on the east bank which he says was uninhabited, rather than the west bank where he records the presence of 'marauding Maasai'. He took this route because he teamed up with an Arab trading caravan for greater protection, and the Pangani was their regular trading route from the coast to the Kilimanjaro region.

When Fischer presented his findings to his financiers – the Hamburg Geographical Society – he pointed out that the transport of goods to the coast could be done in ten days using strong Maasai asses. The direction is important; he was not talking of bringing in supplies, but exporting goods. Soon after, both Britain and Germany established East Africa companies and concluded an agreement ceding Germany influence over the southern half (Tanganyika), and Britain over the northern half (Kenya).

In 1904, in their weakened, desperate state after the rinderpest plague and famine, Maasai leaders were pressured into finger-printing an agreement with the British, which decreed that the Maasai would relinquish all of their northern territory except Laikipia and move into the southern 'reserve'. In his book Thomson described how Maasailand was comprised of two contrasting regions. The southerly region, he says, is 'sterile and unproductive in the extreme. This is owing, not to a barren soil, but to the scantiness of the rainfall, which for about three months in the year barely gives sufficient sustenance to scattered tufts of grass'. Of the northerly region he writes that 'a more charming region is probably not found in all Africa ... there are dense patches of flowering shrubs, noble forests ... great herds of cattle, sheep and goats ... sweet-scented clover, anemone, coniferous trees ... the country is a very network of babbling brooks and streams ...'[6]

To defuse a potential outcry over the signing of the 1904 agreement in London, the Commissioner sent a telegraph to the Foreign Office saying 'All the [Maasai] chiefs readily assented to these proposals which were really their own wishes'.[7] To sweeten the move, the agreement declared that Laikipia and the southern reserve were to belong exclusively to the Maasai people 'so long as the Maasai as a race shall exist, and that European or other settlers shall not be allowed to take up land in the settlement.'[8]

In 1911, the British took Laikipia and sold the land to white settlers.

Together, the 1904 and 1911 agreements reduced Maasai grazing lands to one quarter of their former extent. The fact that the 1911 treaty abrogated the terms of the former added salt to the wounds of the Maasai. Yet the Secretary of State for the Colonies reported to the House of Commons in July 1911 that 'The Masai came to a unanimous and even enthusiastic decision to move to the Southern Reserve'.[9] It is hard to believe that anyone in their right mind would prefer 'barren soil' and 'scattered tufts of grass' to 'sweet-scented clover' and 'babbling brooks'. Political spin was already a practised art, it seems!

Sir Charles Eliot, the first Commissioner of British East Africa, gave his reasons in that uniquely British colonial style that ensured they got what they wanted, yet portrayed themselves as the custodians of fair play:

> The right of the Maasai people to inhabit particular districts is undoubted, but their right to monopolize particular districts and keep everyone else out appears to me most questionable ... I cannot admit that wandering tribes have the right to keep other superior races out of large tracts merely because they have acquired the habit of straggling over far more land than they can utilize.[10]

The latter was a false impression. The problem for the Maasai was that they practised such an environmentally sensitive land-use system that they left no adverse trace on the land which they were using. One could say that their practices were ahead of their time. Under normal circumstances, the Maasai are careful managers of their natural resources. Their traditional semi-nomadic lifestyle ensures that habitats are rested in rotation and given time to replenish. Over time they developed a complex system of rights and governance to ensure sustainability.

Certain nutrient-rich grazing areas were 'closed' during most of the year in order to be available during the dry season; others were held as special emergency reserves to be used only in times of extreme drought. Thus the move to the southern 'reserve' not only reduced their land by three quarters, but abolished their access to vital nutrient-rich 'safety net' grazing reserves.

'It is now recognized that excision of the most fertile moist parts of Masailand ... has had the ultimate effect of precluding the rest of it from pastoral use,' writes Kathryn Tidrick, a social historian who specialises in the colonial period.[11] In other words, pastoralism in the arid southern portion without periodic access to the moist northern portion, was always going to be unviable and unsustainable. Half the puzzle was missing.

Thus the Maasai became a victim of their own enlightened and sustainable herding practices. White settlers quickly occupied the fertile highlands which they lost. Many were British emigrants, but another sizeable group was moving northwards:

> Many Afrikaners were exiled after the Boer war for refusing to take the oath of allegiance to the British Government in South Africa. By ox-wagon they trekked up to Tanganyika where they were received with open arms by the wily Huns, who gave them land at Arusha. This was not as a benevolent gesture, but so that they could be used as a buffer against the savage marauding Masai warriors. They suffered sorely at the time, but after the Germans had tamed the Masai they found they had been allotted the most fertile land in the country.[12]

I remember stumbling upon one of the Boer farms while visiting a land rehabilitation project outside Arusha. On the lower slopes of Mount Meru, the outlines of the settler's fields are still visible, along with an orchard of neglected overgrown fruit trees. The farm is abandoned; the settler's house is derelict but still standing, and commands a breathtaking view to Mount Kilimanjaro and the Amboseli plains.

Sir Charles Eliot also recruited Boer settlers in Kenya. Three hundred of them were granted land permits in 1904. White settlement was pursued aggressively by the British as the main means of repaying the huge debts accumulated from building the Kenya–Uganda railway. Tanganyika was less affected by white settlers than Kenya, but after the British had taken over from the Germans, the Maasai suffered their greatest land losses.

Having deprived the Maasai of their best land, the British declared that the Maasai kept too many cattle; they were the culprits who were decreasing the fertility of the land – such as remained theirs to use. A succession of district officers banged their heads against the Maasai's bond to cattle, and tried various ways to lure or force them into selling their livestock in order to reduce their need for land. The Maasai remained impervious.

In fact, they could not drastically reduce the number of their cattle without compromising their nutrition. Milk is their staple food and the average Maasai needs to consume at least one litre per day to stay healthy. The Maasai told me that they calculate ten cows per capita to meet a family's food requirements throughout the year. Not all cows are milking in a given month; some are youngsters not yet milking, and the milk has to be shared with the young calves. And now, even the best milker in a herd has low milk production due to the poor browsing.

When the Maasai first reached the lush plains lying between Lake Victoria and the crater highlands of Ngorongoro, they named them *Siringet*, which means 'grassland unlimited, without a boundary'. It must have seemed like paradise. It was a place of plenty, and the Maasai co-existed with the herds of wildebeest and zebra and the prides of lion that followed their migrations. In the 1950s the British created the Serengeti National Park and the Maasai lost this massive grassland. Some tried to stay on. Their forced eviction in the 1960s was witnessed by the son of a park ranger:

One day my father said, "We're going down to remove the Maasai from Moru Kopjes" ... I remember that day as hell and bloody fury

– the flames and smoke and dust, confusion, animals and people, shouting and shooting. The smoke and the burning – the horror of it all. The villages were torched and the dogs were shot ... The women and children were rounded up into trucks.[13]

Although conservation is important and imperative, it was not necessary to evict the Maasai. They do not hunt wild animals for food and are natural conservationists, history providing the evidence that they can live symbiotically with wild animals without inflicting harm. In 1901, the Hindes, who were stationed for many years in a Maasai area, recorded that

in former days when the Maasai occupied the whole of the plains of East Africa, the game was quite tame ... it was not uncommon to see antelopes, zebras and gazelles grazing among the Maasai flocks in the immediate vicinity of their kraals. But during the last few years the game has not only been hunted by Europeans but even by Wakikuyu and Wakimba natives ... in consequence [the animals have] become much shyer.[14]

Nowadays even ecologists agree that traditional pastoralism is compatible with wildlife conservation, and some claim that the cattle herds of the Maasai and other pastoralists have actually played a key role in creating the great savannah grasslands of East Africa.

Tanzanian independence in 1961 brought no abatement in land losses for the Maasai. In the Steppe, 124,000 acres of their grazing lands with the best rainfall in Simanjiro District were taken to create around eighty large-scale farms growing cash crops for export. Some of these were established with donor aid and at that time they were run as parastatal farms. However, since Tanzania abandoned socialism they have been sold off to high-ranking bureaucrats, politicians and foreign agro-businesses.

Further valuable grazing land, water sources and drought-refuge areas such as Silato swamp were lost to the Maasai when Tarangire National Park was established. Although it lies on the western border of the Steppe, the repercussions of this loss affected a far wider area, leading to increased pressure on remaining water sources such as Landenai.

Compounding these large land losses, small-scale cultivators have encroached wherever farming is possible. For this, the Maasai themselves are partly to blame. When land tenure regulations were relaxed in the late 1990s, their leaders lacked foresight.

"There was land," Nyange, a son of Sainoi, explained to me, "but the village leaders distributed it to whoever asked. Now arable fields block our routes to water. As we pass through our herds sometimes trample or consume crops. Conflicts ensue. Even battles."

More and more, the Maasai themselves are having to supplement their pastoralism with cultivation. But that, too, is dependent upon rainfall. I was learning that the biggest obstacle to increasing agricultural production in East Africa is not the lack of rainfall, but the unpredictability of it. Cultivation is like gambling. In Tanzania there is an abundance of under-used fertile arable land, but the weather is capricious.

When rain does fall in the Steppe, it tends to come in cataclysmic downpours. I was once caught in a mini-cyclone at Ruvu Remiti, a small settlement on the river. For the first half-hour wind and rain blasted from the west. As I sheltered with others under the overhanging roof of the village shop, the wind suddenly snatched three tin roofs and tossed them into the sky. Children who had been sheltering inside shot out screaming. Just as suddenly, the wind died; the rain ceased. It became eerily still and silent. I said my farewells, but as I reached the door of my car, the roaring gale started again, from the opposite direction, but with equal fury. Those roofs which had withstood the earlier westerly onslaught succumbed to the easterly.

As unpredictably as the storm had arrived, it departed. Leaving the soggy village, with its sodden inhabitants staring at the ruins of their homes, I was amazed to find, not far ahead, that the sandy track became completely dry. Not a drop. The torrential rain had fallen in a band so narrow and so well-defined you could have constructed a boundary fence.

The drought was forcing Maasai to turn to other activities. In Landenai I learnt that some had even turned to mining. Maasai as miners? It sounded extraordinary. I decided to find out more.

In 1967, a previously unknown mineral was discovered at Mererani in northern Simanjiro District. Named 'tanzanite' after the country, it has a dazzling blue colour when cut, and is one of the rarest minerals in the world. In fact, this seam in Simanjiro is the world's only known source of the gemstone.

Mererani is a rough area. The potential value of its gemstones lying below ground – estimated by one mining company to be in the region of one thousand million dollars – has attracted the desperately poor and those who do not hesitate to exploit others in their desire to get rich quickly. The combination is lethal. At the time of my visit in 2000, the artisanal mines were unregulated and relied on child labour. Small boys, known as snakes (*nyoka*) for their ability to squirm along the low, narrow tunnels, delivered tools, food and water to the miners underground. The boys were lowered into the shafts by ropes; the tunnels below were poorly ventilated and the boys breathed in graphite dust. Fatal accidents occurred with horrifying regularity – tunnel collapses, flooding, breakdown of the ventilation system, as well as fights and murder. Above ground in the ugly shanty settlements, girls worked in bars and cheap hotels which functioned as brothels.

It was an area I had been advised to drive through with doors locked and windows closed. The rate of theft, rape and violence was said to be high. While there were global mining companies working there to extract the mineral, most of the bad things – the risky mining, the shoddy tunnels, the excessive working hours – took place in what was termed 'artisanal' mines. A wealthy person would buy a concession for a certain plot of land, not knowing what was there. The concession was then sub-divided and leased out to further middlemen. These people then contracted labourers who were promised a percentage share of any finds which they made. Circumstances varied, depending upon the nature of the 'boss'. Some were better than others. But in many cases the miners were forced to run up tabs at local shops owned by the contractors, and saw most of their income evaporate in the interest they had to pay.

On visiting some of the artisanal sites, I witnessed the truth of the reports I had been given. I interviewed several Maasai who were digging with the most elementary of picks and hoes at the bottom of shafts. In this area the mineral-bearing seam was not so far underground. It was like a quarry which had been divided up into hundreds of small deep pits, none of them shored up with any kind of support.

"This is not what we choose to do. It's the drought. We have to live," one *moran* told me, shame-faced. He hadn't found anything that day or the day before, but three days earlier he had made a find. He pulled out a grubby handkerchief and untied it. In the middle lay a cluster of small, dull-blue chips of rock. He knotted it carefully again.

Maasai women had also come into the area. I spoke to some who were charging three hundred shillings for a container of water which they had brought by donkey.

It was depressing and I didn't stay long. Before the miners came, the Maasai and their herds had inhabited this area. One billion dollars of buried treasure changed that.

Most of the women's groups with whom I was involved lived in the Ruvu valley on the eastern edge of the Steppe, and relied upon the river for their water source.

On exceptionally clear mornings in the Steppe, I could see snow floating in the northern sky. It was this apparition that encouraged the Maasai to settle in the area – a rain-shadow terrain where there are no wells or springs. The Ruvu has certain parallels to the Nile River though on a far smaller scale, for it is a year-round river fed by the high rainfall and melting snows of Mount Kilimanjaro.

I could never get over the fact that there was a river hidden within such an arid landscape, nor that it could have so little impact on the environment. The biggest irony was that although the people and their herds were never short of drinking water, in every other way life was unsustainable in this valley. It was hot and dry, with little vegetation, for the sulphur content of the soil meant that in large areas even grass did not grow. So there was water to drink but no grazing for the herds. Up on the escarpment grass was green from the early morning mist and the cooler altitude – but there was no water to drink. Life was a tension between the two needs, and the herds endlessly migrated between river and ridge.

The majority of settlements were located two to five kilometres distant from the river, to avoid the flat land which was flooded when it rained. If there was time in the early evening, I loved to visit the river. At Ngage the river was close enough to walk there. As one approached, the thorn trees grew higher and thicker, and the graceful green trunks of yellow acacia trees appeared. Close to the water's edge the temperature was several degrees lower. The muddy-coloured waters of the river swirled swiftly by the reedy banks, in a hurry to escape the hot valley without losing too much of its precious load of water. Among the reeds weaver birds built their pendulous nests; egrets and herons stalked fish and kingfishers darted here and there. Normally, I would have been tempted to swim, but there were crocodiles – as large as a man, they told me. I never saw one, but word of their reputation and how they pulled children under as they collected water was sufficient to banish all thoughts of bathing in the river.

If I walked along the thin strip of forest beside the river, after a kilometre or two I came to a hunters' safari camp set at a bend in the river. It was an indication of the presence of big game in the area – lion, leopard and buffalo. I never saw either the big game or the hunter tourists. But they came, apparently. They flew in to one of the vast pans of dried mud where jeeps met them and took them to the camp. I contacted the safari company who said they were happy for Mama Masai members to sell their products at the camp, but when the women turned up one day they were chased away.

If I followed the Ruvu valley northwards towards Kilimanjaro, after fifty kilometres or so I came to what seemed like a mirage – a vast lake. It did not exist at the time of Dr Fischer's expedition. The lake is called Nyumba ya Mungu, which means 'House of God' in Swahili, a translation from the original Maasai name, *Enkaji Engai*. The name originally referred to a grotto in which there was a rock shaped like a throne (*Olorika Lengai*), hence the name. The grotto was located near a low-lying marshy area. In 1965, the government of Tanzania built a dam across the river for the generation of electricity and the area was flooded. So the 'House of God' and its throne now lie below the lake waters, and the Maasai lost another important grazing refuge. Cultivators and fishermen migrated into the area, some from as far afield as Malawi.

The expanse of water was extraordinary. On my first visit I was entranced by the beauty of the lake and the sheer quantity of its bird life. Part of its appeal stemmed from the striking contrast with the brown, parched land surrounding it. It was an oasis for birds of every kind, and completely hidden away. Although much of its shoreline is dry, caking mud or thorn bush, there are some extensive areas of reed beds. No tourist jeeps mar its shores – few foreigners have heard of the place. Driving around its edge I scanned the shores with my binoculars. There were hundreds of geese, ducks, pelicans, fish eagles, ibis, jacana ... The women pushed past egrets as they went to draw water. Trees were jammed with nesting herons, and the water's edge with every kind of wader. Along the shoreline squadrons of turquoise bee-eaters turned on stiff wings like mini-kites. Offshore, among the dug-out canoes of local fishermen, flocks of skimmer birds flew so low they caught small fish in their open bills without getting their feathers wet.

With the snowy peak of Kilimanjaro reflected in its still waters, it was a veritable Garden of Eden for the House of God.

9

'The neck cannot go above the head'

I was lost. I killed the engine and got out. The *engang* where the woman whom Montse had nicknamed the Queen of Sheba lived, should have been visible on the south side of the road. But there was no sign of habitation, only interminable thorn trees. Was there an *engang* hiding among them? Their thorn-brush barriers provided such perfect camouflage that one could easily crash into an *engang* before recognition dawned. I walked a few paces in various directions. The only visible sign of life was a racing hare, the only sounds were the squawks from a pair of hornbills and the frenzied percussion of invisible insects.

Too confidently, I had told Oloserian that I would find my own way from the main road and meet him at Lorimba. I reversed the car and retraced my route. On my third traverse I was relieved to spot a reddish cloud in the distance. The Project jeep arrived with a flourish of dust and Oloserian's smiling face in the front seat. I followed their trail and an *engang* suddenly materialised on the north side, like an occultist's trick.

The Queen of Sheba and her entourage welcomed us.

"*Mama yeyo! Takwenya?*"

"*Iko!*"

"*Sopai?*"

"*Ipa*."

"You've moved your *engang*!" I exclaimed, once the greetings were deemed sufficient.

The Queen of Sheba looked puzzled. "It's where it's always been. Here's the hut where we keep the beads – don't you remember?"

She was right. Inside everything was exactly as before. "But I thought you lived on the other side of the road?" I was truly confused, but Oloserian was laughing. "They dug a new road, Mama Joy! It used to pass by on the north side and now it passes to the south. Look – over there you can see the old track."

By paying a visit to each Mama Masai group *in situ* I hoped to gain some insight into their circumstances and the challenges they faced in making a go of their beadwork business. After a positive start, things were beginning to stutter in the second year.

The fuel gauge on my car suggested that communications were going to pose a major problem. The original groups were located along the Ruvu valley – Lorimba, Engorini, Loiborsoit and Ngage. Then outliers were added at Orkasmet, Namalulu and Landenai, turning the crescent into a misshapen Y with its tail curling the wrong way. Eighty kilometres separated Lorimba, the tip of the tail, from Ngage, while Namalulu on the western axis lay a hundred kilometres from Lorimba. From 2003 onwards, when new groups began emerging in the north around Nyumba ya Mungu, the crescent stretched to 150 kilometres. Linking these points were the most rudimentary of tracks; my average driving speed was thirty kilometres per hour.

There were no telephones. Donkeys carried goods but never people. Maasai men travelled on foot or occasionally on bikes, and once a month a truck ventured from the main road as far as Loiborsoit. The only regular transport was the wind that lifted dust from one spot and deposited it in another.

Why were the groups so dispersed? One reason was that the population in the Steppe is sparse; the environment cannot sustain a dense population of people and animals. But the other reason was that the groups were established only where there was take-up of the idea, where women demonstrated their interest by making the effort to create a group.

Had I fully appreciated the geographical challenges at the outset, I would have jettisoned the whole beadwork idea.

After leaving the main highway at the foot of the Paré Mountains, it took me about half an hour to reach the narrow bridge over the Ruvu at Gunge, which marked the entry-point into the Steppe and Simanjiro District. A line of satiny, grey-barked baobab trees, like scarecrow-sentinels, guided me towards a muddy stretch. After heavy rain this section could be impassable for days, sometimes littered with sunken carcasses of trucks waiting for the mud to dry. The only other river crossing added six hours to the journey time. It was not a problem when entering the Steppe because the texture of the mud could be quickly assessed at the outset. But it was a gamble when trying to leave, for the alternative route lay in the opposite direction and it was impossible to predict how much rain had fallen at Gunge until one had committed to driving there. It was tantalising to be within twenty minutes of the solid tarmac of the main highway yet be forced to backtrack and follow the six-hour loop to the other river crossing.

But usually it was dry. Bumping down the slope to the bridge, the vast Steppe unrolled before me like a grainy photo. It was not entirely flat. A low escarpment dissected the horizon, and here and there solitary summits emerged from the savannah like shark fins. Without these landmarks – remnants of vanished volcanoes – I could never have found my way. Once across the bridge the vista disappeared, and I was submerged in thorn bush.

Half an hour or so beyond the bridge lay Lorimba and the first of the women's groups. I nearly always dropped in on my way through. Greetings were the first task on arrival and could not be rushed. Meanwhile, children gathered like swarms of flies. They gathered around me, my passengers and my car. They scribbled in the dust which cloaked the vehicle. They wiped a viewing patch in the rear door window and peered inside to see what I had brought. "Oranges!" one exclaimed, and word passed down the line from the tallest to the smallest. I opened the door and extracted some from the sack which I had bought at a wayside halt.

Goats arrived and licked at the tyres and bodywork, seeking the taste of ocean salt from Dar es Salaam. When this carwash was complete, they settled in the shade underneath the vehicle. Apart from the austere border around the huts, this was the only proper shade available. The women and I retired to the faint comfort of a 'shade-tree' – a spindly thorn with leaves no bigger than the dung beetles that scurried in the dust beneath. Here they spread out leather skins and one or two brought three-legged stools of a low scooped design, hand-carved, smooth and polished from use.

Business never began right away. Members lived in scattered *engangs*, several kilometres distant. Children were dispatched to spread the word of our arrival, or if the women had been forewarned and on the lookout for my dust trail, they appeared out of the bush, on cue. As they greeted me each woman pulled out the products which she had made. Even if there were other pressing matters on my agenda, first I had to inspect what they had made. This was an exciting moment for all of us. I never knew what to expect. Exclamations and a buzz of anticipation ran through the group as they waited for my pronouncement – *sidai!* or *siyo sidai!* – good or not good, or sometimes *dama sidai!* very good.

To encourage them in the early days, I often bought their good products on the spot. Sometimes they had produced beautiful work – exactly what would sell – or had created a new design, and I would go into eulogies. Other times it seemed that there was an unsalvageable error with each and every item and it was hard on both sides to hide our disappointment. It was important to explain carefully what was wrong so that mistakes didn't re-occur. I tried to be strict and not accept unsaleable items. But there were times when their pleas and circumstances tugged at my heartstrings and I caved in.

"Why are these beaded Maasai men *green*?" I inquired as I inspected the Lorimba group's work.

"Don't you think it's a nice colour?" asked Nemberes, their youthful leader with her gazelle eyes.

"Yes, but ... Maasai don't wear green."

"We ran out of red beads so we substituted green," she explained.

Full marks for initiative but zero for marketing sense, I wanted to tell her. No tourist will buy little *green* Maasai men. But it was bizarre for me to try to explain why to them. To insist that as replicas of Maasai they had to be dressed in red; had to be tall and skinny; had to be wearing dangling earrings and necklaces. They didn't get it at first, this image of themselves. They hadn't chosen it, they didn't own it, and were completely powerless to change it. As an outsider I knew more about it than they did! As I stressed that in future their beaded Maasai men should be red, I wondered what hidden signals this conveyed. Did it suggest that spontaneity is wrong, that individuality is not encouraged? That conformity is more important than innovation? These were not the development messages I wanted them to absorb.

Frankly, they didn't care. They were happy for anything that brought them money.

"Look – this one's a reject, she's missing a leg," I pointed out.

"So she is. But is there a problem with that? Tell your customers that this one is a handicapped Maasai ... she went to the river to fetch water and a crocodile bit her leg off. Maybe you can charge more for a handicapped Maasai?"

If we shared a common sense of humour, patience was a different matter. Theirs was elastic; it could stretch and stretch. Mine stretched a little, and then snapped.

"Next time, you should buy more red beads. Don't substitute another colour. Did you try to buy red beads in the market?"

Silence fell on the group.

"It didn't happen."

"And why not?"

"Because ... we didn't go."

An enigmatic answer. It could cover a multitude of reasons, ranging from cultural taboos and gender roles, to lack of foresight in putting money aside, or simply to lack of interest.

The sustainability of the business depended upon the women procuring their own beads. The Project was due to close in a year or two, and by then they had to be completely self-reliant. Traders brought beads into the area, but their prices were exorbitant and made the Mama Masai products uncompetitive. The closest place where the women could buy them in bulk at a lower price was Arusha. But getting to Arusha could take six hours or more and was also costly.

After our business was concluded the women showed me the primary school they were building with Project support. Until it was finished and a teacher assigned, the closest school was at Ruvu Remiti, some fifteen kilometres distant. "It's too far to walk to Remiti each day. Even the older children can't manage it. Those with money rent lodgings so they can attend," said Nemberes.

This explained why none of the women at Lorimba had been schooled or spoke Swahili. Their lack of literacy meant that they had to rely on memory for all the instructions and management of the group, and sometimes their memory was faulty.

"Are you interested in learning to read and write?" I inquired. "We could request the Project to organise adult literacy classes."

I studied their faces, trying to gauge their interest. It was not clear. But later, when the time for departure came, Nemberes leaned against the open window of my car as though to stop me leaving. "The thought of learning to read and write is sending shivers down my back!" she suddenly confided. "It's been my dream for such a long time." A luminous smile flashed across her face.

Shooing goats from underneath the car and dislodging children from the tailgate, Oloserian and I headed on to the next group. The road was empty save for a few cows. After half an hour we passed the primary school and a solitary shop at Ruvu Remiti. Here the track splits into two. The left fork – with the daily bus – climbs onto the plateau and continues to Orkasmet, the capital of Simanjiro District.

But we took the right fork, which remains low, curving northwards, following the broad flat valley towards Kilimanjaro, the river's perennial source.

From Remiti onwards there were no permanent buildings until the training centre at Loiborsoit, an hour or so further on. Even *engangs* were largely absent, for the Maasai avoided the low-lying, flood-prone land near the river.

Bumping along, I pondered the problems facing rural areas where the population density is low. Living in clusters, in towns, in cities, close to major markets where one can trade, has many built-in advantages. While the Maasai Steppe is an extreme case, population density is low in many parts of Africa, and this has to be one of the reasons why poverty is proving so stubborn to wipe out. Take the challenge of providing schools in the Maasai Steppe. No matter where the primary school is located, many children will be unable to reach it on foot. The distances are so great that primary schools began appearing only in the 1990s, and when I first visited there was only one secondary school in the whole of Simanjiro District.

Julius Nyerere, the first president of independent Tanzania, is still widely revered in the country as a man of ideals and integrity, and fondly referred to as Mwalimu – teacher. He was one of those African leaders who gave himself to his country, and not vice versa. He saw the challenge that the low population density posed to his development vision. His solution was known as *ujamaa*, or 'villagisation'. It involved the relocation and concentration of large swathes of the rural population. Under his government's radical version of socialism, all land and economic enterprises were taken over by the state. New villages were laid out, with schools, clinics, water supply and other services.

The logic was sound, but the relocation was compulsory. Even more controversially, households and communities were sometimes uprooted hundreds of miles in an attempt to mix up tribal boundaries. Nyerere saw a threat to peace in tribal loyalties. Wishing to promote a sense of nationhood that was stronger than tribalhood, and to avoid any one tribe having the ascendancy, he strove to create multi-tribal settlements. Thus, farmers from the interior suddenly found themselves relocated to the infertile coastline where the dominant occupation was fishing, or to a place where the soil and climate were totally unfamiliar to them. That this forced migration on such a vast scale took place without bloodshed, without any kind of major protest, is a tribute to the mildness of the Tanzanian temperament, and to their faith in the inspiration and ideals of Mwalimu.

Nyerere's policies led to economic collapse, but established a strong foundation of peace and a fair degree of social progress. He was able to establish primary schools throughout the country and, during his tenure, school enrolment climbed until nearly every child was in school. In addition, adult literacy quadrupled so that four out of five adults were literate.

But the one tribe that Nyerere did not force into *ujamaa* were the Maasai. He must have suspected that they would never accept it without bloodshed. So they were left in peace to follow their traditional wanderings far from the upheavals and budding urban settlements of the new Tanzania. As a result, while other tribes and communities were stirred into the pot and gained education, most of the Maasai did not.

"You've overshot the turning!" Oloserian brought me to my senses.

"What turning?"

"You turn left here for Engorini and the members of Matonyok group."

"*Here?*"

Oloserian seemed astonished at my poor recall. "Don't you remember that you turn left here? And you've been here before!"

"Hmm ... the turn-off didn't stick in my mind."

I searched the surroundings for a marker of some kind. There were none. The Steppe was too dry for baobab trees. The sandy track was unremarkable, the thorn trees unremarkable, and the clump of yellowish weed at the junction was on the point of dying and not a reliable marker. There were no visible signs of an *engang*. Only thorn trees coalescing, with distance, into an impenetrable barrier.

It took me many trips before I thoroughly mastered the lay-out of the Steppe. I learnt to be more observant of the small details – a particular jolting bump, a nickpoint in the nearby ridge, a strangely shaped anthill, or a trail of cattle hooves which might suggest the presence of an *engang* nearby.

Kaika was a large and imposing man. As he clenched my hand in his, I was doubtful if I would get it back again.

"*Sopai?*"

"*Ipa.*"

"Kaika is the advisory member of Matonyok Group," explained Oloserian as feeling slowly returned to my fingers.

"A pleasure to meet you," I said. But in reality this disclosure vexed me. The primary purpose of the women's groups was for them to do something independently of the men. It was hoped that by running their own small income-generating activities, and managing the income from these, women would gain greater respect, have some money to spend on their priorities, and begin to play a greater role in family and community decisions.

Having a male advisor appeared to run counter to these aims, and Matonyok was not the only group to have given such a role to men. I wondered why. The most obvious explanation was that the women did not feel confident to manage their own affairs. Alternatively, perhaps it was the men who did not believe that the women were competent, or were worried about allowing them free rein. Had they somehow convinced the women to create a role for them? A third possibility was that the women were being savvy and diplomatic, that they had deliberately devised a male role in order to allay male fears and ensure that husbands gave permission for their wives to be involved in the groups. I hoped it was the latter, but with the lesson of the leather-tanning group still fresh, the suspicion lurking in my mind was: *who is controlling the money?*

Oloserian had told me that there was one member of the Matonyok group who was not only literate but had completed the full seven years of primary school. Her name was Magilena and I was looking forward to meeting her, thinking she must be a very useful asset to this group. We found the women already beading, sitting on leather hides in the shade of an acacia. Magilena was tongue-tied when Oloserian introduced me. Quite possibly I was the first *mzungu* she had encountered. Pulling her shawl across her face, she stared resolutely at the ground so that I had to address the shaved crown of her head. I tried my best pidgin Swahili, and Magilena's shawl shook as giggles overcame her. Still a child, she barely reached my shoulder. In another culture she would have been in the pony-riding, pop-idol stage of girlhood, but being Maasai, Magilena had just become the sixth wife of Kaika. The fact that she had actually passed her primary school-leaving exam – few achieved this in 'bush' schools – and therefore been eligible for secondary school made this state of affairs even more poignant.

Since the leather-tanning workshop was still in disarray, the groups were making products solely from beads. As we settled into our discussions, I found myself once again stressing that they should obtain the beads themselves so that their enterprise would not be dependent on me.

"We can't afford to buy the beads!" they protested with one voice.

"Then use the money from the start-up loan you received from the Project."

"It's finished. We bought maize."

The maize, I learnt, was not for personal consumption but for profit. A speculative venture, it was based on the hope that the price would go up as the dry season progressed, and when high enough, they would sell. I was quite surprised that the women were aware of price fluctuations and speculating in the futures market. I suggested it was prudent to diversify their investments, that they might earn a faster and higher return by investing in beads, but blank faces showed me this was a step too far, too fast. They were still learning the feel of money in their hands. Besides, in an emergency, maize could be eaten; beads could not.

All the groups chose to share profits equally between their members, regardless of how much work each had contributed. "A woman may be sick, or her child sick, and she can't work, but still she needs food in her stomach," they explained. This cooperative approach was typical of the Maasai, and in sympathy with Nyerere socialism which still permeated the country.

During our discussion, Magilena did not utter a word. Officially, she was one of their leaders since she had naturally been appointed their secretary and book-keeper. But though she had the education, she was at the bottom of the social pecking order and knew it. Older women had the respect, wisdom and experience to make good leaders, but lacked the literacy skills and awareness of the outside world to manage their small business in a cost-effective way. The two should have been complementary, but I could see that Magilena's potential was untapped. Her large and impressive ledger book was empty even though she had attended a training course on how to keep records. She could only act when instructed by her elders – and they could not begin to imagine the usefulness of written records.

'The neck cannot go above the head' says a Maasai proverb. Education is indisputably an extremely powerful force for change and development. Yet Magilena's case showed me how its value can remain untapped unless the holder is permitted to use it. The introduction of schooling presents a particular challenge to a strongly age-stratified society such as the Maasai, where wisdom and respect are the preserve of the elders since it knocks that system out of kilter for a while, at least until education is achieved by all.

At first, the Maasai were renowned for being 'resistant' to education. There were regular reports in the East African press of Maasai girls running away from home in order to attend school. However, in the Steppe, attitudes towards primary school education were beginning to change. As soon as a school opened, parents enrolled their children, even their girls.

At Ngage, Baba Kicheche invited me to view a new extension they were building to the primary school. He was the councillor for his ward and a member of the district council. "We need education," he told me. "Thanks to education we've already made some changes. We never used to boil our milk. Now we do because we've learnt about the risks. We've begun to build toilets. These things are useful. They improve our health. We're willing to change, providing the change is not in conflict with our tenets and identity as Maasai."

"I've heard that many Maasai don't approve of education. How is it that you're different?"

"I was one of the few of my generation to get an education. I remember them coming. They made all the boys of my age group line up. I was about eight at the time."

"Who came?"

"The British, with the elders and leaders of our Ward. One *mzungu* walked along our ranks and touched some of us on the shoulder with his stick. We were made to stand aside. I stood as straight as I could, with my head upright. I saw that he was choosing those who were tall, confident and alert. I was happy when his stick touched my shoulder."

"And what happened then?"

"They sent us to a mission boarding school – at that time there was no school in Ngage. Everything was paid for. The only condition was that our parents gave their permission. Some didn't agree; they were afraid. But I was lucky – my parents said yes.

"Things are very different now," he went on. "Nearly all our children attend primary school. We have Maasai with secondary education and with degrees who can assume leadership. In the past, outsiders had to bring us new ideas. Now we can develop and promote new ways of doing things ourselves. Responsibility is in our hands. We've Maasai who are agricultural experts. It's much better; we can believe things from somebody we can trust." Yet in this area, schooling remained a distant dream for most girls. Boys were more likely to get an education if the family could afford it. On one visit to Kaika's, a lad in Maasai garb greeted me, and requested in perfect English that I bring him a football on my next visit. He was one of Kaika's sons, on holiday from an English-medium boarding school in Kenya. I was astonished. The rest of Kaika's children were barefoot, and there was not a stick of furniture in any of his wives' huts. Over time I met one or two other boys in other *engangs* who attended schools in Kenya, though their numbers were few. If the family were wealthy and owned many cows, they would sell one or two at the beginning of each term to cover the school fees.

At a later date I attended the circumcision ceremony for the sons of the Project manager. They lived in Arusha, attended private English-medium schools, and made only occasional visits to their grandparents in the Steppe. But their father made sure that their two lower teeth were removed and that they went through all the Maasai rites, such as circumcision.

As I travelled around the timeless Maasai bush I wondered what the future held for these boys. Would they become proud cattle-herding *morani*? Or would they be lost to their own culture forever? And how did they reconcile the two worlds in which they lived?

There are some who believe that to maintain their culture, Maasai children should not be encouraged to pursue education. But I have never met a Tanzanian child who did not passionately yearn to attend school, even while their parents might be antagonistic. Who can deny children their right to choose? And when the rest of the world is changing fast, and encroaching on their territory, one could argue that they need education more than ever in order to figure out how best to adapt to the challenges of the modern world.

"I want to build a secondary school here in Ngage!" Baba Kicheche exclaimed one day. "We want our children to be participants in the world." This, from a people dismissed in a colonial report of 1921 as 'primitive savages who have never evolved and who under present conditions, in all probability, never can evolve.'[1]

Time and again the scale of the upheaval taking place in the Maasai Steppe was brought home to me. Old values pitted against a new order: education, climate change, environmental degradation, land encroachment, population growth, social disintegration. The wrong sort of change has a way of infiltrating even the most traditional and remote cultures. Given this, it seems better to accept that change is inevitable and to let go of some traditions while holding fast to a few really important values.

The last thing I would ever wish to see is for the Maasai to be relegated to reserves, provided with assistance but deprived of their traditional livelihood, obliged to stifle their memories of the days when they once roamed freely.

10

Overexposure

As the bus from Arusha pulled into Ubungo station in Dar es Salaam, I spotted shaved heads and colourful robes on board. Representatives from each beadwork group were visiting the city for what Oloserian termed an 'exposure' trip.

For the Maasai women, it was the trip of a lifetime.

To save costs we had agreed that they would stay at my home. I had stressed to Oloserian: *no more than six women*, and I counted them as they dismounted. There were indeed six women: Esta, Raheli, Anna, Mama Kicheche, Mama Baraka and Mama Nyeyesu. But in addition there were three babies – Jaki, Baraka and Nyeyesu – plus Sion, Esta's ten-year-old daughter whom she had brought along to help take care of Jaki.

I decided the accommodation would stretch. Two women plus babies could sleep on the beds in our guestroom, while the rest would have mattresses on the floor of the old storeroom which we had converted into a TV room. The storeroom dated from the 1980s when these were a standard necessity in houses rented to foreigners. This was the period of economic austerity when Tanzania's experiment with socialism collapsed, and the expatriate community survived by shipping in container-loads of toiletries and other sundries. Now the policies had changed and the economy was liberalising fast. In fact, the pendulum had swung so far to the right that the government – still the same revolutionary socialist party – seemed to be begging capitalists to come in and exploit them.

Exhausted from their journey which had begun the day before, the women were nonetheless in high spirits. At my house they received a boisterous welcome from our Rhodesian Ridgeback and Alsatian, both of whom went mad with the exciting smells of cattle and savannah-dust that they brought with them. Most Tanzanians are fearful of dogs, and usually I had to chain the dogs before they would step inside the gate. But the Maasai women were fearless and did not flinch. They were the only locals ever to visit our home who did not cringe at the sight of the dogs. When I commented on this fact to Oloserian, he was offended at the very suggestion that they might be frightened. "We Maasai are afraid of *nothing*! Least of all an animal."

During the tour of our house, I introduced them to my husband and two children, to Mama Laddie who worked for us, and her husband Moses who was our guard-cum-gardener. I explained the sleeping arrangements and how to control the air-conditioner. They were fascinated at the blast of cold air which came out of it. Then I introduced them to the bathroom. It was a tight squeeze, but the six of us just fitted inside. I showed them the shower and the wash basin and how the red-knob tap produced hot water and the blue-knob cold. They were amazed.

"What's this?" they asked, pointing to the final object in the room.

Esta had seen one before, though it had been a squat design. Ours had a seat. I did my best to explain. "You sit on it to pee ..."

"*Sit* on it?" they exclaimed. "Surely not ...?"

"Like this," I said, obliged to give a demonstration of the position.

"How can you? Surely you can't do it ... while you're sitting down? It must be very uncomfortable!"

"We can. We do," I said, restraining my laughter as each in turn practised the seating position and pushing the flush lever.

None of the women had ever been to the city before. My plan was to work on improving the quality of some of their products in the mornings, and in the afternoons to introduce them to handicraft shops which might market their products. I would also show them where to buy beads and other materials at discount prices, and generally orientate them to the city, with the idea that in future they could do these tasks themselves.

But it quickly became apparent that they had a completely different agenda. Not only had they come with a long shopping list, but they were a walking compendium of medical complaints, all needing urgent attention by paediatricians, gynaecologists, ENT specialists and so on. Of the two who did not have a baby strapped to their backs, one was pregnant, and the other wished to find out why she was not.

They assumed that I would organise all of this.

My marketing strategy was to identify three to four handicraft emporiums willing to stock their products on a regular basis. Selling at seasonal craft fairs was an interim rather than a long-term strategy; the women needed a regular market throughout the year. I drew up an itinerary and we did the rounds.

One of the handicraft boutiques was inside a swanky five-star hotel. The women stared at their reflections in the plate-glass windows that stretched from floor to ceiling, craned their necks upwards to the soaring arches and cupolas, and followed me in single file across the vast marble atrium, past splashing fountains.

"Is this water for bathing or for drinking?" asked Esta, breaking their speechlessness.

"It's for looking at."

"Simply to *look* at? Not to use?" They fell silent again.

The woman who ran the handicraft boutique was courteous and sympathetic. She purchased some products, paid the money up-front, and offered to put only a low mark-up on them. Most shops liked their products because they were slightly different to the run-of-the-mill Maasai beadwork, but almost none were willing to pay money on the spot. They wanted the items on a 'sale or return' basis or payment three months later.

The reception in one handicraft emporium was far less friendly. This was the largest store with the most extensive collection of arte-facts, and the one which I hoped would be the key outlet for the women's products. It was owned and managed by a foreigner, and was stylishly laid out. I could see his eyes light up as the women displayed their products and Esta did her sales pitch. Then he engaged in inten-sive bargaining. The prices he offered were less than the cost of the beads and leather in the product; nothing at all for the labour time of the women. I had to intervene before Esta said 'okay'. I knew the cost of the materials and the time taken to make each product. We had agreed to base the labour cost on the legal minimum wage for Tanza-nia. I explained their situation to the owner, their need for a more sustainable income and fair prices for their work so that they could afford to send their children to school.

Turning to me, he said in English, "You haven't been in the coun-try long enough to know. Maasai are rogues; they always try to cheat. They will be happy with a few cents for they have nothing better to do with their time."

Stung by his blatant prejudice, I could think of no suitable retort. I gathered up their products, stuffed them into the bag and stalked out. The women followed me.

"What happened? What did he say?" pestered Esta once we were outside.

"He was rude."

"Didn't he like our things?"

"Yes – but he didn't like the prices."

"I know that, but what did he say?" she persisted.

But I refused to tell.

On the hospitality side, things began to go awry on the second day, when chicken was on the menu. I had asked Mama Laddie to cook them some African dishes. The first meal she produced was rice and beef, but on the second day she cooked chicken. When it was served, they informed me that Maasai never eat chicken! They never keep poultry. How could I not have noticed? Looking back on my visits, I realised there was no memory of a chicken pecking in the dirt, no clarion call of a cock crowing at dawn. But an absence is a harder thing to register than a presence.

Esta ate the chicken, and even seemed to enjoy it. Anna valiantly ate a few mouthfuls; Mama Nyeyesu and Mama Baraka refused to try it, and Raheli took one mouthful and had to rush to the bathroom. Without much hope I looked in the pantry for alternatives. As a family we were largely vegetarian and the only alternatives I could offer were vegetables, bread and eggs.

Eggs? *No!* For these were laid by chickens and were equally abhorrent. Fish was also banned. They preferred to eat bread with margarine – a product introduced by the British and now a staple of the Tanzanian diet.

Mama Laddie, who came from Malawi, was highly amused. Quickly she became friendly with the Maasai and when I returned from a trip to the Steppe, she would ask after each by name. She approved of the fact that they said grace before every meal, but she rolled her eyes at the mess they left everywhere. Housework does not feature among the chores of the Steppe. You cannot sweep up sand. Goats and wind tidy litter away.

During the mornings, we worked in the shade of our terraced porch. Baby Baraka was a cherub; he never cried, rarely complained. But the plan for big sister Sion to take care of Jaki was not working out. In the strange environment, Jaki demanded her mother's attention or screamed incessantly. It was frustrating for Esta, and left Sion without much to do. Seeing Sion wandering in the garden one day, and thinking she might be lonely, I asked my daughter if she would entertain her for a while. They were not far apart in age.

"*Mum*! I'm not going near her. She's *scary*!"

"What do you mean? Surely you're not frightened of her?"

"She *bites*!"

"Don't be ridiculous. She's smaller than you."

"*Mum*! I'm *serious*. You don't believe me – *look*!" She pointed out a bite mark on her arm.

"Why would she bite you? You must have been doing something to her?"

"I wasn't doing anything! She just walked over and bit me without warning."

"And then what happened?" I asked, trying to fathom out the cause of this strange incident.

"She bit me a second time, even harder!" She showed me a second bite mark.

"I don't believe you! How could you let her do that?"

"It's true," said my son, laughing helplessly; "I was there. I saw her do it!"

I left the two of them giggling.

After that I looked at Sion with a new respect. She and Jaki were two of a kind. What was the word Jacopo had used for Jaki? *Mkali*. Fierce. Like the dogs inside the compounds which had a notice on the gate stating: *Mbwa mkali*.

Curious to know more, I mentioned the incident to Esta at the end of their visit, and she in turn questioned her daughter. It transpired that Sion had wanted to see if *mzungu* children cried tears like Maasai children. When my daughter hadn't cried the first time, she had bitten her a second time, harder than the first, to make the tears flow. It was all quite logical.

In the afternoons we toured the city. Esta was an enthusiastic tourist. She wanted to see *everything,* and the others followed her lead. They adored the luxury of travelling in my air-conditioned car – somehow twelve of us managed to squeeze inside.

We toured the harbour, the downtown area, the hotel boutiques, the supermarkets and Coco Beach. I got some strange looks as I parked the car and one white woman and a crowd of Maasai women and babies clambered out. What the women commented on was interesting. Skyscrapers they passed without a murmur. But a neighbour's front garden drew a long discussion. It contained three jersey cows with massive udders. They wanted to know how many litres of milk they gave daily, what food they ate, where they came from, and asked many other detailed questions.

But without a doubt the sea came top of their list of wonders. On the first evening I took them down to Oyster Bay and we walked along Coco Beach. They were mesmerised with the size of the ocean and its restless waters, puzzled by the fact that the waves came constantly towards them yet the water never advanced. Only Esta was bold enough to lift her skirts and paddle in the water.

"Look! Here are your shells," I pointed out, fingering a small cowrie. These form a distinctive part of Maasai designs, and they were using them as fasteners on some of their leather bags.

Half way through their stay I decided it was time they started to find their way around the city by the local *dala-dala* buses. These are small mini-buses, their nickname a corruption of the word 'dollar'. Empty seats are rare, but if you are small or a competent contortionist, they are a cheap way to get around the city.

Each *dala-dala* has its start and end destinations painted in large letters on its front and sides. In addition, each is colour-coded: one half of the bus painted the colour representative of its start-point, and the other half for its destination. This is helpful for those who are unable to read.

I gave Mama Kicheche some money for their fares and dropped the women at Ubungo bus station with instructions on how to reach my area of town. Oloserian and I drilled them over and over again. "What colour *dala-dala* are you going to take?"

"Red and purple," they answered.

"That's right – Maasai colours! Easy to remember."

Oloserian and I drove back to the crossroads near my home and waited. One after another, crowded *dala-dalas* screeched to a halt, split their sliding doors like overripe fruit and spilled passengers onto the pavement. No sign of Maasai women. I was beginning to be concerned, when finally another red and purple mini-bus pulled up and

Maasai women appeared in its doorway. All the babies, even placid Baraka, were bawling their heads off. The last person to dismount was Mama Kicheche. Her eyes and forehead were clenched with worry, and she looked ready to burst into tears. When she spotted me, her jaw dropped and she locked me in a hug.

"I thought we were lost forever. I thought I was never going to see you again. Never going to return to the Steppe, my home, my husband, my children!" she wailed, clinging to me like a drowning woman.

I took them home and soothed nerves with large mugs of tea.

Time rushed by. By the end of their stay I was exhausted from my multiple roles as hostess, caterer, trainer, chauffeur and tour operator, not to mention walk-on parts as medical advisor and consumer guide. On their final day we spent the afternoon buying leather and kilos of coloured beads in Kariakoo market, together with flour, sugar, oil and an array of pots and pans to take back with them.

One item remained on Raheli's shopping list. Each day we had hunted for it in vain. I rolled down the car window and called out to another shopkeeper. "Excuse me, do you know where we can buy cow-fat?"

He regarded me oddly, and shook his head. It was not an item that was normally sought on the urban pavements of Dar es Salaam.

In the back of my car, six Maasai women were holding an animated conversation.

"I don't think we're going to find it," I said.

"We must," begged Raheli. "I need ten litres to take back with me."

"Won't butter or margarine do? Or sunflower oil?"

"It must be cow-fat," Raheli insisted. "I'm pregnant, and supposed to drink a cup of it every day."

She was astonished when I explained that cow-fat did not feature on my regular shopping list, that it was not a common consumer item for urbanites. We had already made a fruitless – or rather, fatless – tour of the supermarkets and the container shops. We had then headed to the central Kariakoo market where I thought it might be plentiful, but this market was just as fat-free.

"Let's give up and go home," I said, wondering how I had allowed myself to be lured into this quest.

"Not yet!" pleaded Raheli.

"Let's find some Maasai men and ask them," suggested Esta. "They should know where it's available."

So we drove around and wherever we spotted one, Raheli rolled down the back window to ask. But the answer was always negative. We covered every neighbourhood in the city where Maasai hang out, but with no luck.

"You should have brought some with you from home," I told Raheli.

"We don't have any at home. We sent our cattle to Handeni because of the drought."

"Sorry, it looks like you're going to be unlucky. When I was pregnant, I was told to eat green leafy vegetables."

Raheli gave me a look of horror and disbelief.

Laden with shopping and exhausted with the heat and noise of Kariakoo market, we returned to my home. As I opened our front door I found our sitting room transformed into a discotheque with loud music and strobe lights.

"You haven't forgotten we're having a party, Mum? You agreed it was okay!" my daughter greeted me.

I *had* forgotten. And my husband was away. I dumped the beads and the Maasai women and rushed out to buy crates of coke and pizzas. By the time I returned there was a line of 4x4s parked outside and a group of Tanzanian drivers patiently whiling away the hours, waiting for their young passengers. Our sitting room was heaving.

That evening passed in surreal confusion as I tried to keep half an eye on the party. For much of the time the Maasai and I huddled in the relative quiet of the TV storeroom counting beads and money. The beads were sold wholesale in long skeins; 120 skeins of the same colour came knotted together, so each colour bundle had to be carefully untied and counted out – so many to this group, so many to that group. Inevitably, threads broke during this process and beads went skittering to the far corners of the room. The Arusha bus left in the early hours of the morning and it was essential to have everything packed and ready the night before. Money transactions – additions and subtractions and multiplication went on late into the night.

Our sitting room lay at the entrance to the house so that when I took the women out to eat at a local restaurant, or when they wanted to access their bags in the spare bedroom, or visit the bathroom, or I needed something from the rest of the house, there was no avoiding passing through the centre of the disco party. As we paraded back and forth I peered into its semi-darkness with motherly concern. Was that really my daughter kissing in the corner? Surely that couldn't be my son with a girl on his lap instead of a football? They were growing up in a single evening.

What did the disco dancers make of the file of Maasai women passing by, the strobe lights catching a wayward nipple peeping out between their robes? I don't believe they even noticed. As for the Maasai, I have no idea what they thought. I was too tired to make any effort at explaining. I could only reflect what a strange schizoid world we live in. One half struggles with empty stomachs and unmet basic needs; the other half with having too much and too little in the way of needs to give direction to their lives.

When I drove the women to the bus station early the next morning, I could barely hide my pleasure at their imminent departure, and nor could they. The city had exhausted them. They pined for the peace of the Steppe.

"Goodbye" ... "I hope you had a lovely time" ... "Do come again".

What stories would they tell to their friends and family? "Give my greetings to everyone!" I yelled as the bus took off and its rear slogan 'IN GOD WE TRUST' grew smaller and smaller as it carried the women from one epoch to another.

11

A jealous husband

Heavy rain had fallen recently. As I left the main road and entered the Steppe, I noticed that the dry bulbous stubs of the desert rose had burst into bloom, and bordering the track, thick leafless stem buds of an amaryllis-type flower were powering through the sandy gravel like rockets ready to launch. I never saw them again, and had I not chanced to drive through on that particular occasion I would never have guessed that such secrets hid beneath the arid soil.

Guided by Oloserian, I was on my way to visit Esta's group in Namalulu for the first time. Namalulu was like a distant outpost. To reach it we had to leave the river valley crescent, climb up onto the plateau and pass through Orkasmet, the capital of Simanjiro District.

'District capital' suggests a certain cachet that Orkasmet did not possess at that time. It was hardly a town, more a straggling village with a single row of shack-like shops, and a few spartan government offices camping in a half-derelict building. There were no paved roads, but there was intermittent electricity, a health post, the one and only secondary school for the district, and a couple of bars serving chicken and chips, maize and beans, beer and coke.

The government officials whom I met all indicated a preference to be elsewhere. They regarded their assignment as a prisoner regards a jail sentence. Simanjiro was an almost brand-new district, carved out of the over-large district of Arusha. It had miles to go to reach the standard of other district capitals. Some of the government offices had desks, but several did not.

The creation of Simanjiro District in 2002 was meant to facilitate greater government investment in the area. But when the political map was reorganised, a stroke of a red pen by an overzealous administrator had excised Simanjiro not only from Arusha District but also from Arusha Region, assigning it instead to Manyara Region which was created in the same year. A government official once disparagingly described Manyara as a rhinocerous with a severed head. Simanjiro is its backside; the small town of Babati, its regional capital, lies in its head just above the extremely thin neck. As the crow flies, the distance between Babati and Orkasmet is only 160 kilometres, but the only negotiable road between the two is the road that goes north to Arusha. Anyone from Orkasmet wishing to consult superiors in the Manyara regional office had to drive six rough hours northwards to Arusha, travel past the Arusha regional office, resisting the urge to drop in, and continue south-westwards for a further four hours. The road map ruled out a day return trip and obliged travellers to stay overnight. It guaranteed that few could afford to do business at regional level, and condemned Simanjiro to remain an isolated, empty and disregarded spot on government maps.

Oloserian's sister had just been hired as a secretary by the district government. She showed us the list of government posts for the district – over one hundred in total, ninety per cent of the vacancies unfilled. The tour of the administrative headquarters demanded a lively imagination, for most of it was at the conceptual stage and presented an unremarkable vista of thorn bush.

As we drove westwards from Orkasmet on a jolting road of the plateau terrain, the thorn bush became slightly greener, slightly more generous in the number of leaves allotted to each shrub, and as a result there were more animals. A group of kudu galloped across the road and there were zebra browsing in the bushes. Arriving at the village of Namalulu, we passed a row of shops selling shawls, soap, rice, torches and other basic items. Turning off the main street we entered a small compound, and there under a shady tree awaiting our arrival patiently – as always – were the Mama Masai women, with Esta and Gloria their leaders.

Namalulu group had been the best and most reliable of the groups. But suddenly their production had taken a dip in quality and I wanted to understand why.

After the customary hugs, handshakes and greetings, they spread out a cowskin and showed me their latest products. They resembled the tangible outcome of a game of Chinese whispers, where a message started at one end becomes ludicrously distorted by the time it reaches the other end. In this case, while each modification had been small, the end result was some way from the specifications we had developed in the training. According to the women, they lacked a set of samples to copy.

"Where are the samples you brought back from the workshop?"

"Esta has them."

"So what's the problem?"

"Esta's moved away and she's taken the samples with her."

Esta explained that she hadn't moved, but her 'village' had relocated. It was now situated in a place called Oromoti, thirteen kilometres from Namalulu. Too far for Esta to walk the round-trip each day. Without her guidance and initiative, the group had gone into decline.

Unfortunately, she had taken the samples with her, leaving the rest of the group with some beads and a bag of rejects. They had been faithfully copying the rejects.

While explaining the need to get correct samples into everybody's hands, and how Esta might best continue to provide leadership and supervision, my words became engulfed in a maelstrom of Maa jabbering.

When the storm died down, Oloserian translated: "Esta's husband moved their village because he was jealous."

"Jealous of whom?"

"Jealous of the time that Esta was giving to the women's group."

"And *for that* he moved the entire village?"

"Yes."

Silence followed as I mentally revised my previous assessment of Maasai gender relations to accommodate this new finding. It was disturbing, and exposed the fragile support on which the women's groups rested.

Esta was the most dynamic and educated of the leaders, and her enthusiasm was infectious. Her group had had success in their sights, and Esta had begun devoting more and more time to their activities. According to Oloserian, Esta's husband felt she was neglecting him and feared he would lose men's respect if he failed to assert control over his wife and her affairs. I did not imagine that she had neglected his physical needs in any way; rather, it was the threat she posed to his status of head and decision-maker in the family as her gift for leadership flowered. Possibly they had had some arguments, and Esta would have had the self-assertion to defend her rights – she was, after all, Jaki's mother.

His solution was crafty. By relocating their community to Oromoti, he had dissected Esta from her group, without having to raise his voice against her activities in public.

The sun was swelling and sinking. I offered Esta a lift to Oromoti, and she offered me hospitality for the night at her new *engang*. To Oloserian's dismay, I accepted her offer with alacrity. Esta normally wore a shining smile, but now her smile split her face in two, wrinkling the tight, shaved skin on the crown of her head.

At her *engang* we drove around the circular barrier until we came to the entrance. The dwellings were different to those of the eastern Steppe. Each *enkaji* was ellipsoid, with a flattish, slightly bulging mud roof, resembling a legless hump-backed elephant, and in size not much bigger.

It was odd that they should have flattish roofs when this area had higher rainfall than the eastern steppe. "Don't they leak when it rains?"

"We add anthill deposits to the mud – it makes them strong and waterproof. They don't leak if we keep them well maintained," Esta replied.

Oloserian explained that all Maasai dwellings used to be like these, but some decades ago there was a serious epidemic of meningitis on the eastern side. The government declared it was due to the cramped living space and lack of ventilation of the *enkaji*. They launched a health campaign, urging Maasai to build huts with higher, peaked roofs for better ventilation.

Esta pulled out two chairs and Oloserian and I were obliged to sit upon them. A horde of children held us hostage while Esta made tea. I recognised a familiar face among them. Jaki! She was taller and skinnier than when we last met, but with that assertiveness that was easily recognisable. She greeted me with a smile that was an echo of her mother's, and climbed trustingly onto my lap. Jaki on her home turf seemed an altogether sweeter child than I remembered. But there was no doubt that she was 'boss', the gang leader of the little girls. We played some clapping games, while the older children played their version of hopscotch. Another game which the Maasai played was *bao*. Under a shady tree near a settlement, one might find sixteen small depressions scooped in the sand, with nuts or small stones lying in each. It is a game which is played in myriad variations across Africa.

As the sun touched the earth, the reddish sand and mud huts of the *engang* began to glow and long fingers of shadow stretched from every spindly thorn tree. In a cloud of dust and clanging bells, the cattle came home, shepherded by *morani* in their fiery red cloaks. The women sallied forth from their huts, carrying their bottle-shaped gourds to begin the process of milking. Then the calves were locked into small pens, the goats corralled into a separate pen, and the cows settled down in the heart of the *engang*. An inner barricade of thornbrush was pulled into place around the animals, while an outer barricade protected the whole *engang* from predators. Here, it was necessary, for they were closer to the game areas. Occasionally, there were lion, but the main predators were hyena and leopard.

With the darkness, we moved inside. The interior design of Esta's *enkaji* followed the pattern of all Maasai homes. First, an entrance chamber, a curved space where grain or tools are stored and where guests might be entertained. At the far end of this chamber a doorway with a threshold led to a small room. Here, there was a hearth where there may be a fire, and a couple of three-legged stools or upturned buckets to sit on. Filling up half the room was the Maasai equivalent of a double bed: a raised platform of interwoven branches, about two feet off the ground, with the ends of the branches embedded into the mud walls on three sides. This is where children or guests sleep. A small adjoining room offered greater privacy and was filled entirely with a sleeping platform. Since this room lacks a door in its frame, the edge of its sleeping platform can be used as additional seating by those gathered around the hearth. This bedroom is barely long enough for a Maasai man to lie lengthways, and only just wide enough for a husband and wife to lie side by side on the nights when he visits.

Oloserian and I settled ourselves on buckets and stools by the hearth. A short while later, Esta's husband, Lemberes, joined us. He turned out to be a likeable and charming man, and I had to jettison my prejudice. Maasai men are unfailingly courteous, and I was often struck by their affability, their lack of airs, their straightforward manner of speaking to strangers. They were neither offhand, nor overly polite or obsequious.

We talked about the water scheme for Oromoti and Namalulu. Lemberes had visited the water project at Landenai mountain, and subsequently had pestered the Project to survey the smaller Namalulu hill in the hope that it could yield enough water to be worth piping. The community had cleared a track for transporting construction equipment to the site. When finished, there would be a chain of standpipes.

His elderly mother expressed her delight. "Can you believe it? There will be piped water, close to our *engang*!"

"Things are so different now," she went on. "Less than ten years ago we had no place we called 'home'. We were continually on the move, a few months here, a few months there, following the rain and the grazing. And now look at us. Here's our *engang*! Here's our water supply! These are my grandchildren *who go to school*!"

She had decorated her hut with designs in red and white mud, and messages which said in Swahili: WELCOME ALL GUESTS TO GRANDMA'S, WE WELCOME YOU IN THE NAME OF GOD. The pleasure of having a place called 'home' was evident.

"We've even learnt how to cultivate maize!" added Lemberes, as though such an activity was a shameful joke.

"And did you have a successful harvest?"

"Fifty kilos," he answered with a smile.

I knew that Oloserian was encouraging Maasai to try cultivation where feasible. It was not easy. Farming is a body of skills and wisdom that accumulates in a community over generations. Cultivation demands access to land with sufficient moisture and reasonably fertile soil to support a crop, in a location protected from foraging herds. Oloserian was teaching them how to train their donkeys to pull a plough, instead of digging the soil by hand. Weather was the biggest challenge. The upland area around Namalulu did not lack rainfall in an average year, but it was unpredictable. A farmer never knew whether to risk planting at the onset of the rains or to wait.

But Lemberes had harvested a bumper crop that year. When Esta served the food, there were two steaming mounds of rice with pieces of meat and potatoes poking through, each with two spoons embedded in the mound. One for Esta and me to share and the other for Lemberes and Oloserian. Before eating, she gave thanks; not a rote grace, but a sincere expression of gratitude.

Amen! I was starving. Regardless of one's religious beliefs, the sense of being grateful for daily food is a sentiment that people in affluent countries have largely lost. We take food for granted. My spells in the Maasai Steppe made me think again. I considered myself lucky if the first meal of the day appeared before the sun set. Normally, we survived on mugs of tea. Although I carried some snacks with me, they never lasted long. It was rarely possible to eat in private, and since everybody else was hungrier than I, these snacks had to be shared. Even the largest bag of peanuts or tin of biscuits, divided between a women's group and their children, disappeared in seconds.

After supper, the men retired to sleep in another *enkaji*, while Esta, her children and I remained in the hut where she had done the cooking. With the insulation of its mud walls, the hut retained heat like a tandoori oven. There was a handkerchief-sized window but otherwise no ventilation. Esta pulled the door closed behind us and settled herself with the children in the inner sanctum, while I lay down on the other sleeping platform. With its covering of smooth leather hides, the 'bed' was more comfortable than I had anticipated, once I had shifted slightly to avoid a knob of wood.

But the heat was stifling. I got up and touched the stones on the hearth – they were burning hot. For a while I wandered outside. The stars were like a cloak across the sky. All was quiet except for soft sniffs and bursts of steamy breath in the cattle pen. Eventually, I retired and drifted off to sleep, only to wake around midnight with the sensation of crawling skin. Must be mosquitoes, I thought. I switched on the torch but saw nothing. I lay down again. The tickling and itching grew worse. Sleep became impossible. Something was scurrying over my tummy and in the warm crevices of my body. *Fleas!* I leapt off the leather-skin bed and collided with the goats which were tethered beside it as I fumbled for my torch. Fleas and more fleas ... on the hop everywhere! It was a banquet. Exotic white flesh was on the menu, and they were feasting in relays.

I stripped and sprayed every inch of skin with mosquito spray, but the damage was done. During the following days, I scratched myself bloody. Thus ended my romance with Maasai *engang* life.

Still itching furiously, I awoke the next morning to find my car had a flat tyre. Some men offered to change it while Oloserian, Lemberes and I walked up the Namalulu hill to inspect the water project. The pipeline was only half-laid but already in use, and at its temporary endpoint a crowd of women and donkeys with water pots had gathered.

It was mid-afternoon before we left Oromoti. Oloserian estimated it was a four-hour drive from Namalulu to Ngage, where we were headed, with no habitation between the two where we could stop for the night. Driving after dark is hazardous, largely because it is hard to see the road and stay on it. I allowed Oloserian to take the wheel. It was a jolting journey, for most of it was on the rocky plateau top, without the cushion of sand.

The Project was also going through a bumpy patch. One manager had been fired and another was sought in his place. The vacancy notice urged Maasai women to apply, but to find such a person was probably not much more than a dream. Meanwhile, Oloserian had received a promotion and a new staff member called Frida hired to take his place. I was on my way to meet her for the first time. She was not Maasai, but she was a woman. I was not unhappy. Oloserian had been invaluable as a translator and an informant on Maasai culture, but I sensed that women came low on his list of priorities, definitely below cattle. After all, he was a Maasai man.

The sun sank lower. By the time the road flattened and softened, indicating that we had reached the Ruvu valley plain in which Ngage lay, it was truly dark with the particular pitch-blackness of a moonless night in the Steppe. Entering Ngage village, the car suddenly plunged on its side and I banged my head on the door.

I assumed we had driven into a ditch or suffered a blowout to the front tyre. I scrambled out on the driver's side as the passenger door was embedded in sand. There was no pothole, and the tyre was in good shape. But it had rolled to a stop some distance from the car. With dismay, we stared at the wheel-less axle buried in the sand, and realised we had forgotten to check that the nuts had been fully tightened after the tyre was changed. They must have slowly worked loose during our jolting journey and dropped, one by one. Our chances of seeing them again seemed remote – they could be lying anywhere along the rocky trail from Namalulu.

Tired and hungry – no food had appeared that day – I feared that we would have to abandon the car and walk on. Then suddenly there was an excited cry from Oloserian. He had found one of the nuts. I rustled in my bag for my torch. Retracing the car tracks, we searched inch by inch and managed to recover five of the six nuts. It seemed miraculous. They could have fallen off anywhere, but they had chosen to hang on until we had reached our destination. I shuddered to think what might have happened had they worked loose when I was travelling at speed on the tarmac highway.

The next day we dug out the sand in which the wheel axle was buried and managed to get the jack in place. With the wheel on, and the five nuts as tight as we could get them, we drove on northwards to Nyumba ya Mungu to meet up with Frida, the newly hired Project employee. There was no immediate answer when we knocked on the door of her house, but we could hear murmurs and laughter within. The door finally opened a crack, and five faces peered around its edge at varying heights. "*Mama hayupo*," the highest face informed us. "She's attending a training for census enumerators at the school."

We waited at the school. The woman who slipped out to meet us during the breaktime was young and attractive, with a striking resemblance to the faces in the doorway, though she seemed barely old enough to be their mother. Like Oloserian, Frida was trained in livestock management and was working for the district government. They had agreed to second her to the Project for two years. Frida would receive a top-up salary from the Project, which was greatly welcome – after fifteen years of government service, her basic monthly government salary was a meagre US$80. "I don't know anything about beads, but don't worry, I'll do my best," she assured me, as I finished the long list of problems connected with the women's groups. She leaned forward and whispered: "My husband doesn't like this place. He wants us to leave. The Steppe isn't meant for humans, he says. But I like it. I love the Maasai. Their lives are full of hardship – who will help them if we don't?"

We said goodbye and retraced our route. As we passed through Ngage for a second time, a small boy flagged us down, shouting and waving.

In his hand was the missing sixth wheel nut.

12

The beacon

The girl blinks, mesmerised and blinded by the brilliance of the sunlight reflecting from the tin roof of the school. It shines like a blazing beacon. It is new, and she can hear the tap-tap-tap as workmen hammer it into place. Last year, classes met under the trees; the year before that there was no school, no teachers, no pupils.

"Nilolei! Move – it's your turn!" Her friends have scratched a framework in the dirt and they are hopping from square to square, their loose robes flying open. Their bodies are lithe and frail, the dusky skin on their legs and buttocks powdered with cream-coloured savannah dust from where they have lain on the ground.

She swivels on one foot and tosses her stone into the next square of the frame. Hop, hop, jump-hop-jump. She throws her stone purposefully and thinks: now that there is a proper building, with a proper roof, perhaps ...

Nearby, a boy is engrossed in trimming a forked stick. He is smaller than her but skilful with the knife. He shaves the stick smooth of thorns and chops the ends short. Then he carves a small hole on the inside end of each fork. Selecting another smaller stick, he shaves this thin and straight and slots it between the twin forks, noting with satisfaction how it fits snugly into the two holes, closing the triangle. From a knotted corner of his orlokaraha, he takes out six bottle caps and hammers them flat with a rounded stone. Choosing a sharper chip for a chisel, he hammers a hole into each one. Finally, he threads each onto *the straight stick of the triangle and slots it back into place. He shakes it and strums his fingers against the bottle caps so that they spin and make a satisfying rattle.*

"Do you know where I can find more bottle caps?" he asks his sister. "I need ten."

"Why?"

"For my abacus."

"What's that?"

"Nothing to do with you. It's arithmetic. Addition, subtraction."

Seizing a stick, he scratches numbers in the sand. "See – this is 1, that's 2, that's 3, that's 4 ..."

"I know how to count!"

"But you don't know how to write!"

"Yes I do." She snatches the stick from him and quickly works it through the sand.

He laughs and taunts her. "That 3 is facing the wrong way, and the 4 is upside down."

"So what if it is! You beware! You get education and you won't be a Maasai. You'll be too weak to herd cattle. That's what they say."

"Soipei! Where are you? It's time for school," their mother Yeyo calls out.

She watches her mother help her younger brother don his new school clothes. The shorts look uncomfortable; they must chafe your legs when you run, and the buttons on the shirt are strange. A button pops off his shirt, and Yeyo scolds, "Pick it up, don't leave it in the sand – I'll sew it on later. Run, or you'll get caned for being late."

"Yeyo – have you seen – there are rainclouds in the distance?" She hopes her mother will smile, but Yeyo merely grunts and says, "Have you gathered wood for Koko? She can't cook till she has some firewood."

Not today. Perhaps tomorrow, Nilolei tells herself.

From the rocky outcrops where her search for firewood takes her, she notices the school roof shines even more brilliantly, like an enormous sequin. It marks our place, she thinks. You can see it from everywhere. I will never get lost again. If people ask me, I will say, "I live near the shiny roof."

Back in the engang *she throws the wood down outside Koko's hut. One of the pieces catches her eye. It is gnarled and knobbly, like a twisted body. There is its head, its neck, its trunk, and that small branch could be an arm. With coals from Koko's fireplace, she draws two eyes and a mouth onto the head.*

Her doll comes alive, and demands clothes. But first some beads. She steals a few from her mother's pouch, threads them into a necklace and slides it over the head of her new friend.

On the thorn barricade there are some scraps of cloth. She wraps a strip of red around her doll and ties it in a knot over one shoulder. But then, spotting a scrap of blue cloth, changes her mind. She takes off the red, and fashions the blue scrap into a school skirt, stapling it with thorns. Her baby will go to school. To the school with the shining roof. Her baby will be modern. She will learn to read and write. She will speak Swahili and every language in the world.

Engrossed in dressing her dolls she hardly notices that rain is falling. In no time it is sluicing down in sheets. A fragrant scent rises from the dampened earth. Shrieking with excitement, the toddlers chase through the puddles that are forming. She ties the doll onto her back and races with them until, out of breath, she pauses, and arching her body and neck backwards, allows the rain to splash onto her upturned face and open mouth.

Suddenly, there is commotion in the engang. *People are running to the exit. She watches them stream past her.*

"Run! Run! To the school!" shouts her older sister, tossing her a bucket.

She races after them, uncomprehending. As they approach the school, the noise of the rain drumming onto the tin roof adds its cry to the urgency. Children are darting in and out of the rows of water-spouts that shoot from its unguttered corrugations. Her sister shouts, but she cannot hear; the noise is deafening, like thunder. She stares where the water-spouts from the roof are drilling a straight line of holes into the dust. Copying others, she shoves her bucket under one of these, and the gush of water onto plastic joins the percussion. In no time her bucket is full. She lifts it onto her head. Water slaps and splashes from its rim as she straightens her knees. Steadying the bucket with one hand, she sways until she finds the position in which the bucket stays balanced.

With straight shoulders and a smooth stride, she leaves the school, homeward bound.

13

●○●○○●○●○○●○●●○●○●○○●○○●●●●●○○●○○●●●●○

Five pigeon eggs

Kaika's *engang* invariably gave me a warm and enthusiastic welcome. The moment my red car entered their homestead, an astonishing number of young children would swarm from its nooks and crannies and envelop my car, buzzing excitedly. It was like stepping into a crèche. Dressed in nothing but a loose cloth knotted over one shoulder, they approached me like a ragged, barefoot army, their feet peppered with wounds from the stabbings of thorns. As we became more familiar, they would proffer their heads as a sign of respect and I would lay my hand on the cropped, textured hair of each. If Kaika was at home, he would stride over to greet me. Everybody, far and wide, seemed to know Kaika as he was an elected government leader for this area. As such, it was his business to keep an eye on everything, to liaise with the district councillors, to arbitrate disputes and deal with other matters like that.

Kaika and his wives had built a special *enkaji* solely for guests. It was even equipped with a bed and mattress, and a hole-riddled mosquito net. Thus I was spared the fleas, but still had to find a thick thorn bush for a toilet. Over the years, I slept in this room on various occasions. It was not uncomfortable, and a framed photo of Mwalimu Nyerere kept me company, but the *enkaji* had modern-size windows with bars but no glass, and it was impossible to escape the eyes of the children who peered through to spy on everything I did, including my bedtime routine. "*Koko* – what's that garment you're taking off?" ...

"What's in your bag?" ... "Can we play with your camera?" ... "You left your pen on the ground, can I keep it for school?" My presence provided free entertainment.

But sleeping in the *engang* allowed me to observe life going on around me, to see the dynamics of a large Maasai family. Which is how, rather belatedly, I discovered that Kaika had six wives, all of them members of Mama Masai.

Each of the wives was quite different. There appeared to be no common criteria in their selection. Some, like Anna, his fifth wife, appeared more favoured than others. She had been the group's spokes-woman on my first visit – it was she who had talked of stepping stones. She had deep-set, twinkling eyes, an unflinching serious gaze when she spoke and dimples when she smiled. Though a junior wife, she often seemed to take control when there were practical matters to be arranged, decisions to be taken. Kaika appeared to consult her more frequently than any of his other wives. He clearly respected her opinion and enjoyed her company. When they spoke together, she looked him straight in the eye and did not act inferior or reticent in any way. Their relationship appeared relaxed, based on mutual respect. It was Anna whom Kaika brought with him later, on a unique private trip to Dar es Salaam, to find a cure for her distress over a series of miscarriages.

Another favourite was Magilena, his youngest wife, the educated young woman I had met when I visited the Matonyok group. Possibly each wife had been the favourite when she first arrived. Within a year of her marriage Magilena had produced an enormous baby boy, the splitting image of his father. In her arms, his head dwarfed hers. Like a cuckoo in a warbler's nest, he had a bottomless appetite and Magilena was constantly breast-feeding. As the baby grew, Magilena seemed to shrink. Thereafter, new babies appeared on her hips at almost yearly intervals.

Two other wives were both called Raheli, adding to my confusion. One was plump and vivacious, and the traditional midwife for the community. The other was Kaika's oldest wife. I would have expected her to be the most respected, the matriarch of the family, but she was a quiet, unassuming woman with slightly shabby robes and no appearance of taking precedence in any way.

Kaika's marital relationships were surely more subtle and complex than this thumbnail sketch suggests. But I did not delve deeper until I had known them for a much longer time.

If Kaika's *engang* resembled a crèche, the children at Sainoi's homestead at Engurashi would easily have filled a whole primary school. Their *engang* was on a grand scale, double the size of others. For Sainoi's husband had no less than twelve wives. Even Oloserian found this remarkable, although I heard stories of men with twenty wives or more.

One day I asked Nyange, one of Sainoi's sons, how many brothers and sisters he had. He replied that he didn't know. "Can you calculate the number?" I pressed him, proffering my pen and notepad. He jotted numbers down, going through his father's offspring, wife by wife. The total figure stunned him. His father had sired 87 children, of whom 66 were still living. This came as a revelation to Nyange. He murmured the number several times to himself. "I'd never thought about it before you asked me. Can my father really have had 87 children? It's hard to believe. But it's true!" He stared at the figures on the notepad and relapsed into silence.

Among the 87 siblings, Nyange was one of the few to attend school. He speaks good English and holds a university degree. Yet he has chosen to return to his roots and serve his community, and when I encounter him he is always dressed in traditional *illkarash* and *orlokaraha*, never in trousers and shirt.

The number of women a man marries depends largely on his ability to support them and their offspring. In other words, on the number of cattle he owns. With milk as a major staple in their diet, a sizeable herd is required to maintain the family with a year-round subsistence milk supply. Based on the ratio of ten cows per capita that Kaika had quoted, I calculated that his family needed around three hundred cows to ensure food sufficiency and other basic needs. The number for Sainoi's extended family would have to be double that figure.

When looking for a new wife, there were other factors to consider besides cattle.

"I begin by asking questions about her family," Kaika explained. "Are they good people? Are the men in the family physically strong? Is the mother hospitable, does she have a good heart? Are they true Maasai – or Ndorobo?"[1]

Kaika's cousin Moses said he looked not at a man's wealth, but at his behaviour and attitudes, when searching for a husband for his daughters. "He should not be too big a person. By that I mean he shouldn't have too many cattle or he will be too full of his own importance and act like a boss." The common practice is for the man or his father to visit the girl's home and express interest to her parents. "Initially, I went alone," continued Moses. "But I always consulted my daughters before concluding an arrangement. If they were happy, then the marriage went ahead."

I have never had the opportunity to attend a wedding. They tell me there is little ceremony, nothing to compare with the rites for circumcision or eldership. The dowry cows are paid in instalments. Some are presented at the time the wedding pact is sealed, and the remainder up to several years after the event. On the day of the wedding, the groom goes to the bride's home, accompanied by other men from his community. The bride is dressed in wraps made of soft sheep's leather sewn with criss-crossing strips of beads and adorned with layers of beaded *esosi* neck-plates. She should not show her face, so it is shielded by a beaded crown from which hangs a spider's web of chains and sequins across her face. The women prepare their wedding garments themselves – the ornaments, the beaded wrap of skins, the leather thong shoes. The bride and groom sit together on stools. They might drink some beer made from honey or aloe vera roots. One by one, the elders give them advice. To the groom they might say: "You have the power to control this woman completely; use it wisely"; and to the bride they might say: "Protect your husband; make him happy." Meanwhile, the bride's father will plead for leniency: "Don't punish my girl too severely; she is still young!" The bride and groom, and their companions, return to the man's *engang*. That night they still sleep separately. The next day there is dancing and beer drinking, and on the following night the man may sleep with his new wife.

Having several wives was the norm among men in the communities which I visited. But there was one marriage that was even more unusual than Sainoi's. This was Jacopo's. Jacopo was the night-guard at the Loiborsoit centre. An archetypal Maasai in looks, big and strong, he was in fact a gentle and sensitive man. His only wife, Elisabet, was a classic Maasai beauty – slender, tall and ebony-skinned. Jacopo adored Elisabet and vowed that he would never marry another.

'So disregarded are women, that in some Maasai districts five large pigeon eggs, blue or white, green or amber coloured glass beads will purchase a woman, whereas it takes ten of the same beads to purchase a cow!'[2] records May French Sheldon, a female explorer of the nineteenth century.

Sheldon herself experienced enormous male prejudice when she set off on her expedition, leaving her husband behind. 'Do be reasonable and abandon this mad, useless scheme,' friends and acquaintances begged her at Charing Cross Station.[3] *The Spectator* decried her journey as having no scientific goal, motivated merely by 'feminine curiosity ... hardly a useful and laudable one.'[4]

But her covert goal was to prove that women were the equal of men in every way. 'Having ever flouted in my face the supercilious edict that it was outside the limitation of woman's legitimate province, I determined to accomplish the undertaking,' she writes.[5] Her expedition was the culmination of eight years of preparations to realise her ambition 'to personally lead and command an independent caravan of blacks – solely at my own expense, without the assistance or companionship of white or black men or women above the rank of servitors – through a much-reviled section of East Africa among alleged hostile as well as some peaceful tribes'.[6]

Her purpose was to observe and write a less prejudiced account about the people, particularly women and children, unhampered by the desire to remould them in her own image. She suspected that earlier accounts written by male explorers were biased and superficial since white men were not permitted an intimate acquaintance with the lives of East African women. Sheldon desired to study the locals in their homes, 'to know the women as wives, mothers and sisters; to know the men as husbands, fathers, brothers, and lovers, and see the children as they were'.[7] Consequently, she never refused an invitation to enter a home, however small and dilapidated it might look.

When her boat arrived in Zanzibar, she was greeted by a barrage of ridicule from the British. She writes:

> The bare idea that a woman should be foolhardy or ignorant enough to dare to enter Africa from the east coast and attempt to penetrate [the] interior as far as the Kilimanjaro district of the late Masai raids, at a time when great disturbances had been provoked by the Germans and a revolt was brewing, and essaying thus to do as the sole leader and commander of her own caravan – the thing was preposterous, and the woman denounced as *mad, mad* ...[8]

The British warned her that native porters were untrustworthy, lazy, vagabondish, and did nothing without compensation. On the point of departure, even Sheldon experienced a wobble in her confidence as she reviewed her caravan of two hundred ex-slave porters.

> When I looked with amazement over all these strange black and every conceivable shade of brown faces of my caravan, discerning much brutality imprinted thereupon ... I marveled if I should always be able to control them and make them subservient to my commands, and for a moment was somewhat dubious as to my ability, however, after experience with them, when I had to trust my life to them, they proved faithful, uncomplaining, chivalrous, and marvels of patience, endurance, and consistent marching day after day.[9]

Sheldon was a colourful character: determined, brave, entertaining, and delightfully eccentric. Perhaps being American helped her to be unconventional. On one occasion she entertained local children by cutting a segment of orange peel into a set of false teeth and putting them in her mouth. Delighted with the trick, a local elder withdrew from the crowd and returned, bloody but smiling, to present her with one of his own teeth, just extracted, with a hole bored through it so that she could string it round her neck. In all she did she tried to show the locals 'that I did not spurn becoming acquainted and was most interested in everything they did'.[10] 'I found the people and conditions very much what I aspired to make them, and certainly the natives are not so black as painted, and are peculiarly amenable to gentleness and kindness ... They are all on one piece of a common humanity'.[11]

'In fine, without bloodshed ... it has been my privilege to traverse the country of thirty-five African tribes, and return to the coast with all my porters, leaving behind a record women need never blush to consider.'[12]

Sheldon's bride-price of five pigeon eggs or glass beads suggests that Maasai women were treated as chattels, and not very valuable ones. But if one considers how much the average man elsewhere spends on dating his girlfriend, and how much he spends on buying a new car, then it may well be the equivalent of five glass beads.

Maasai men still pay a bride-price, but in cattle, not beads. If in Sheldon's time, one wife was the equal of half a cow, then the value of women has risen considerably since then. Kaika paid Anna's parents eight cows for the right to marry her. "I felt very proud that I was worth eight cows. I don't see the custom of dowry cows in a bad light at all," Anna told me.

There are few outward signs of women's subservience. Though a bride price is negotiated, I never observed women being treated as chattels. They do not avoid looking at the men when they speak, or cover their faces or look at the ground, as they do in some cultures. One time I overheard Anna giving Kaika a list of instructions of what needed to be done while she attended a training workshop, and one time an argument between them which she appeared to win. I noticed that the women were very relaxed with Oloserian. During workshops, they kept up a continual chatter, "Oli, can you help me?" ... "Oli, look at this." Not a vestige of subservience related to his being a male Maasai, nor to his education and status as a livestock officer.

When we talked about marriage, the women invariably declared that they liked being one of many wives. Polygamy was the norm for them, so naturally they were primed to accept it, but they had their reasons for liking it too.[13] These included never being lonely, female company and support always close by, child care on tap, by pooling resources, labour saving in many ways. At the same time, each wife has a fair degree of autonomy. They cook and sleep in separate huts with their respective children. Each builds her own *enkaji* within the *engang*, alternately building to the left and to the right of the main entrance, according to their marriage order.

"Anna is going to build herself a new *enkaji*," Kaika informed me proudly one day. "It's going to have a tin roof!" He didn't say "I'm going to build Anna a new *enkaji*." It was her own decision, one which she and she alone was entitled to make, but from which her husband derived a certain pride in having a wife who was progressive and capable of managing her own affairs. I watched Anna's new abode going up. It was still made of wattle and daub but larger and higher than her old one. When the walls were completed, she added its crowning glory and became the first of Kaika's wives to sleep under a tin roof.

Jealousy is the usual argument put forward against polygamy, and to a degree jealousy existed. A husband had to be wise and fair, and possibly a little crafty to keep his harem happy and content. After a few years the Matonyok group grew too big and splintered into two, and I noticed that some wives stayed with the old group, while some went with the new. But from what I observed, jealousy among the wives was not as strong a force as solidarity.

The colonial administrators did not care much for the Maasai – and their regard for women was even worse. To them, the Maasai had an attitude problem. They were frustratingly conservative and intractable. They kept too many cattle and too many wives. The British wanted them to reduce both, and their secret tactic to achieve this was taxation. For several decades the Maasai not only had to pay a tax on their cattle but an extra-ordinary 'hut tax' which became known as the 'plural wives tax'. They justified the double taxation by portraying the Maasai as being very wealthy due to their large cattle herds. Even in its time, the tax was controversial since it placed women in the same category as other taxable property. Yet the plural wives tax remained in force until 1950.

If a Maasai man derives his status from the number of his cattle and wives, a Maasai woman derives her status from the number of children she bears him.

As we worked together there was time for chatter, and I would ask each woman how many children she had. For older women, the answer was between five and ten. For younger women, they commonly responded: "I've three children at the moment, but when my family is complete there will be six." I never requested this expanded answer, but it was clearly important for them to stress that their child-bearing was an unfinished task.

"You don't think three is enough?" I would ask.

Appalled at such a suggestion, they sucked their breath in through their missing bottom teeth. Six children was the minimum number a respectable woman should have, but the more children the better, providing the family had sufficient cattle to support them.

"How many children do women in your country have?" asked Anna.

"I've got two. One or two is common. A few have more, but it's rare to have as many as six."

This puzzled them. There was further racing and rolling of Maa syllables. "How can a woman be renowned if not through having many children?" Anna wanted to know.

I tried to convey to them the lives of women in my culture, the things which we value, and the things on which our prestige is based, and some of them seemed less meaningful and more harmful than having many children. For a while they were silent as they assimilated this information.

"For us, if you bear many children, it shows that your husband loves you," Esta interjected.

I had not considered that perspective before. Suddenly, the high birth rate in Maasai families made sense to me. If a husband is shared between many wives, it is natural to assume that the woman who bears the greatest number of children is the most favoured wife and, as such, has greater prestige than the others.

But it was not simply prestige the women were after. They clearly adored children for their own sake. And so did the men. They might love their cattle, but they also loved their children. 'A woman without children is like a wilderness', went the words of a well-known Maasai proverb.

"I was married for four years before I fell pregnant the first time," recalled Nasujiak, an old grandmother. "At that time, it was the custom to give your firstborn to another Maasai to bring up, usually to your mother-in-law. But when my son was born I was so overjoyed, I loved him so much, I couldn't bear to be parted from him and I refused."

"What happened?"

"They didn't press me. They saw how much I loved my baby. It's good that practice has disappeared. Back then a mother was not supposed to let her firstborn see her face as she was breast-feeding so that that the baby could bond when it was given away. We no longer believe that way nowadays. It's better."

"I think women love their husband more than their husband loves them. Especially when we want another baby!" said Sainoi with a mischievous chuckle. "If a woman is still breast-feeding and her husband wants to sleep with her she can refuse and tell him to come back later when her child is bigger. One time, I remember my husband pleaded to sleep with me and I said, 'No, it will disturb the children; I must be alone to comfort them in case they wake up.' He argued that he was the one in need of my comfort! But still I sent him away. 'My babies need comforting more than you!' I told him."

"My husband treated all his twelve wives well. He loved us all," she went on. "He would give us money when we begged for it, unless he genuinely had none to give. Of course, he beat us when cows went missing, or when we didn't report a missing cow. Sometimes the boys brought the cattle back and we didn't count them carefully enough to spot a missing animal. But he never caned us without good reason. I was happy that my husband was an important and wealthy man. He was a good provider. He had more cattle than anyone else I knew. We always had enough food to eat, and he started cultivating land some time before any other Maasai. When he was over ninety years old, he could still walk from Engurashi to Pangalala or Orkasmet.

"When he died, we buried him inside the *engang* within the cow enclosure because he was a man of such stature. People came from far away, from Arusha and beyond. It was a big ceremony and we killed many sheep and cows. I wept for days and days."

When I consider the status of Maasai women in today's Steppe, the only certainty is that their situation is more complex than the price of five pigeon eggs or eight cows suggests.

The relationships which I observed between men and women were complex, multi-layered and often inconsistent. Love and respect existed – on both sides. At times, women showed an equality and autonomy that was unexpected. Yet somewhere under the surface lurked an unyielding rock of male authority, at least as far as cattle were concerned.

The more I learnt from them the less I was able to sum it up. To view polygamy as intrinsically demeaning to women was oversimplistic. As in monogamous relationships, the success of a marriage and the happiness of its participants depended as much on the attitudes and expectations of the individuals involved. As I watched Mama Masai members fraternising and fellowshipping together (where are the feminine terms?), my dominant impression was of the strong bonds of sisterhood and camaraderie. The air around them was commonly filled with joking and laughter and ripostes. They did not come across as unhappy wives, gnawed by jealousy; they did not appear to be systemically downtrodden or living in fear of their husbands.

Yet the fact remained that women's status was low and they complained privately of their lack of freedom to make expenditure decisions, even down to a bar of soap. Esta's story was a warning to wives who did not toe the line; so too were the references to being caned by their husbands. These things disturbed the positive picture I had built.

How to harmonise these conflicting images? It was beyond me.

14

—•◦◦◦••◦•◦◦•◦•◦•◦•◦•◦•◦•◦•◦•◦◦◦•◦•◦◦—

Business as usual?

"We don't know how it happened," recounted Mama Kicheche. "Probably the kerosene lamp was not thoroughly blown out. Maybe a wind knocked it over. We couldn't put the flames out because we didn't have any water. And we couldn't rescue our goods because we didn't have the key."

Arng'ariat group had decided to establish a small shop with their start-up loan. Ngage was a slightly larger settlement than others, worthy of the label 'village'. It was composed of nearby Maasai homesteads and the dwellings of some non-Maasai people since it was the headquarters for a division of Simanjiro District. As such, it had a small office with a solar panel and a short-wave radio, a primary school, a few shops, a couple of bars serving food and drinks, and the staff quarters for a health organisation working in the area. There was thus a small community of people with a bit of cash in their pockets, which made running a shop a viable business.

Their shop was modest – a cubicle with a grille in the wall through which they traded a stock of school materials, sugar, flour and other consumables. Business was not bad as most Maasai chose to patronise their shop rather than those of the competition. Instead of serving in the shop themselves, the women had apparently hired a young Maasai man. After locking up the shop that evening, he had gone out with his mates, taking the key with him. By the time he had been located – and long before their donkeys returned from the river with water – their shop was a pile of cinders.

The loss of their shop with its stock was a serious blow, but worse was the revelation that all their funds from the shop and their beadwork had been stored inside. These cash notes of Tanzanian currency were now – alas! – a pile of unspecified ash.

"You had stored *all* your cash savings in the shop?" I repeated, aghast.

The women smiled sheepishly. "But we managed to salvage these," said Mama Kicheche with a positive spin, placing a sack in front of me. Inside were thousands of soot-stained beads. Their plastic bags and threads had melted away, but the beads had survived and were quite useable once cleaned. Their indestructability was a positive feature of beadwork that I had not previously considered.

Keys were causing problems. At Pangalala group, the women were dispirited and not working. Their beads and samples were locked in a chest, and their leader had vanished with the key.

This had been the state of affairs on two previous visits, so I was disappointed to find the leader and the key still absent. After further questioning, they divulged that their leader had permanently moved away and was unlikely ever to return. It had not occurred to them to select a new leader, or to break open the chest.

But their main challenge that year was cultivation. The first year they had harvested a decent crop of maize, and encouraged by that small success, they had planted a much larger area. When the maize was knee-high, the rains abruptly ended. Clouds passed by overhead, thunderbursts and rain fell elsewhere in the Steppe, but none in the particular spot where their maize was planted. The crop shrivelled and died.

Planting maize in the Steppe was always going to be risky. What puzzled me more is that they had hired migrant labourers to do the work. "Couldn't you have saved that cost by doing the work yourselves?"

"We know so little about farming, and our fields are so far to visit every day. We've cows to milk, children to feed."

They waved their hands vaguely towards the escarpment. "I'm a good walker," I said as I proposed a visit to the site. Further conversation revealed it was a full day's walk to reach their fields.

"Isn't there anywhere *closer* you could farm?"

"There's no moisture in the soil down here."

"Why live down here then, if there's better grazing for your animals and the possibility to cultivate up there?"

The women replied with the same gentle patience as when they responded to children's questions: "There are no water sources up there. Rain falls, but only occasionally. The grass is green from cloud mist. We must live here, close to the river, where we can carry water to our homes."

A fire was burning in the entrance chamber to Magilena's hut at Engorini. Inside the inner chamber it was hot, dark and smoky. The book-keeper was sitting on her cowhide bed wrapped in blankets, damp with perspiration, a newborn baby sucking at her breasts. This was the finance office of Matonyok group.

I peered at the bundle in her arms. "Girl or boy?"

It was a boy. "I envy you!" exclaimed Frida, who was accompanying me . "What herbs do you Maasai use to make it a boy?" A small smile hovered momentarily on Magilena's glum face, but she denied taking any such concoctions.

"I've five children, and all girls!" Frida explained. "My husband wanted a son, and each time I prayed for a boy. After three girls I thought, 'How are we going to feed them? Three's enough. No more.' My husband agreed, but later he changed his mind: 'Let's have just one more; maybe it will be boy this time.' So we had another. Again it was a girl! And I told him, 'Now we definitely stop. No more. We can't afford another.' But after some time he pleaded and pressured me, saying, 'Mama, *please,* just one more. I *know* it will be boy this time.' So we had number five – and it was a girl. I cried, and my husband cried! But even he agreed that five children was too many, and we stopped."

Despite the soft bloom of motherhood in her face, Magilena was thoroughly jaded with her incarceration. Following Maasai custom, she had to remain inside her tiny hut for three months, being fed the best food but never going outside. It is a precaution which Maasai take to protect the life of the newborn and the mother.

So we were obliged to do our business inside her hut. We found her ledger book stuck in the rafters. Frida produced a torch and we peered at its pages in the smoky darkness. There were scribbles at odd angles to the page, a few figures scattered here and there, none of them inside the columns, or dated. Sweat trickled down our faces as we struggled to make sense of the accounts. When the torch batteries packed up, I leapt at the opportunity for some fresh air and went to dig mine out of the car. When I returned, Frida was expounding the importance of written records and the proper way to keep them. But had I been confined to Magilena's hot smoky prison, I think I would have ripped the ledger book to shreds.

Managing a business was a steep learning curve for the women, and it was not surprising that their zest for Mama Masai income activities waxed and waned. Esta's forced removal from her group had demonstrated their gender boundaries. But there were many issues lurking under the surface which I knew nothing about.

From my viewpoint, the biggest challenge was figuring out how their beadwork business could function independently of assistance. The Project was due to close soon. Dependency was a common syndrome in Tanzania, which scuttled many well-meaning attempts to help. Even where keys were not missing, a group's refrain was inevitably: "Our beads are finished. Have you brought us more?" No matter how many times Frida and I explained that it was up to them to put money aside and go and buy the beads, and they agreed to do so, it never happened.

Maybe you should drop the beadwork idea – perhaps there's better income in something else?" I suggested several times. But they were adamant they wanted to continue. "*You* bring us the beads and *we'll* make you your products," they declared, making it sound like they were the ones doing *me* a favour.

Remoteness was our main challenge. It was a day's journey to reach a town where beads and wire could be purchased at prices that were not highly inflated. With no local transport the first part of the journey had to be on foot. Cultural factors added to the challenge. To make any kind of a journey they needed permission from their husbands. Some had never been on a bus; they were unfamiliar with the layout of the towns, and totally inexperienced with the business of making purchases and sales.

Were we being hopelessly ambitious? Expecting that they could leapfrog from being dependent wives of subsistence pastoralists to being independent businesswomen?

The curious thing is that historical records show that Maasai women were not stay-at-home wives in the past.

'By a strange reversion of the conventions of civilization,' writes Sheldon, 'the men do all the needlework, and embroider their own and the women's bead and metal belts and ornaments, and also do the fighting; and the women are the unmolested purveyors between hostile tribes when they are at war.'[1]

So it was the women who were the business people of the Maasai, fearlessly trading with 'hostile tribes' while their young men beaded ornaments and played battle games! Though men were the guardians of the cattle, it was the women's responsibility to milk the herds, cure the hides into leather, and trade animal products to supply their other needs. Bunches of grass – a symbol of peace – were a necessary accessory to Maasai women's attire on account of their dealings with hostile tribes.

Other accounts corroborate that the Maasai used to trade extensively with neighbouring tribes, and it was solely women who conducted this trade. The explorer, Thomson, describes one as 'well-dressed in bullock's hide and loaded with wire, beads, and chains, driving a donkey before her as she wends her way fearlessly towards Kibonoto to buy the vegetable food eaten by married people and children'.[2]

Merker 1904 ethnography of the Maasai is considered the best study of its time. Captain Moritz Meker was a German colonial administrator stationed in Moshi, and the value of his ethnography is that he was able to study the untouched and uncolonised Maasai who lived to the south of Arusha – that is, in the same part of the Maasai Steppe where the Mama Masai live. And quite possibly the Mama Masai women with whom I have dealings with, are direct descendants of those whom Merker describes in this way:

> What is not used in her own household in the way of milk, meat, and skins is her housekeeping money, with which she buys vegetable foods and such household objects as she does not make herself. She is not supervised in this in any way by her husband. It is beneath his dignity to interfere in these affairs.[3]

Maasai women would either travel alone or in small groups to market-places such as Moshi and the settlements of other tribes, where they purchased foodstuffs such as maize, bananas and sweet potatoes. Mercker records their donkey caravans travelling distances of up to five days, trading goods along the way.

But there was one difference from the present situation. This trade was barter, not cash.

'The Maasai must learn to use money and learn soon. His need of money to pay tax is a main incentive at the moment to induce him to bring his cattle in person to an auction where he sells for cash and is introduced to the mysteries of competition in prices ...' wrote Baxter, the British colonial Maasai district officer in Tanganyika, in a report dated 1933.[4]

The colonial 'monetisation campaign', as it became called, aimed to alter Maasai culture by replacing the traditional barter trade with cash so that the Maasai would view cattle as commodities rather than as symbols of God's blessing. By requiring their taxes to be paid in cash, and by dangling imported items in front of them, the British hoped to lure the Maasai into selling more cattle and reducing their need for land.

But the Maasai were not interested in becoming consumers. They had no desire for non-living possessions; they were not attracted by the status symbols which others pursued. The monetisation campaign was a dismal failure with regard to the colonial aim of lowering cattle numbers. 'The Maasai is a miser of cattle. He allows his herds to increase indefinitely and will only sell sufficient slaughter stock to pay his tax and satisfy his very moderate requirements in cloth and wire,' records another frustrated district officer.[5]

Yet the monetisation campaign had far-reaching consequences for Maasai society.

Cattle were returning for the night. The setting was perfect: a red globe sinking into the fiery horizon, red-cloaked Maasai *morani* running here and there, and a herd of long-horned cattle kicking up dust. I stationed myself by the entrance to the enclosure and stared into the camera screen. A large cow with impressive horns approached. As I clicked 'video mode', I realised the cow had the wrong organs. Through the screen, I observed it lower its head and charge me. I dived for cover, and the onlookers burst into laughter. They loved it when I made a fool of myself.

"*Koko*!" called out Mama Kicheche. "What are you frightened of? The bull won't harm you! He's just curious. Trust me."

Could I trust her? Should I trust her? I was outside my comfort zone; I had no experience with cattle. My fears in this regard mirrored Mama Masai's distrust of money, and their inexperience at handling it, which was the root cause of many of their management problems.

Money tends to slip into our lives at an early age. Without a qualm, we accept a currency note as a substance of value, never sparing a thought as to its phony nature, rarely regarding it as a worthless scrap of paper masquerading as something of value. In fact, we are such fundamentalists concerning money, that we are ignorant of the sheer amount of faith we employ each time we handle it. I believe that this was largely the cause of Mama Masai's reluctance to handle money or to put income aside as cash savings. Unable to read and write, figures in ledger books had no meaning for most of them – they had to take things on trust. Even a wad of cash notes had little resonance for they were used to operating in a largely cashless economy. Currency they could appreciate were numbers of cows or sacks of maize. If income was not immediately translated into these, then they felt it had disappeared, or that their leaders had cheated them. Despite the monetisation campaign, even the men, when they earned cash, preferred to convert it into four-legged currency which providentially bestowed a daily dividend of milk.

For the rural poor in Tanzania, market transactions are conducted in small coins – 10, 25, 50, or 100 shilling coins. One thousand Tanzanian shillings is roughly equivalent to 40 pence (GBP) or 60 cents (USD).[6] For the Mama Masai women to earn significant income from their beadwork, they needed to purchase beads with Tanzanian shilling notes that had a serious number of zeroes after the digit. Although they had chosen a traditional skill and product, unfortunately it depended on imported beads which were expensive and not available locally.

What had happened to the women that they no longer had the freedom they once enjoyed? Why did they no longer travel and trade? What had caused their economic disempowerment so that now they played a supporting role to their husbands rather than the independent role they had enjoyed in the past?

The culprit may have been the monetisation campaign.

British colonial officers unconsciously brought with them a sense of masculine superiority, the dominant gender attitude of British culture at that time. Since they were exclusively male, they chose to deal with Maasai men. Thus when they began to lure the Maasai into the cash economy through taxation, money and all trade conducted in cash became viewed as the exclusive property and domain of *men*, argues the anthropologist Dorothy Hodgson.[7] Maasai women were hardly visible to the colonials, except as chattels. Indeed, Baxter's memo quoted above, is notably devoid of female pronouns.

As Maasai men began, albeit reluctantly, to integrate themselves into the cash economy, and money started to penetrate the thorn barrier around their *engangs*, women found themselves excluded. Men positioned themselves as the guardians of money, with the result that women were slowly dispossessed of their trading role and shared rights. As money gained currency, the women had less and less say in matters of household income and expenditure, thus losing their economic status and skills.

In this way, during the latter half of colonial rule (1930–1961), a female-dominated barter economy slowly gave way to a male-domi-nated cash economy. And women, who had once travelled and traded, became confined to the homestead.

My own observations supported Hodgson's theory. Bereta, one of the oldest members of Mama Masai, could remember participating in such trading. "We used to go to the camps of the *mzungu* to barter milk," she told me. "They gave us kerosene and sugar in return. But we never sold them cows – that was the men's right."

It seemed likely that the women's reluctance to handle money was partly due to this perception that cash was the property of men. Any cash that the women earned was vulnerable to being appropriated by men, which explained the women's desire to convert their money earnings as quickly as possible into maize – a foodstuff, the rightful property of women. In social interactions, men and women appeared to be on a fairly equal footing, but when it came to cash earnings from their animals, the men had absolute control and the women had none. There were no longer any forays to marketplaces, no barter of milk or hides as in the past.

This theory may be only part of the explanation for the low economic status of women. Nonetheless, understanding how recently even Maasai men had been introduced to money, helped me to see the beadworkers' challenges in perspective. To deal in money required faith and trust. The coins or notes in the women's hands were not alive, as were living, breathing cows that they could milk each day.

On the other hand, translating money into beads would appear to be culturally appropriate and acceptable. As a trading currency, beads have a long history in Africa. However, there remained the fact that to get the beads they were obliged to travel outside their community, and women had lost the right to do this. And unlike sacks of maize, beads were not instantly convertible into food, should the need arise.

Lack of trust or confidence – or both – were probably the main factors which moderated the women's engagement in income-generation activities. It was not surprising when I thought about it. Why should women trust this idea of cash-generation? Why should they invest the effort to make it work? To me, an outsider, it might seem obvious: "You are struggling to make ends meet. Your herds are adding to the destruction of the environment, the very thing on which your livelihood depends. The reduction in your grazing lands and global warming are placing your lives in jeopardy. Here's a different way to earn a living. Here's some training for the new skills you'll need. Here's a loan to get you started. Don't worry – there are no risks!"

It was like asking me to herd their cattle. They might offer assurance that the bull isn't going to gore me, but could I trust their words? Why on earth should they invest their time, their skills, even some of their own scarce resources, into this crazy scheme? When viewed from their perspective, their lack of commitment was not surprising – on the contrary, I was amazed at their degree of perseverance. We had no assurance that the idea would work. Nobody knew. Something might work in one community and fail in the neighbouring community. Projects such as ours were like doctors trying to cure a stricken patient: "Here, try this treatment ... oops sorry, that didn't work! Why don't you try this one next?"

After a while the patient begs to die in peace.

Nonetheless, there was evidence that the groups were making money. Not yet in a sustainable way, but enough to make them reluctant to abandon the idea.

"I bought myself some soap and a hurricane lamp," one woman testified. "I bought some material to make myself and my daughters new robes," said another. Others had spent their income on household utensils; some on food treats such as rice, biscuits and fruit for their children. One mentioned that she had been able to buy medicine for her children; several mentioned buying school books.

Mama Kicheche had bought herself a goat. Not good news for the environment, but this one was her own. "I wanted something alive," she explained, "so that whenever I see it jumping around my *engang* it reminds me that this is *mine*! I did something on my own!"

Even more encouraging was the report that Esta had taken some of her group's products to an agriculture fair in Arusha. The Regional Commissioner liked her beaded leather bags so much that he ordered some more. Esta asked people in Loiborsoit to send her some more leather from the small tannery. When none was forthcoming, she had not been deterred but had gone to Dar es Salaam, bought leather in the Kariakoo market, made the bags and delivered them to the Commissioner. Although her costs must have far exceeded her income in this particular case, the fact was that she had used her initiative. I feared for the state of her marriage! But this effort, more than anything else, encouraged me to persevere.

Frida's arrival also triggered a burst of new progress in the groups. She was dedicated and extremely hard-working. Over time I came to appreciate that the gender bond, the common understanding and experiences which women share, more than outweighed the fact that she was not Maasai – and quite quickly, Frida picked up Maa language.

Carrying out her livestock responsibilities, Frida faced tremendous male Maasai prejudice. The Maasai looked down on her disdainfully from the height: "You think you can treat my cattle? *Ho*! I will sit back and watch the spectacle, for surely you are not up to the task!"

At first, they would not let her near. "I wasn't even allowed to touch their cattle! I could only advise from a distance," she told me. But slowly she proved her worth. The breakthrough was a particularly difficult case where a large calf was stuck in the birth canal. After a long struggle Frida delivered the calf, alive. Word got around, and soon the Maasai were calling on her veterinary skills.

The Project supplied her with a motorbike – a *piki-piki* in Swahili language. I had never seen a Tanzanian woman riding one. Frida did not define herself as a feminist, but neither did she turn her back on a challenge. Mastering the *piki-piki*, she took the spills in her stride and became familiar with basic maintenance. Driving on the sandy tracks was not easy. She had a helmet but no goggles, so she would wrap her scarf turban-style around her face. One time I was driving behind her in my car, when a massive dust-devil crossed our path. For several minutes I stopped driving as I could see nothing. I was worried for Frida on her *piki-piki*. Eventually, she emerged, dusty-red like an anthill, but still smiling.

When I complimented her on her motor cycling skills, she responded: "Riding *piki-piki* is *much* easier than castrating bulls!"

Under her direction and energy, the Mama Masai groups began to flourish. New groups sprouted spontaneously, like desert flowers after rain. How word spread I did not know. A cluster of groups emerged in the north-east, around the shores of Nyumba ya Mungu lake. In Orkasmet, the district government was actively promoting women's groups. They even employed Esta as a skills trainer in one of their workshops.

"Did you train them in beadwork – in the same products?" I asked Esta the next time I saw her.

"Yes."

"And how are *they* going to do their marketing?" I inquired, thinking that the existing groups could plug into the government's marketing plan.

"Through you," she answered, puzzled by my question.

My elation evaporated.

15

Kariakoo

The answer to any question beginning "Where can I buy ...?" was invariably "Kariakoo."

Kariakoo is the most authentically African part of Dar es Salaam. It is rare to see any white faces among the thronging crowds, but if one can face the chaos and heat it is an Aladdin's cave of treasure at half the cost of the upmarket shops. Pyramids of aubergines and towers of tomatoes spill onto the pavements around its covered market. Along its clogged streets vendors display an eclectic mélange of pots and pans, *kanga* cloth, carts of vegetables, rice and beans; garish calendars, prayer rugs, mobile phone covers, farming implements, dog chains, key rings, coils of wire, skins of leather and skeins of beads, to mention just a few.

Thanks to my involvement with the Maasai women's groups, I learnt to find my way around this quarter and came to appreciate its rich diversity. Here, peacefully nudging shoulders on the same street, one might see a Maasai in tribal dress, a Muslim man in his *kanzu* and *kofiya*, or a woman shrouded in a black *burka*, mingling with women in vivid *kanga* cloth printed with Swahili proverbs or political slogans – some with crosses around their necks; or a traditional medicine practitioner dressed in an animal skin and, hanging out on street corners, the modern youth: girls in high heels and mini-skirts, boys in sagging denims and cut-away T-shirts.

When I first arrived in the city, I was warned never to go to Kariakoo alone. In the hustle and bustle of its crowded streets, pickpocketing did not require great skill. But I followed some basic ground rules and the worst that ever happened to me was to be jostled, finding a hand reaching into my already empty pockets. If one came by car, the first rule was to park the car outside one of the smarter looking shops and pay the shop assistant a few coins for keeping an eye on it. The second rule was to have a firm grip on one's purse. The pickpockets' tricks were ingenious. A common one was to knock on the window of a car and point at one of the tyres. The driver's typical reaction was to jump out and inspect the flat tyre, leaving the door open, handbags and shopping exposed.

With due precaution, I would wend my way to a pedestrian alleyway off the main Msimbazi thoroughfare that slices through Kariakoo. Along this alleyway a huddle of unemployed young men would be sitting on the pavement or leaning against the wall, threading beaded trinkets as a way of earning their sustenance for the day. The shop at the end of the alley was adorned with strings of glass beads of every colour. Usually, there would be one or two Maasai customers at its counter. After I had made my purchases, the shopkeeper would wrap the beads in newspaper and kindly carry them to my car.

Beads could be purchased in Simanjiro, but at treble the cost, and the range was limited and availability unreliable. I was aware that buying raw materials for a women's handicraft enterprise located five hundred kilometres into the interior broke several basic rules of business and development. Every step I took around Kariakoo market, I was wondering how the women's groups would be able to manage this supply line without me. I was not the first to be concerned about the supply line. The name Kariakoo is a corruption of the term Carrier Corps and dates from the days of World War I, when Germany was fighting Britain for control of East Africa. To feed their troops they needed a vast supply line and recruited a corps of several hundred thousand porters. The Kariakoo area – close to the port of Dar es Salaam – was their base and starting point.

Beads and the Maasai. The two are firmly wedded in the minds of most visitors to East Africa. Yet how did it come to pass that the decoration for which the Maasai are famous is dependent upon imported materials? I was curious to know when the Maasai first started wearing beads. Was it a recent fashion, something they had adopted since the first explorer-tourists arrived, or were they already clothed in beads when they began their southward push out of the Nile Valley?

On her 1891 expedition, Sheldon records: 'A Masai woman's regulation dress consists of four metal spiral coils for the legs, four similar coils for the arms, and a metal coil collar supplemented by brass and pewter collars or necklets ... to which is added several pounds in metal and other beads.'[1] She also mentions brass Catherine-wheel earrings and blue and green glass rings embellishing a cowhide hood.

Their ponderous coils of iron, copper and brass weighed up to fifty pounds and resembled exaggerated, multifold, continuous bangles or car springs, according to Sheldon, and their enormous weight and pressure deformed the bones and muscles of the young women. Thomson, too, describes these coils as being 'so awkward that the wearer cannot walk properly, she cannot sit down or rise up like any other human being, and she cannot run'.[2] Sheldon was such an ardent collector of tribal handicrafts, she even stripped the iron coils from the corpse of a Maasai woman that her expedition came across in the bush: 'I nerved myself to the removal of her leglets, which had become so imbedded into the flesh and muscles of her legs, amputation was necessary.'[3]

All the early explorer accounts agree that coils of wire and chains of metal beads were the main decorative material of the Maasai. Male Maasai were basically nude, though they sometimes wore a short leather cape over their shoulders, while the women wore 'a bullock's hide from which the hair has been scraped, tied over the left shoulder, passing under the right arm. A beaded belt confines it round the waist'.[4]

Their dress has not changed greatly. Cloth has been substituted for the leather robe, but it is worn in the same style over one shoulder and contained by a leather waist belt, often beaded. Some women still wear coils of copper on their legs or arms, but most have abandoned this custom.

At the time of the explorers, many other tribes were wearing similar quantities of metal and beads, but only the Maasai have maintained a semblance of their traditional dress and decor. Perhaps this illustrates the conservatism of the Maasai. To me, however, it speaks more of the strength of the threads in their social fabric – to the point that they have been able to maintain many of their traditions, against all odds.

Although these historical records exist, it cannot be assumed that either the beads or the metal ornaments pre-date this time. The reason is that these same explorers came to the shores bearing quantities of both to ensure themselves a peaceful passage among potentially hostile tribes. Thomson, for example, carried 44 porter-loads of iron, brass, and copper wire and 22 porter-loads of beads, alongside a mere 11 loads of stores and 8 of ammunition. Upon reaching the border of Maasai territory, Thomson writes:

I now found I had a work of no small magnitude before me, which I had not anticipated. The whole of my beads had to be restrung into the regulation lengths of the Maasai country. Unless in this form they would not be accepted. Before I could leave Taveta, therefore, 60,000 strings had to be made up.[5]

I was amused when I read this. I knew what it was to while away the hours unstringing and restringing beads into quantities which each women's group required. Thomson, however, was able to set a hundred of his porters to work on the task. He describes how the beads were measured out to each and the headmen employed as detectives, with fearful penalties to minimise stealing. 'I was doomed to bitter disappointment. Not a man brought back the amount he received. Out of about four loads distributed, nearly an entire load was wanting,' he went on.[6] He had my sympathy! No matter how many beads I carried into Mama Masai land, their bead chests were always empty, with too few products to account for them. Beads seemed to leak out of their hands, just as in Thomson's day.

Sheldon not only carried in wire and beads of every variety, but also trinkets, music boxes, kites (shot down by children with their bows and arrows), wind-up flying birds (she was accused of black magic) and – incredibly, eccentrically – her court dress! It was of white silk with silver netting and a long train, and she modelled it to impress the various sultans and chiefs she met along the way. 'The large crystal multicoloured stage jewels covering the gown were, one by one, removed to bestow upon covetous natives, until not one remained,' she recalls.[7]

In her book, she provides fine sketches of all the artefacts she collected. Among the materials used for beads and body ornaments, she lists iron, silver, gold, brass, copper, pewter, ivory, bone, horn, glass, amber, wood, animals' teeth, porcupine quills, musk, vanilla, goatskin thongs, and beads made from beans and sweet grasses and from peculiar black pine-like needles obtained from a huge forest tree. She talks of earrings five inches in diameter, of dark blue and red small beads called 'sem-sem', and of 'green and blue grass rings' that were 'prized by the Masai'.

Around Kilimanjaro, Sheldon encountered Chagga tribe blacksmiths who were skilled in making not only spears, knives and agricultural tools, but also necklaces, bracelets, leglets and other ornaments. She describes how the dainty, slender, link chains and metal beads worn by Maasai and other tribes were made from coarse wire

by repeatedly drawing when heated with long slender pincers through perforated metal or stone screens of various sizes in order to reduce to a delicate size ... and the many sizes of metal beads they manufacture by cutting from wire cubes of certain length, then by beating them thin and flat, turn them into little cylinders, pressing the edges so close the union is scarcely noticeable, at the same time keeping them round.[8]

From these and other descriptions, it appears that metal was the main decorative material of the Maasai at that time, with other beads made from organic matter such as horn, bone and seeds. All were manufactured locally and almost certainly pre-date the nineteenth-century explorers. But during this period, foreign beads began inroads from the coast. Red glass beads from Holland are recorded in Maasai necklaces as early as 1850.

Beads have been a trading currency since ancient times. Like gold and silver, they are adaptable and indestructible. They can be bought and incorporated into necklaces and other ornaments, and when the need arises, broken apart, traded, and re-used. In the seventeenth century, European vessels heading to the East Indies traded glass beads from Venice and Holland for food along the African coast. It was only with the rise of the slave trade during the eighteenth century that beads were displaced by silver coins.

Recent research is bringing to light the extent of early trading links along the East African coast. Trade beads of red coral or glass were in use in Madagascar from the twelfth century. Before the Portuguese and Dutch, there were Arab traders, and before them came Indonesian and Chinese vessels. I like to think that the Maasai might have been wearing glass or gem beads long ago. Not garlands of them, but a few choice ones perhaps.

Professor Chami, an archaeologist at the University of Dar es Salaam, told me that he had discovered glass beads of early Roman origin on the coast just south of Dar es Salaam.[9] If beads were on the coast, they could have been traded inland, to the upper Nile Valley, to northern Kenya, and elsewhere. Ancient Egyptians also had glass-blowing skills and were fond of wearing beads, and the Maasai originate from the Nile Valley. I am not the first person to be struck with how the Maasai women's *esosi* neck-plates resemble the broad, beaded necklaces of ancient Egyptians. Some sources suggest that small quantities of Egyptian and Roman beads were traded across the Sahara rather than by sea. The evidence, however, is elusive.

While much of the evidence is lost in the dust of time, it is well established that the beads which the Maasai wear today were first brought to the region by Europeans from the late nineteenth century onwards. These are small, pressed glass beads of very even dimensions, with perfectly drilled holes, originating from central Europe. Glass beads have been made in Bohemia since Roman times, but the industry really flourished from the sixteenth century onwards. By the outbreak of World War I, Bohemia was the world's largest exporter of beads. That war not only ripped apart and re-named Bohemia, but forced Germany to cede Tanganyika to Britain under the terms of the Armistice. In Czechoslovakia, the bead industry declined under communism, but it later revived, and the packs of beads which I bought in Kariakoo all bore the stamp 'Made in the Czech Republic'.

The arrival of Bohemian beads radically transformed Maasai jewellery and stimulated their creative talents. The uniformity of the beads enabled the women to weave the striking geometric designs of their *esosi*, for which they are famous today.

There are rules about the placement of colours, the women explained to me. Blue beads have to be accompanied by white; major bands of different colours are separated by thin strips of a third colour. Some say there is meaning embedded in their designs. Blue to represent the sky and *Engai*, green the grass which supports the cattle, red for their blood, and white for their milk. It is also said that their beadwork carries messages about where they come from, and to which age group they belong. Possibly they do. But the women I worked with insisted there is no underlying meaning, it is just a matter of taste – what you like; what looks good on you. In other words, it is fashion. And fashions could change quite rapidly, even in the Maasai Steppe. Colour choices varied greatly from Kenya to Tanzania, and even within Tanzania. During my years visiting Simanjiro District, the women's *esosi* shed their colours and became more and more minimalist in style, until they consisted almost entirely of white beads, inset with an occasional narrow oblong of transparent lemon or turquoise beads. Strikingly different to the styles in Kenya where, judging from photos, they favour red beads and strong colours. Clearly, if one kept abreast of current fashions in different districts, one could discern from where a woman originated and her likely age, depending on whether her *esosi* was in the latest fashion or slightly dated.

After purchasing beads, I headed to the leather section – a row of low shacks on the edge of Kariakoo. None of the leather on sale was produced in Tanzania; most came from Zambia. The Maasai told me they sometimes traded their raw hides into Kenya. This convinced me there was business potential for the Loiborsoit tannery if they could only improve its management and the quality of its products. It did seem ridiculous to import leather to pastoralists!

Over time, the supply of leather in Kariakoo proved unreliable. The groups were forced to stop their leather bag production and switch to items they had never heard of such as coasters and placemats. These maintained traditional elements in the design, and wiring the beads was the primary method of construction.

It was then that a new problem appeared. Rust. Maasai women had no scruples about a touch of rust on their *esosi* necklaces, but foreign customers pointed in horror at its traces on their beaded placemats. The problem was exacerbated because the products were largely marketed in Dar es Salaam. While the Maasai Steppe is bone-dry for much of the year, the air in Dar es Salaam is humid and ocean-salty.

So the third item on my list in Kariakoo was stainless steel wire. On my first recce, I found a roll of super-fine stainless steel wire in my closest local shop in Msasani village. Assuming it to be a commonly available item, I used it to design a series of beaded animals for Mama Masai to produce. I had no idea what the locals were using it for; it never occurred to me to consider why it might be available in Msasani village in particular. I was never to find it in any other retail store in the country.

The Msasani peninsula, north of Dar es Salaam, is largely the luxury residential area. Colonial bungalows with shady verandahs dot the area, which was favoured by the British for its cool winds and palm-fringed bay. Nowadays, modern and far grander houses and apartment blocks have sprung up, almost entirely housing expatriates or Tanzanians of Indian origin. From our house I could walk north, east, or west and still hit the coastline. If I walked east I reached the lush gardens and grand houses facing the breaking surf of Oyster Bay and Coco Beach, but if I walked west I reached the local village of Msasani, the original settlement on the peninsula, which overlooked the much more tranquil waters of Msasani Bay, protected from the swells by offshore islands and reefs.

Here, there was a mosque whose loudspeakers summoned me to prayer several times a day. Nearby was a path that led through a waste patch of ground overgrown with palms and tropical weeds. Hidden in the vegetation were several tall stone pillars, inscribed with writing, from the seventeenth century: the remains of one of the oldest Arab settlements on the East African coast. Beyond this lay the beach. It was not a beach for bathing. The water was too shallow, and its muddy, gravelly sand was clogged with the litter of fishing – dead shells, stinking fish-heads, sea-bleached rope ends, old rubber tyres, plastic bottles which the fishermen used as buoy markers for their nets and lobster pots, and mounds of flotsam and jetsam from the Indian Ocean. My dogs revelled in the place.

Pulled up on the beach or moored just offshore, or plying the waters of this bay, were a fleet of *mashua*, *dhow* and *ngalawa* fishing boats. These boats with their lateen-rigged sails and outriggers have hardly changed in design since the Indonesians first brought them to East Africa seven hundred years ago. It was this fishing business that led to the presence of thin stainless steel wire in my local Msasani store. Fishermen used it to fix their hooks. When this shop ceased to stock it, I spent months scouring Kariakoo for rust-free wire. Eventually, I located an Indian wholesale supplier. Most of the shops in the old city centre are owned by Indians who have lived there for generations. Their business-minded forebears had arrived in East Africa some decades before British or German explorers realised the business opportunities that East Africa might offer.

Msasani village was a lively, bustling little market – like a mini Kariakoo – its streets filled largely with the local Muslim population of Wa-zaramu, but in amongst their long white *kanzu* dress and *kofiya* caps it was hard to miss the brilliant red shawls of Maasai men. Along the main 'high street' of Msasani village there was a building which the Maasai used as a resting place. Several Maasai women had followed their menfolk to the city, and they were commonly outside this building, sitting in their L-posture on the edge of the road, occupied in beading. This area was so popular with off-duty Maasai night guards that its Muslim shopkeepers stocked a wide range of Maasai wraps and blankets. It was an eclectic and unexpected mix – Muslim and Maasai. For me, it was one of the things I appreciated most about Tanzania – Muslim, Christian, Maasai and tribal cultures mingling without animosity.

From Msasani village, if I took the road heading north towards the point of the peninsula, I soon reached the well-known social spot called The Slipway. It looked out onto the same fishing boats on the same bay, but as one sat in the shade of its Mashua Bar, sipping a cold beer and watching the sails of the *ngalawa* float past against the scorching-red sunset, it presented a totally different world and outlook. The Slipway was the dream-child of an Italian immigrant. It was an old boatyard built by the Chinese. It still housed the decaying hulks of some boats that the Chinese had failed to make seaworthy, as well as one or two luxury speedboats, and plenty of navigational scrap. On the marshy spot next to the boatyard, the Italian had built sea dykes, raised the level of the land, and created a hugely successful plaza area, surrounded by small shops and restaurants. There was a feeling of space and light, a hint of Saracen style in the architecture, and the Indian Ocean lapping at its edge.

The place came into its own once the baking sun was preparing to depart for the day. In the evenings, The Slipway displayed an even greater concoction of cultures and nationalities, albeit a far more wealthy clientele, than that found in Kariakoo or Msasani village. This is where the wealthy and upwardly mobile could share a beer, a passion juice or a bottle of coke, depending on their culture. Much favoured by the international community, it was a cosmopolitan mix of black, brown and white, and sitting at one of its tables one could hear snatches of conversation in scores of different languages, the dominant ones being Swahili, English and Gujarati. On Sunday nights it would be packed with people of all ages, from teenagers in the skimpiest of garments to women of the *Mubarikiyah* sect, in satiny, nightgown-style dresses with hooded capes.

Although it was rare to see a real live Maasai at The Slipway, their iconic presence was everywhere. They featured on T-shirts, on carvings of ebony wood, on the canvases of Tinga Tinga paintings, as motifs in restaurants and on the glossy covers of volumes in the bookshop. Every Saturday, The Slipway hosted a handicraft bazaar, where local artisans could bring their wares. Business was thriving. Producers paid good money for a table at The Slipway market and foreigners thronged to the place to buy their gifts and furnish their rooms. There was a range of tie-dyed textiles and clothing, oil paintings, wood carvings – and a host of stalls selling beadwork!

On the surface, it seemed the ideal marketplace for Mama Masai products. Yet so far I had been reluctant to pursue this option. As The Slipway gained in popularity, the market drew in more and more customers, and more and more producers applied to sell their wares. The competition became intense; the foreign clientele became more adept at bargaining and the prices dropped lower and lower. Knowing the hours it took to thread beads onto wire and create their designs, I was a good judge of the labour-cost as well as the purchase-cost of the imported beads. With the added transportation costs into and out of the Maasai Steppe, it was impossible to compete, price-wise, with producers in Dar es Salaam. In fact, much of the beadwork on sale at The Slipway market at that time did not originate in Tanzania at all, but was imported from Kenya. While the beads cost less in Kenya, the products would have to cross the border and pass through at least one, and probably two, 'middle' hands. I calculated that the actual producer – whether they were youth in the Kagera slums of Nairobi, or genuine Maasai of the Rift Valley – got nothing more than a few cents for a day's work. A pittance, even by African standards.

Mama Masai did not need large profits, but they needed a fair income. While privately I questioned whether the beadwork idea could ever be viable and sustainable, I hated to admit defeat, and so

I continued to try to find the right connection point with the affluence which inhabited the Msasani peninsula.

There was a large, imposing Maasai woman who sold beadwork at The Slipway. She was an urbanised Maasai – or even a fake Maasai – for though she dressed in Maasai garb, she did not shave her head. During their 'exposure' visit, I had taken Esta and the others to The Slipway market, and this Maasai woman had accused them of coming to steal her designs. I was amused, though it was not a joke. My own reluctance to exploit this market was for the same reason – fear that Mama Masai's designs would be stolen and their prices undercut. But since it was proving hard to develop sales through other retailers, the scale of The Slipway market now seemed worth the risk of copycat designs.

My acquaintance with Tumaini, a woman from Malawi, was based on other connections, so it was a while before I realised that she had a stall at The Slipway. Tumaini was petite, half the stature of the aggressive Maasai at The Slipway market, but she was not intimidated by the cut and thrust of Slipway bargaining. I was happy when she agreed to trial Mama Masai's products at her stall, and to pay for them on delivery.

As I prepared to leave The Slipway, a slanging match broke out between the urban Maasai and her neighbours.

"You steal my customers!" she shouted at the pair of slim young girls managing the stall next door.

"How much you pay?" she demanded, grabbing the arm of a South African customer. "I give you best price! I trouble myself for you. I open up my things. I show you this, I show you that. Why you no buy?!" She tried to wrench the purchase out of his hands.

I crept away. I did not have the guts to wheel and deal in such a place.

16

-●○○◎◍●◉○○●○●●◉○●◐◉○○◎◍◐◐●◉●●◉○-

Warriors or orators?

Tumaini sat in the passenger seat clutching a box of solar-powered calculators that I had bought in Kariakoo in the forlorn hope these might prove the solution to Mama Masai's money-management problems. After successfully piloting two consignments of their beadwork in her shop, Tumaini wanted to establish a direct link with the producers. I was delighted as this was a step towards our goal of making Mama Masai independent and sustainable. During the drive, she regaled me with stories about the Maasai, mostly with the moral that the Maasai are not to be trusted, they are arrogant, aloof, dangerous; they steal; they attack; they kill.

But once in the Steppe her attitude changed. As each day passed and brought us to another cluster of Maasai *engang*, I witnessed Tumaini's fears and prejudices peel away like sunburnt skin.

"These people are good people; they are not bad," she exclaimed with a note of surprise. "The women are serious in their efforts. They try very hard. But they are so poor. Where I come from there are poor people, but these Maasai have nothing, nothing, *nothing!*"

For their part, the Maasai welcomed anybody who bothered to travel to their neck of the thornbush. They towered over diminutive Tumaini who came from a mountain people near Lake Nyasa – about as far away as one can get from Maasailand. At each *engang,* she gathered together the women who could read numbers and taught them the mysteries of a calculator. When she saw that the Maasai women gave thanks to God for every meal, and even for every mug of tea, the last shreds of any prejudice with which she had been reared were obliterated.

She was so captivated by them that she even came with me on a second trip.

Over the years, a number of people accompanied me to the Maasai Steppe, and I observed that the charm of the Maasai, close-up in person, quickly won over compatriots as well as foreigners.

Compared to its neighbours, Tanzania has few tribal tensions and is a remarkably peaceful country. This is partly due to the tolerant nature of Tanzanians, but also to a deliberate policy by President Nyerere who sought to replace tribalism with a sense of national identity. While the loss of much tribal history and tradition has taken its toll on the Tanzanian psyche, there is no denying the value which peace and political stability have brought.

But the movement towards greater social cohesion largely bypassed the pastoralist and indigenous people. The Maasai live in the interior, but they remain firmly on the fringes, and have become more marginalised than they were in the past. Government functionaries commonly perceive the Maasai to be backward and inferior to arable farmers, a hindrance to progress, an annoying conundrum from the past.

Years ago, when I was travelling in that mini-bus which rammed through the herd of Maasai goats, I had no inkling of what might lie behind the driver's behaviour. But now I saw the incident as indicative of the prejudice which exists against the Maasai in their fellow East Africans – the lack of understanding, even the contempt with which their way of life is viewed. It was as if the bus driver hated the Maasai because of their refusal to embrace the modern era, which by association tarred all Africans with the brush of 'backward savages'. Or perhaps he was driven by his tribe's collective unconscious to punish the Maasai for whatever they may have inflicted on his ancestors in the past.

Undoubtedly, the Maasai did their share of cattle raiding and fighting in the past. But so did other tribes. The Maasai just happened to be better at it than most, thanks to their superior organisation and the morale of their warriors. Yet the people of East Africa owe a debt to them: the Maasai never condoned the slave trade. Their fearsome reputation and distribution in a north–south band blocked the slave-traders' access so that many tribes in Kenya and Tanganyika were spared.

The irony today is that although the Maasai remain adamantly independent, intent on following their own destiny, their lives are more governed by the image which others have created of them. Who they are, and who they want to be, has become overshadowed by the persona other people perceive. The history of their image is inextricable from the story of colonialism and the attitudes that white people brought with them. Like it or not, the *mzungu* is irretrievably embedded in their history and, the Maasai have been shaped and redefined by the encounter.

The stories of the early explorers, their descriptions on first meeting the Maasai, the adjectives that they used to portray the Maasai, make fascinating reading. They have been admired, dreaded, worshipped and reviled, but rarely have they left a white person unmoved. Reading these accounts, I was intrigued to compare their impressions with my own, to reflect on what had changed and what had endured, what rang true and what did not.

When missionaries and explorers set foot in East Africa in the second half of the nineteenth century, they referred to the Maasai as a force to be reckoned with. Arab slave traders gave them a wide berth. Tribes of the Bantu group lived in fear of them. There are various references to their fighting ability, though few by eye-witnesses, and much of the raiding and fighting appears to have been between rival Maasai clans, not against others.

The earliest description in English is probably the one by Dr Ludwig Krapf, who arrived on the coast in 1843 and describes the Maasai as:

These worst of heathen, these truculent savages who conquer or die, death having no terrors for them ... They are dreaded as warriors, laying all to waste with fire and sword, so that the weaker tribes do not venture to resist them in the open field, but seek only to save themselves by the quickest possible flight.[1]

Krapf never travelled far enough to penetrate Maasailand. He may have had informants, but he is quite possibly repeating hearsay and hyperbole from other tribes. Raised as a German Lutheran, Krapf was sent to East Africa by the Anglican Church Missionary Society and set up his base on the coast, at Mombasa. Almost immediately, he lost his wife and baby daughter to malaria. In 1846, he was joined by fellow German, Rebmann, who became the first European to set eyes on Mount Kilimanjaro. Alas for Rebmann's fame, the story of snow on the equator was too fantastical for the Victorians to believe at the time. Krapf also reached Kilimanjaro, but never passed beyond this point into Maasai territory proper. Livingstone does not appear to have encountered the Maasai, neither did Burton or Speke, for their journeys from Zanzibar followed a wide loop south of Maasai territory.

Thus it is the explorer Joseph Thomson who provides us with the first detailed eye-witness accounts of the Maasai – and the name for the small graceful gazelle species. His book *Through Masai Land*, published in 1885,[2] became an immediate bestseller, with Victorians avid to know more about the 'dark continent' and its fabled tribes. Thomson primes the reader to expect the worst. The frontispiece shows an etching of a dark, devilish-looking Maasai warrior with the caption 'On the warpath in Masai Land'. The term 'dreaded warriors' is strewn through its pages. In the introduction he quotes from Krapf; he describes expeditions such as Baron von der Decken's, which set out to enter Maasai country but 'at the very threshold, they were met by several thousands of the dreaded warriors, and compelled to return to the coast'.[3] He explains that Arab traders never dreamed of entering Maasai territory with less than 300 men, while he, Thomson, had only 150, and by the time his caravan was on the verge of Maasai territory, his porters 'had heard so many dreadful stories about the murderous propensities of the Maasai that they were electrically charged with fear'.[4]

As Thomson ventured into Maasai territory, he learnt that the expedition of the German explorer Dr Fischer was a few days ahead of him, and had just had an encounter in which three Maasai had been killed and the tribe thrown into a state of 'profound excitement'. When word then arrived that a great war-party of two thousand Maasai warriors lay on his path, Thomson considered his options. Would they attack? Should his party retreat? Thomson had sixty thousand strings of beads with which to negotiate peace, but who would dare to make the first move? The Maasai warriors with their spears and shields – or Thomson's party who had guns?

Neither, as it happened. It was Maasai women!

They entered Thomson's camp, unarmed and unannounced, 'with a mincing, half-dancing step and peculiar motion of the body, chanting a salutation all the time. Each one carried a bunch of grass in the hand, a token of peace and goodwill'.[5] I love this story. I can picture the scene, see the way the women moved, hear their high-pitched voices chanting. And the fact that they came bearing green grasses. It took courage on their part, given that a Maasai woman had been one of the three killed, and they must have felt extremely vulnerable to enter the white man's camp with its guns and enormous retinue of male guards and porters.

The women informed Thomson to expect a deputation the next day. Thomson describes how excited and nervous he felt as he walked to the assignation: 'Passing through the forest we soon set our eyes upon the dreaded warriors that had been so long the subject of my waking dreams, and I could not but involuntarily exclaim, "What splendid fellows!" as I surveyed a band of the most peculiar race of men to be found in all Africa.'[6] After sticking their spears in the ground and resting their shields, a spokesman arose from the Maasai,

> leisurely took a spear in his left hand to lean upon, and then using his knobkerrie as an orator's baton, he proceeded to deliver his message with all the ease of a professional speaker. With profound astonishment I watched this son of the desert, as he stood before

me, speaking with a natural fluency and grace, a certain sense of gravity and importance of his position, and a dignity of attitude beyond all praise.[7]

After many speeches and other ceremonies, Thomson agreed on a payment of cloth, wire, chains and beads. Despite this peace-offering, a day or two later he beat an undignified retreat under cover of darkness when he learnt that the whole country ahead of him was up in arms to revenge the Fischer affray. He later regrouped and returned in a convoy with an Arab caravan for greater protection. As the caravan neared Maasai kraals on this second foray, he describes how *morani* began to appear: 'they do not hurry themselves. They survey us leisurely, and by neither word nor sign betray any feelings of astonishment'. Gravely, they introduce themselves and Thomson confesses himself 'greatly struck by the unusual manners of these savages, so different from the notion we have formed of them'.[8]

Later, he relates another anecdote which illuminates the Maasai character. A donkey had been stolen from a Maasai warrior and sold to Thomson's party. The plaintiff, chancing to recognise his donkey in Thomson's camp, seized it and tried to carry it away. A cry of 'guns!' was given by the guards and scores of armed porters streamed out of Thomson's camp to form a ring around the disputants. Elsewhere in Africa, such a demonstration would have produced panic among the natives, says Thomson. Not so with the Maasai who, although few in number, 'remained as cool and indifferent as if they were quite unaware that they were surrounded ... An orderly and calm discussion ensued, and ended with an arrangement agreeable to both parties'.[9]

I have chosen these three anecdotes from Thomson because for me they sum up the character of the Maasai as I have seen them: their essentially peaceful, courteous, and even gentle nature, their love of talking and ability to debate, and their fearlessness, which I feel is the more apt word for a quality they possess than the commonly applied 'fierce' or 'warlike'. In my experience, they are neither naturally aggressive, nor inclined to hatred.

As for the women, Thomson writes that they 'had all the style of the men. With slender, well-shaped figures, they had brilliant dark eyes, Mongolian in type, narrow, and with an upward slant. Their expression was distinctly lady-like (for natives) ... Obviously they felt that they were a superior race'.[10] He concludes that the damsels would have been without fault, 'if they had only discarded clay and grease and used Pear's soap'.[11]

Naturally, the explorers wished to portray themselves as exceedingly brave and courageous and this required exaggeration to make the Maasai more warlike than was the case in reality. Thomson is torn between stressing the dignity and forbearance of the Maasai and exaggerating their arrogance and physical power. 'They indulged in none of the obtrusive vulgar inquisitiveness or aggressive impertinence which makes the traveller's life a burden among other tribes ... I began almost to like the Masai, for troublesome and overbearing as they were, they displayed an aristocratic manner, and a consciousness of power ...'[12]

After another incident he writes about 'the cool manner in which three or four elders came into camp without a trace of fear, though their people had been murdering the traders time after time ... They were magnificent specimens of their race, considerably over six feet, and with an aristocratic savage dignity that filled me with admiration.'[13]

Despite some hyperbole, much of Thomson's account rings true for me; it is a relatively balanced one for its era if one reads it carefully, and he supplies a great many details about their customs and social organisation.

For some time, Thomson managed to negotiate his way through Maasailand with copious gifts of beads and wire, and 'medicine-man' acts which were based on Eno's fruit salts and a false tooth which he could take out of his mouth and flash at the Maasai when trapped in a dodgy situation. But he was exposed as a fake when he was unable to cure the rinderpest plague which was beginning to ravage the herds of the Maasai: 'Round the kraals the scene was simply fearful – hundreds of animals dying and in all stages of decomposition ... a fearful stench prevailed, and the people were in helpless distress. They chanted from morn till night an incessant prayer ... The country seemed to be full of lamentations and despairing cries.'[14]

They pleaded with Thomson – believing him to have supernatural powers on account of his false tooth and Eno's fruit salts – to stop the plague. When he was unable to do so, their mood turned dangerous and Thomson made a hasty departure.

From Krapf and Thomson it is apparent that the Maasai already had a certain reputation among other tribes, and when white people arrived, many unwittingly became subscribers to that viewpoint.

A few came with open minds. A missionary who travelled through Maasai country in 1882 recalled that the Maasai were very kind in their manner to him and he enjoyed 'hours of pleasant conversation' with elders.[15] The Hungarian explorer, Count Teleki, found his fear of the Maasai to be unfounded as he made his way up the Ruvu River, and described the Maasai as friendly, peaceable, charming, helpful and by far the most interesting and most powerful people he met. He remarks on their love of talking and listening, their 'great command of dialectics' and the 'parliamentary etiquette' evident in their debates. Sidney Hinde, who was 'Resident to the Masai Chief', also mentions the Maasai's 'undoubted gift of oratory ... keen perception of justice ... and considerable reasoning faculties'.[16]

I was disappointed that Sheldon, the American adventuress who set out to straighten the record of men, is quite derogatory about the Maasai. She appears to fall prey to the prejudices of her Zanzibari porters. A few days into her expedition, Sheldon is startled by the cry of 'Stop, Masai, Masai!' from her porters who 'launched forth into a voluble, rapid gibberish ... pointing to certain vague objects far away in advance of our line of march, and manifested unfeigned alarm and fear'. It turns out they were not Maasai in this case, but after this scare Sheldon says 'I could not but experience a qualm of insecurity, and for the first time fully realised the terror the African bogy-man – the Masai – struck to the Zanzibaris heart'.[17]

145

Sheldon writes that Maasai women lack comeliness, their brass and iron coil adornments are hideous, and the men are belligerent, braggarts, mirthless, never exhibiting signs of affection, having no songs but those of war. I cannot recognise in her descriptions the Maasai whom I know. How many did she meet in person? Her route barely brushed the edge of their territory and she is possibly recounting what her faithful Zanzibari porters told her. It is noticeable that her descriptions of the Maasai are of a more general nature than her accounts of the other tribes she meets.

She describes only two incidents at first hand. In the first, a group of Maasai warriors appear with uplifted spears and demand payment but 'were soon appeased with a few lumps of bluestone'.[18] Perhaps it is this incident which led Sheldon to write 'Blusterers that the Masai are, they cannot be seriously looked upon as true warriors, or as possessing real bravery; but rather as African Jack Shepherds'.[19] But this incident is believable. I can imagine the gang of *morani* lads saying to each other, "C'mon, let's have some fun with this white woman; let's go harass her and get us some beads and stuff!" They would not have intended her harm, merely a bit of sport, I imagine. In the second incident, when several Maasai women approached her with their grass in their hands, Sheldon thought it 'one of the daintiest exhibitions of symbolical friendliness I had ever witnessed'.[20] But she concludes: 'Rather an impossible barbaric people to effect much by way of civilization upon, for a long time to come, meanwhile they may be annihilated.'[21]

What happened to their annihilation? Perhaps it has not come to pass because of their civilisation. In Sheldon's time, the Maasai already had monotheistic beliefs, a highly organised social structure, a democratic governance and justice system, and were skilled speakers and negotiators. This may help explain why they remain distinct today, whereas other tribes have lost their heritage.

As shiploads of colonials took over East Africa, the word 'Maasai' became more and more embellished and enmeshed by the attitudes, prejudices and misconceptions which the immigrants brought with them.

Within a decade of Thomson's and Fischer's expeditions, both the British and the Germans were forging railway lines through the heart of Maasailand. Commerce was the reason. The British desired to link Uganda to the coast. The construction crew suffered from attacks by 'man-eating' lions and on at least one occasion by Maasai warriors. But the surveyor-in-chief describes how the Maasai became so friendly that when an Indian surveyor went missing, the Maasai found him, 'fed the wanderer like a fighting-cock, and three days later brought him back to the depot'. [22]

In Tanganyika, the Imperial High Commissioner Carl Peters claimed that 'The Maasai were not impressed by anything except the gun, and then only if you used it on them'.[23] Peters shot and killed 120 locals during his expedition around Kilimanjaro and became known as 'bloody hands'. In a 1903 memorandum to the Foreign Office, Sir Charles Eliot, the Commissioner for British East Africa, described the Maasai as the most important and dangerous of the tribes with whom he had to deal.[24] He started the trend of mixing admiration with denigration when talking about the Maasai: 'They resemble the lion and the leopard, strong and beautiful beasts of prey... they have hitherto done no good in the world that any one knows of; they have lived by robbery and devastation, and made no use themselves of what they have taken from others'.[25]

It suited the agenda of the early colonials to define the Maasai as indolent, warlike and uncivilised, so they had no scruples over seizing their land. It comes as no surprise to discover that both Carl Peters and Charles Eliot were strong subscribers to the notion of white supremacy. Peters had to flee Tanganyika after ordering the hanging of his mistress and her native lover; his damaged reputation was later rehabilitated by no less a person than Adolf Hitler. Eliot never married and spent his leisure time studying molluscs. If only he had stuck to malacology and had not meddled with the Maasai.

Eliot did more than anyone to demolish the Maasai. 'I have no desire to protect Masaidom,' he writes in a letter to the British Foreign Secretary. 'It is a beastly, bloody system, founded on raiding and immorality, disastrous to both the Masai and their neighbours. The sooner it disappears and is unknown, except in books of anthropology, the better.'[26] It was Eliot who forced through the two land agreements which set in motion the steady erosion of Maasai livelihoods, still rolling one hundred years later. These agreements had to be fingerprinted by the Maasai, in neither case by someone who could claim legitimate political authority over the tribe since their democratic organisation did not comprise overall chiefs. In fact, the fingerprints on the 1911 agreement are those of a thirteen-year-old boy. Sympathetic colonials such as Dr Norman Leys, tried to blow the whistle on British seizures of Maasai land, but his voice fell on deaf ears and he lamented that the true story would never come out.

The Maasai were shunted around. In the first agreement, they were removed from the Rift Valley for the sake of European farmers and the security of the new railway. They were sent north to Laikipia, which they were promised 'in perpetuity' since the land was 'not tempting to settlers, though it was quite possible that when the Masai had grazed down the grass and got it sweet, envious eyes would be cast on their lands',[27] writes another colonial officer. Sure enough, a few years later, with the land sweetened by their cattle, the Maasai were ordered out of Laikipia and sent south again, this time to far less salubrious pastures – ostensibly so that they could all be together in one reserve. Suicidal for traditional pastoralism and for the environment.

It is not surprising that the British feared armed resistance from the Maasai. But the Maasai chose far more civilised means. In 1913, they hired lawyers to sue the British government for illegal land acquisition. They lost on a truly serpentine legal technicality. Defence lawyers for the government argued that since the Maasai had had sufficient sovereignty to sign the land treaty, they were therefore an autonomous foreign power and hence the British legal system could not answer their case. In bringing the lawsuit, the Maasai were the first people in sub-Saharan Africa to use the colonial justice system to challenge colonial actions. This pours scorn on the image of them as uncivilised backward-looking savages. Their spokesperson Ole Gilisho may have been illiterate, but his skills and belief in peaceful advocacy are evidence of the value which the Maasai accorded to non-violent negotiations, and the wisdom and knowledge imparted through their informal education system. The passive resistance led by Ole Gilisho has been described as extraordinary for its time and place but also consistent with Maasai customary justice.[28]

It is impossible to reconcile this capacity with the Maasai Reserve Annual Report of 1921, which records that 'the Maasai are a decadent race and have only survived through being brought under the protection of British rule ... They remain primitive savages who have never evolved and who under present conditions, in all probability, never can evolve.'[29] Lady Cobbold probably puts her finger on the underlying reason for the colonial adminstration's blatant blindness when she writes that the Maasai, 'while deferring to armed authority in the most courteous way made it clear they considered themselves the Englishman's equal if not superior'.[30] The British sought control, but the Maasai remained elusive. If they were sent to jail – cattle raiding was the common crime – they simply died. Such an extraordinary number of them died when placed in confinement that the British had to stop using this method of punishment for them.

The Maasai puzzled and challenged the colonial administrators. They were courteous like gentlemen, articulate like intellectuals, preferring peaceful negotiations but unwilling to kow-tow to the colonials, and fearless enough to fight for their rights if necessary. The British admired and feared them, but also scoffed at them. An ambivalent or dualistic 'love or loathe, admire and deride' attitude enveloped them.

Karen von Blixen is one who appears to have suffered from the invented affliction of Maasai-itis. In *Out of Africa* she describes some Maasai *morani* who drop in on a dance at her property in the Ngong Hills:

These young men have, to the utmost extent that particular form of intelligence which we call chic; daring and wildly fantastical as they seem, they are still unswervingly true to their own nature, and to an immanent ideal. Their style is not an assumed manner, nor an imitation of a foreign perfection, it has grown from the inside, and is an expression of the race and its history.[31]

How have the Maasai coped with the mystique and the contempt which surrounds them? Victor Kimesera, a Maasai historian, spoke these words:

We were photographed and drawn; written about and analysed to be finally categorized as pampered noble-savages of the plains – austere and dignified but savages all the same. Meanwhile we, unaware of the intense interest being taken to keep us as items for study and amusement, went about our usual business of tending our families and our cattle and keeping out of harm's way – out of the way of other strange cultures we neither understood nor wanted.[32]

During my visits, I saw no sign whatsoever of their alleged warlike qualities. They no longer kill lion, or hardly ever. Their warriors are more acquainted with the routine of security companies.

Given their history, I found the Maasai remarkably free of prejudice against others. There were one or two members of the Mama Masai groups who were not Maasai and it was encouraging to find that the women were not clannish.

The Maasai's love of talking and debate is still evident. Their accumulated wisdom and value system still holds and helps them to be strong and maintain their distinctive identity while under pressure from all sides. I cannot imagine how they were ever labelled 'savages', and when you read the nineteenth-century accounts of Maasai women with their symbols of peace and trade with hostile tribes, it seems it was never a justified appellation. On first meeting, they come across as very courteous, warm yet refined, not overbearing in their curiosity, and modest with their pride. They are not obsequious, or patronising or pestering; there is neither hostility nor suspicion when black meets white, and this was one reason why I could feel so relaxed among them. We were different, but we met as equals – or so I felt.

In our interactions I found myself constantly reminded of a conversation I had had with Baba Kicheche. It had taken place on my first trip to the Maasai Steppe, but his words stayed fresh in my mind.

"It's true we are conservative," he had said, "yet we are willing to change some of our traditions and beliefs. But there is one principle which we will never change, one tenet which carries all the others within it: we want to be ourselves. We Maasai don't copy other people. We will cooperate with you, but we will always be different. We are proud of our separateness. We shun the behaviours associated with the towns – stealing, rape, bad language, things like that. We want to be the sort of people who when you see us in a crowd, we will stand out, and you will respect us. You will look at us and say, 'He is really somebody. *He* is a *man*.'"

17

Crocodiles and zebras

Sitting on the terrace of our home enjoying the early morning coolness, I wondered if my affair with the Maasai was at an end. And whether I would miss them and the dusty scrub of the Steppe.

Our garden was a verdant, dripping green. I could see the gardener busy with the hosepipe from our rainwater tank. Large seed pods hung from the baobab trees like fruit bats. The golden nuts of the palm trees nestled in a cocoon of green fronds. Shiny, richly coloured aubergines and tomatoes bulged in the vegetable patch beside a crop of weeds and green beans, and along the perimeter fence, bougainvillea spilled its confetti onto the pavement.

In the Steppe, the Drought Rehabilitation Project had closed down. As the year 2004 began, Oloserian went off to search for new employment and Frida returned to her government job at Nyumba ya Mungu. It seemed doubtful that the women's groups had gained sufficient confidence and momentum to continue their handicraft business independently. Our efforts had been too feeble, the strategies unable to overcome the forces we were up against – a coalition of geography, history and culture. To my chagrin, the women showed little interest in taking over the purchasing and marketing functions. Had history ingrained on their minds that it is white people who come bearing beads and carrying away artefacts?

The geography remained insurmountable – the vast distances, the sparse population, the lack of everything which might ease their lives.

As for culture, just as I thought progress was being made, old values clicked into place to resist it. I began to feel a sneaking sympathy for the frustrated colonial officers of the old Maasai districts! They too had tried every ploy to wean the Maasai away from their dependency on cattle. Were the Maasai impossibly stubborn, closed to change? I didn't believe so. It was more likely a failure on our part. We had failed to convince, failed to find the key that fitted.

At the same time, I considered the competing explanation that, frankly, they truly didn't need the income that badly, didn't have a use for these women's groups. That their cows and goats were sufficient, that they were happy the way they were, content with their thornbush horizon. There was more than a grain of truth in this, I felt. They were happy people for the most part; they did not yearn for much. They were not beguiled by capitalism.

But when I put everything together and gave it a stir, what came to the surface was a lack of faith. In themselves, and in others. Over the years, there had been so many broken promises, so many tricks by those who claimed to be working in their interests.

To build faith in the business, Mama Masai needed to demonstrate conclusively that it could deliver reasonable economic benefits for its members. But it could only deliver these if the women decided to invest greater effort. It was a Catch-22 situation. It seemed to me that the women were hedging their bets, waiting to see which way the wind was blowing, just dipping their toes in the waters of self-help enterprise. Like the novelist, it was necessary to suspend their disbelief. The longer I worked with them the more my eyes opened to the size of the risk they were being asked to take. Most people are risk averse, particularly those who have very little. They cannot afford to fail. It is only at the point of drowning that we throw all caution to the wind and clutch at anything that promises rescue.

I considered whether I could continue to help them, alone. As a breeze rustled the fronds of the palm trees and my eyes rested on the abundant greenness of the garden, I decided regretfully that it was not feasible, given the lack of communication means, their lack of faith in the idea, and my other work commitments. I prepared myself to accept that the venture called Mama Masai had failed. We had set off on a journey that had not gone according to plan. We had taken too many wrong turns.

For many months there was silence. I was busy with other work. Then one day, out of the blue, the phone rang.

"This is Muzee," said a voice. "Are you still in contact with Mama Masai?"

"Sort of," I answered. "Why?"

"We've just received an order for five hundred of their crocs and zebras."

I almost dropped the phone.

"Are you still there?" Muzee's voice went on. "Can I tell the client yes?"

Muzee was the director of a fair-trade handicraft agency. We had talked extensively, and at one time I had hoped they might become the marketing partner which Mama Masai needed. Nothing had come of it, mostly because they focused on the international fair-trade market and didn't have a local retail outlet. International demand is largely for high-quality, functional handicrafts, not traditional artefacts and beaded trinkets. But unbeknown to me, Muzee had placed photos of some Mama Masai products on his website. Hence this order for beaded zebra earrings and crocodile keyring tags.

"Are you still there? What's the answer?"

I pondered what to say. How honest to be? I didn't want to deny Mama Masai this opportunity, but didn't want them to wreck the agency's reputation in the international fair-trade market.

"What country is it from?" I asked, playing for time.

"Sorry. I can't share that with you. It's from one of our regular customers in the Far East. We'd like to please them, so what's the answer?"

"It's possible but – *um* – there are a number of *challenges* ... I think you should visit the groups and make the decision yourself."

"Fine. What's their number?"

"They don't have phones."

"Okay. So where are they? What bus do I catch?"

"You take the Arusha bus to Samé District, but then you need your own transport. The groups are one to three hours' drive from the main road. Around eight hours total from Dar."

It was his turn to fall silent. "I don't have that kind of time to spare," he muttered.

After further discussion we agreed that he would send his assistant, and I would drive her there. As soon as I put the phone down I set about trying to make contact with the groups to warn them that we were coming.

Just before the Project closed down, Oloserian had introduced me to a truck driver called Charles who owned a mobile phone. Every few weeks Charles drove along the Ruvu valley to his home at Loibor-soit. He knew where all the Mama Masai groups were located. I sent Charles a text asking him to notify the groups and pass on the date of our visit. There was no mobile network in the Steppe, but he could receive it when he next passed within reach of a signal. It would be a miracle if the communication link worked, but it was worth a try. A week later I got a text saying that he was in Moshi and would be returning to Ruvu in a few days' time.

I packed the car with rice, beans and vegetables, plus packs of tea and sugar for the groups. I had agreed to pick up Muzee's assistant Happiness at the last major road junction on the outskirts of Dar es Salaam. I hoped she would be there on time. I liked to get an early start. One never knew what breakdowns or other delays would be in store.

Although it was only half past six, rush-hour traffic was already streaming from the hills to the ocean-side downtown. I quickly spotted Happiness standing on a traffic island. She was impossible to miss. Every male driver had spotted her, and traffic slowed as their eyes swivelled in her direction. She was dressed in skin-tight white shorts, a skimpy white top and high-heeled sandals.

155

If I had tried to imagine an outfit as inappropriate to the Maasai Steppe as possible, I might have dreamed up this combination. And such was possibly her aim – to signal to the Maasai, and to me, how immeasurably far she had moved from her tribal past. Happiness was the modern face of Tanzania. A professional young woman with good education and employment, fluent in English, and able to afford a night out at clubs like the California Dreamer. I wondered how Mama Masai members would react to her, and she to them. It had never occurred to me to offer dress advice to a Tanzanian. But I bit my tongue and recalled that African tribes had wandered happily naked until white foreigners found their nudity embarrassing.

The traffic lights turned green, and we left the city behind us, rising up into the lush green hills lined with coconut palms and mango groves, she in her spotless white shorts and heels, and I in an old T-shirt and sarong.

It was good to be back in the Steppe. I felt a sense of ease as soon as we left the main road behind and the vast space stretched before us. It was uncluttered and uncomplicated. A space where the sky seemed to lift, where one felt a sense of release and the freedom to think one's own thoughts.

We found our way to the women's group at Lorimba without incident. I wondered if they had got my message; whether anybody would be at home. I had forewarned Happiness that this was a risk. At first glance, the *engang* appeared deserted save for some toddlers and an old woman who spoke no Swahili. Then to my delight the Queen of Sheba appeared, followed by Nemberes and Mama Baraka. They were expecting us. The message system had worked.

"*Koko! Takwenya?* How good to see you! It's been a long time. We thought you'd forgotten us!"

Mama Baraka pushed forward a young child. "You recognise him? I wanted to leave him behind in our *engang*, but when he heard I was going to meet you, he insisted on coming!" It was Baraka, the angelic baby, now grown into an equally placid little boy.

Their warm welcome brought home to me all the reasons why I could not possibly abandon these women without trying one more time. As I had feared, their group had become almost defunct. Their bead stock had finished, and true to form, they had not tried to buy more to continue production.

Without more ado, Happiness got down to explaining our mission. The women became animated. They were adamant they could make their share of zebras and crocs. And I knew they could. This was exactly the sort of order that was easy to do. Large-scale, but with a limited selection of designs to remember, and for a single customer who was 'producer-friendly', with everything taken care of, including an advance payment to buy the beads. On this occasion I had decided (foolishly!) to buy the beads in Dar es Salaam and bring them with me. This was a last-ditch stand, and if it should be successful and further orders followed in the future, then *badai* – meaning later, from the same root as *bado* and just as popular as a vague delaying response – we would address how they could take on this role themselves.

Happiness sat with the women and made them count the number of beads of each colour in each and every row. "I want the same as this," she said, holding up the sample, "No more, no less. *Exactly the same.*"

"*Exactly the same*," repeated the women, in Swahili.

Her white shorts were sprayed with savannah dust, but I was impressed with Happiness's attention to detail. The women had some understanding of the importance of maintaining quality, but not on this level. Did they understand what Happiness was saying? Knowing how weak their Swahili comprehension was, I went off in search of someone to translate. I found William at home. He was a local itinerant pastor. From time to time he had helped me with translation, and I liked his respectful manner towards the women. Before we left, he translated everything that Happiness had said about the number of products, the designs and the way she wanted them done. The women repeated it back to him, and he repeated it all over again.

"*Seri*! See you soon! Work hard!" we shouted out as we headed on to the next group.

I rolled up the windows and switched on the air-conditioning. What a luxury to travel in this way, free of dust, in the cool. It had been sweltering in the *engang*, hotter than I had ever known it. I could measure the heat by the number of goats that gathered under my car while it was parked. Normally, there were two to three, but on this occasion I had to chase out twelve. Twelve-goat heat was a record.

Over the next few days, we repeated the same instructions to each of the groups. Happiness abandoned her white shorts and put on denim jeans and even added a *kanga* cloth over the top.

It was the rainy season and the weather continued blisteringly hot and unusually humid. Our stocks of bottled water diminished rapidly. I thought I had calculated more than sufficient for the two of us for the duration of our trip. But it was impossible to avoid sharing the bottles with the women. Some of them walked quite long distances from their *engangs*. Until the evening, when they sent the donkeys to the river, they had no water in their homes. If children were thirsty they were offered the breast or a calabash of milk. Nobody had food in their homes. We subsisted on a large mug of tea in the morning, another in the afternoon, and finally a meal in the evening.

By the third day, I was longing for a wash and pinned my hopes on the training centre at Loiborsoit. But arriving there with the dusk, we found the centre abandoned and dilapidated. The stench of bat guano hit us the moment we stepped out of the car. The water tank was bone dry. For the first time, I realised how much effort the Project had put into taking care of its visitors.

"Don't worry," I said to Happiness. "We'll go to Sinyati's *engang*. We should be offered some tea there." Sinyati's group was the closest to the centre, and during training courses I had often wandered up to her place in the evenings.

We began walking, and quite soon on the footpath we encountered Sinyati, Elisabet and Kikama rushing to greet us. They had spotted my car's dust trail. The greetings were joyous and prolonged, accompanied with big hugs. "We thought you'd lost your love for us," complained Sinyati.

Over the years, this group had had their ups and downs. Some members were not happy with Sinyati's leadership, and the group had splintered into two. Much as I liked Sinyati, I could understand why. She was such a lively person that she was usually too busy chattering to listen carefully to instructions. Her Swahili was weak, and she invariably carried on a second or even a third conversation in Maa while I was trying to speak with her.

But she was irrepressibly cheerful. No matter how many of her products I marked as rejects, Sinyati responded with a smile, "*Hamna shida* – no problem. *Badai* we'll do them just as *Koko* likes!"

"It's not what *I* like, but what will sell," I would correct her, but of course she was never listening.

Sinyati was inseparable from her close friend Elisabet, wife of Jacopo, the night-guard at the centre. They complemented each other. Where Sinyati was loud and slapdash, Elisabet was quiet and meticulous.

"We waited for you up here because of the stench at the centre," said Sinyati with a laugh. We settled down to business under a small shade tree beside the cattle enclosure. It was one of the rare trees which was not a thorn tree and had leaves which actually gave shade, although the tree itself was not much taller than a Maasai *moran*.

When the sun disappeared behind the ridge, the members departed to their own homesteads. Sinyati's husband Mboi appeared along with Jacopo and they seemed genuinely happy to see me. Both of them squeezed me in a bear hug and wanted to know why I had stayed away so long. Jacopo promised to clean one of the guest rooms at the centre.

Sinyati prepared food for us, and afterwards Jacopo escorted us back in the starlight. He unlocked the door to one of the guest rooms. We recoiled as a blast of bat odour hit our nostrils. The ceiling had sagged so badly that its unsavoury contents had spilled onto the beds. We tried the second guest room. This was cleaner, but invaded with the smell of its neighbour.

Happiness and I decided that we would prefer to sleep on the wide porch area, where wafts of fresh air might reach us.

Jacopo was alarmed. "You can't sleep on the porch! There's no fence around this building any more. There are wild animals! *Lions!* Aren't you scared?"

"Should we be?"

"You're *women.*"

"So? Are you suggesting that lions prefer to eat women?"

Jacopo caved in and offered to help us move the beds. There was plenty of space for them on the wide porch, but no matter which angle we turned them they would not fit through the doorway. Both had a fixed high frame for a mosquito net, and this must have been built inside the bedroom.

Jacopo made a second attempt at convincing us to sleep inside, but Happiness and I were adamant. "We'll risk it," we insisted. So we lifted the mattresses off the beds, and Jacopo positioned four chairs at the corners for a makeshift frame and rigged a mosquito net.

"I'll be right here," he assured us. "Don't worry. I'll stay awake all night. If anything happens, I'll hear your calls and run to your rescue." He clutched his spear and gave a demonstration of how he would deal with the lion or hyena.

"Have you ever killed a lion?"

"Long ago. When I was a *moran.*"

We told Jacopo we would sleep well knowing that he was on guard. It was a long night. Even on the porch the stench was so bad we hardly dared to breathe. Mosquitoes buzzed in our ears and found their way through the cracks and holes in the net, as though guided in by GPS. Around midnight, sleepless and hot, I decided I absolutely had to scrub the sweat and grime off my body. To this end, I sacrificed half a bottle of Kilimanjaro mineral water and enjoyed a flannel bath under the canopy of stars, trusting that Jacopo would not rise. I could hear him snoring in the training room. The volume of his snores suggested he would not wake up even in the unlikely event of a lion attack.

After the wash, I felt much better and drifted off to sleep. In the morning I inspected the track outside. No trace of lions. However, since there was no water in the tank at the training centre, it seemed pointless to battle with the bats. I suggested to Happiness that we should visit Engorini in the hope that we could stay in Kaika's guest room.

But we found their *engang* in disarray. They had not received word of our visit. Anna was absent; she had had another miscarriage and Kaika had taken her to get medical care. The rest of the women were sick with malaria.

We persevered from group to group, distributing crocodiles and zebras, and swatting flies from our faces. Finally, with our drinking-water supply down to its last drops, and the heat unrelenting, Happiness and I cut short our visit. We were exhausted with the heat and lack of water, exhausted with the effort of talking above talkative Maasai women. Hang the customer in the Far East – they might get their crocs and zebras or they might not. One thing was certain: they would never know the stories behind them.

Feeling slightly guilty but hugely relieved, Happiness and I tossed our dirty laundry into the car, switched on the air conditioner, and fled back to the city.

A week later I came down with malaria. It was not the lion which had pounced in the night, but the mosquito.

18

Layoni

At a sign from his father he pulls aside the thorn barricade. Immediately, the narrow exit is filled with a stream of hooves kicking up a dust cloud which smothers their shapes but not the music of their bells. Young bullocks buck and ride on one another's backs at the pleasure of going out to graze.

"Out of the way! Don't blame me if you get pounded like maize flour!" he shouts at a group of small children who stray too close. As the cattle thunder past, he murmurs their names: Rusty, Stripey, Cockeye, Knock-knee; each is different, each one he knows. All of them carry on their hocks the double-slice scars that mark them as belonging to his father. Fifty-six in total. Last year, one died and three were slaughtered or sold, but there are eight new calves this year. He hurries to replace the thorn barricade so that the calves cannot follow the herd. They are too small, too vulnerable to predators.

The sun has not yet risen, but slanting spokes of dust-laden haze radiate from an outcrop of rocks on the ridge, marking the spot where it is about to make its entrance. It is still cool; he wants to reach the grazing before the heat, while there is still some dew on the grass.

Outside the engang the herd begins to fragment, threading their individual routes around the thorn bushes, their bells growing fainter. He ponders whether to lead the cattle up the escarpment of the Laitema hills. There is long grass in the shadow of the trees on the summit, but scant foraging on the scree-clad slope. There would be only an hour or two of browsing before they would have to descend. No – he would save the hills for the worst of the dry season when the plains had been nibbled so raw that they were drained of green.

He knew the riddle: 'How many types of tree are there in your country?' and its answer: 'Two: the green tree and the dead tree.'

He decides to head Remiti-way. A few days ago he had spotted a cloudburst in that direction. He chivvies the cattle along; if there is fresh grass, his herd will be the first to arrive.

His premise proves correct. New shoots are poking through and there are some taller trees for shade. Positioning himself on a rocky point, he allows the herd to roam. He is proud of his herding skills. He observes carefully which plants the cattle like to eat. He knows that orpalakai plant is good for milk production, and omuketya fattens those that have ceased milking. He is determined his father's cattle shall be the best in the area. Every lesson his father has taught him he can recall: where butterflies settle, the earth is moist … where yellow acacias grow, the ground is dry, but the ficus tree conceals water. Searching, he discovers a patch of orpalakai and selecting only those cows milked by his mother, herds them to the spot.

As the heat builds, the cows settle in the shade of an acacia. He is tempted to join them, but decides to stay on his rock where he has a good view, ready to chase recalcitrant strays. His father would give him a beating if any were to be lost or harmed. He scours the land for predators. A secretary bird strides across the pan. When a troop of baboons appears, he gives chase; they are competition for the green shoots. The chase leaves him thirsty. Selecting a cow, he seizes a teat and directs a squirt of milk into his mouth. Hunger and thirst satisfied, he rests against a boulder and stares into the horizon, trying to make out the shape of the great white mountain. It is hidden in haze. His dream is to one day go there and see for himself the mysterious substance which falls from the sky like drops of milk.

Drowsy with the heat, he is on the point of sleep when a painful sting causes him to jump awake. Warrior ants – black ones – the worst *kind! He stamps on their column and watches them scatter. His sandals of old tyres leave tracks as though a bicycle has hopped along.*

Belatedly, he realises the cattle have wandered too far. He makes a wide detour around the herd, chasing the fringe animals back to the centre, and directs the herd into a small clearing further on. To keep himself alert, he draws pictures in the sand with a stick. He writes his name, and then some numbers and some sums. He enjoyed going to school, but herding cattle is better. It makes him feel like a man. Now he feels ready; he is strong and brave. Strong enough to bring down a bull by its horns – the test for young candidates.

And finally his father has agreed that he is ready. This year, after the rains have fattened the cattle, he is to be circumcised. He will no longer be a lowly layoni; *he will become a man, a* moran.

A sound causes him to look up and tense. It is not the sound of cattle; they are more distant. He sees a slight movement of grasses, between him and the trees. His heart pumps. His hand clenches his stick. He can sense an animal of some kind. Its colours are hard to make out, but something is moving through the strands of browning grass; it is low to the ground, not tall like cattle.

Lion! As the word materialises in his mind, his courage flees. His breathing quickens. His legs feel like lumps of ugali. *Is his test to be now? Here, where he stands alone, the unimaginable is about to happen. Only once has he seen lion, and then he was with his father and the lion was distant.*

Here alone, unarmed, responsible for the cattle, terror floods his body. His legs cramp, muscles deaf to his brain. How could he claim he is ready to be a moran? *A clot of panic plugs his throat, bottling the scream which is rising. The animal is coming his way. Should he run? He takes a couple of steps backwards, and stops ... braces himself ... He is a Maasai! If he is to die, he will at least put up a fight.*

He thinks how best to use his stave. Ram it between the jaws? Will he be able to dodge the flailing claws? He swallows hard, strives to control his racing heartbeat and remember what his father has taught him.

With a roar, the animal rises from the stand of grass and charges.
Its roar dissolves into laughter. Its four legs into two. Its fur into the
nude, dust-coloured skin of his friend. "Ha ha! I scared you! Admit it
– you were terrified! I saw your legs trembling. I bet you peed on your
legs, you flighty white-skinned coward! What kind of cattle-herder are
you? You didn't see me coming until too late!"

He is speechless with relief, scarcely putting up a fight as his friend
pins him to the ground. Then laughter bubbles up, and the two of them
roll in the dust, locked in each other's arms.

▲ My car in the Maasai Steppe

▲ My first glimpse of Maasai women: brewing tea for the 'labour party' with Mama Kicheche looking at the camera

▲ Girls learn beadwork skills by watching their mothers *(Photo credit: Dominque Weihe Gibson)*

◀ Mama Masai members in the courtyard of the training centre at Loiborsoit, leather tanning shed in the background

▲ Beading a traditional leather belt

▲ Beading an *esosi* necklace with coils of wire

▲ Magadini group members sporting mobile phones around their necks, bought with income from their Mama Masai products

▲ A typical scene in an *engang* – women beading, and *morani* posing

▲ Checking the quality of finished products

▲ Literacy class at Magadini

▲ New literacy skills: Namunyak reading a story book to her grandchildren at Pangalala

▲ Magadini Mama Masai group *(Photo credit: Dominque Weihe Gibson)*

▲ Elisabet, Jacopo's only wife, who died in the aftermath of the 2006 drought *(Photo credit: Dominique Wiehe Gibson)*

◄ Mama Masai members at Loiborsoit with Jacopo modelling a Maasai ostrich headdress

◄ Anna modelling the beaded leather robe she wore for her marriage to Kaika

► Esta outside her new *enkaji* at Oromoti

◄ Church service at Engorini, near Kaika's *engang*

► Kaika directing the treatment of a sick cow in his *engang*

▲ Kaika with some of his children and grandchildren

▲ An overflow class at Ngage Primary School

▲ Cattle and people waiting their turn to descend into the wells at Orkasmet

▲ Young Maasai shepherd boys

▲ Start of the drought in 2005 – cows on their way to drink at the Ruvu River

▲ Worried by the ongoing drought: Mboi and his family in late 2005 (right to left: Mboi, Sinyati, third wife, Kikama, daughter, Mboi's mother)

▲ Frida

▲ Frida entering sales of Mama Masai products into her ledger

▲ Frida on her *piki-piki*, wrapped up against dust-devils

▲ Frida crossing one of the mudpans of the Steppe

▲ With Frida and members of Magadini group

▶ With Sinyati

▲ With members of Mama Masai at a circumcision ceremony

▲ Newly circumcised boys wearing black garments and face masks. After completing their initiation they will become *morani*.

▲ Maasai elders, the democratic governance system of the Maasai
◄ Young *morani* pose for the camera during an *orpul*, or meat-feast, in the bush

▲ *Morani* at a circumcision ceremony

▲ Decorated women dressed in their best for a circumcision
ceremony

◄ Maasai woman dancing

▼ Women on their way home from a market

19

A mathematical problem

I named it the great unsolved equation of the Steppe. As I drove the endless miles between Dar es Salaam and Simanjiro, and the even greater distance which separated the modern from the traditional, I tried my best to solve the puzzle.

The practice of polygamy is widespread among the Maasai. Twelve wives in the case of Sainoi's husband was unusual, but three to six wives appeared to be the norm. So the problem was this: if every Maasai man marries several wives, how can there be sufficient women to meet demand – assuming equal numbers of girls and boys are born? Whatever way I rearranged the sexes, the numbers did not add up.

"Is it sometimes difficult to find a woman to marry?" I asked Jacopo as he drew me some water from the cistern. The journey had left me covered in a film of dust, like make-up powder for a stage performance.

"Not at all. Why do you ask?" he responded, emptying the bucket on a string. The substance which he poured into my pail was almost opaque, but its gurgling noise already made me feel refreshed. If I had to name one thing which the Maasai Steppe had taught me to appreciate, it was water.

"You've only one wife, haven't you?" I persisted, delaying my wash in the hope of learning more.

"Because I don't want any more. Most people like to have many."

"Are there some men who want to marry but can't find a bride?"

He stared at me as though I was daft, as though I had asked if rice could grow in the Steppe. "Never!" he replied emphatically.

Perhaps the solution was that as men grew old and died, their widows remarried, I thought, as I sluiced the dust off my body with jugfuls of water. But this was not the case, I learnt. Widows remain widows; they did not remarry.

Kaika stared at me in the same way as Jacopo had, when I asked if he had had any difficulty recruiting his six wives. "Finding a bride is no problem for a Maasai man; there are plenty of girls to choose from."

In Loiborsoit, preparations were in swing for a circumcision ceremony. Sinyati beckoned me into her *enkaji*. Elisabet was inside, holding a set of Maasai robes. The two women collapsed with laughter. They wanted me to dress appropriately.

I submitted to a heavy royal-blue wrap, trimmed with white appliqué. A large clip held it in place at my left shoulder, and a beaded belt provided me with a fragile degree of modesty. On top of this, two colourful shawls were knotted over each shoulder. Then came the beads! One ring-plate *esosi* after another was slipped over my head or clipped around my neck. Bangles and arm-bracelets followed, and finally, they proffered a beaded crown with a jutting prong of bead-encrusted leather that dangles chains of beads and sequins across the face. Fortunately, it was too small to fit my head.

A rehearsal in dance steps came next: how to jump on the spot with my feet together and legs straight ... how to shrug my shoulders so that the beaded ring-plates hit my chin in rhythm to their song. Satisfied that I would not embarrass their troupe too much, we set off.

Wafts of singing led us to the circular *manyatta* that had been specially built for the occasion. At the entrance, we formed a crocodile and with Elisabet in the lead we broke into our song and dance routine. Other women came dancing over in formation to welcome and escort us inside. With their faces half-obliterated by loops of beads and sequins which hung across their cheeks from the 'crown' head-dresses, it was hard for me to recognise the members of Mama Masai among them. But they looked splendid. Some had smeared patterns of red and white ochre over their faces. Coils of brass and copper snaked up their legs and arms. All were sporting several kilos of beads. I realised I had got off quite lightly.

The elders were gathered on low stools under a spreading thorn tree. On the opposite side, young girls were singing. Around the perimeter, a small circle of huts had been built and outside one of these, four branches of the *enoilalei* tree were stuck in the ground. Inside, were the boys awaiting circumcision. One branch for each of the initiates. Just outside the enclosure, cowhides had been spread on the ground and here two elders were preparing their knives.

Circumcision is a coming-of-age rite which all Maasai boys undergo somewhere between the ages of twelve and eighteen years. The precise age, or even the degree of physical maturity is not as important as the boy's emotional maturity and determination to take up the spear and shield of a *moran* and defend his family and herds.

"It's the boy's decision to declare when he's ready to be a *moran*," Nyange explained to me. "His father asks him if he's sure that he's strong enough, and brave enough, and dedicated enough to be a *moran* – to defend the cattle from wild animals. He interrogates his son. He tests his weak points, his fears, tries to dissuade him, suggests he should wait another year or two. If the son remains firm in his resolve, then preparations begin."

Circumcision ceremonies are usually held just after the long rains, when the weather is cooler and the pasture is good so the cattle are fat with plenty of milk. The family may consult the *loibon* for their area to see if the omens are good. If they are, he tells the parents to select a cow of a certain colour, kill it and skin it, and instructs the boy to rub fat from the dead cow on his body. The boy lets his hair grow long. To test his resolve, he is taken to a waterhole where wild animals come and ordered to stay there alone for two nights to test his bravery, or a group of candidates might be asked to demonstrate their strength by bringing down a bull by its horns.

The ultimate test of his fitness to be a *moran* is for the boy to go through the circumcision without expressing pain. In the days leading up to the ceremony, their older brothers and friends, even their mothers and sisters, subject the boys to insults and taunts. We say things like: "You're a coward! You're a cry-baby! You won't have the courage to go through with this! You'll let the family down by whimpering!" continued Nyange. "These insults make the boys angry and strengthen their resolve to prove us wrong and to suffer the ordeal without a jerk or a cry."

Sinyati's husband Mboi arrived. He wanted me to witness the actual circumcision. In fact, he was insistent that I should, and strode off to sort it out with the elders. Women are normally banned from the operation itself, for fear their presence might cause the boys to break down and cry. Mboi returned smiling: the elders had agreed on condition that there were no photos, and that we stood at a distance, behind some bushes.

The first boy was led out of the hut. He was wearing black robes and his hair had been shaved. His eyes were wide and staring, as though he did not see the small knot of men waiting for him. They made him sit down on the hide with his legs straight. One man sat behind the boy and grasped him around the chest and arms; two other men pinioned his legs. The elder with the knife moved in. The boy's body went rigid but no sound passed his lips. It was quickly over. Blood was wiped from the knife, and the boy helped to his feet. An elder supported him as he hobbled back to the sanctuary of the hut. It was clear that every step was agony. One after another the four boys were led out and the knife went to work. None of them flinched or made a sound.

The celebrations could begin in earnest. The boys had been brave. Now they were men. Their families were proud of them.

Maasai circumcision ceremonies have received considerable coverage in the media, yet circumcision is only one of the markers of something less visible but much more important. If I asked a group of Maasai what they thought was *the* most important feature of being Maasai, they invariably answered: "*Olaji.*"[1]

Olaji is the over-arching framework of Maasai society. The word is commonly translated as 'age-set', but is better described as a 'generation peer-group'. They provide an identity and guide one's trajectory through life, defining who one is and what one can do. They confer authority and respect, assign roles and responsibilities, and generally ensure that tribal traditions, wisdom, values, and above all, pride in being Maasai, are passed on from one generation to the next.

Every male Maasai is assigned to the *olaji* current at the time of his circumcision. It is not a single-year grouping but a period lasting at least a decade. Every twelve to fifteen years one age-set is declared closed and after a few years a new one is opened by the chief *loibon*. The *loiboni* are traditional healers, recognised for their special power of divination. There are two chief *loiboni,* one in Tanzania and one in Kenya, though this is by chance and their areas of influence are cross-border. After a new age-set is declared and named, every newly circumcised boy will belong to that age-set, regardless of his age or location.

There had been many circumcision ceremonies during my initial visits. The ghost-like masks of young initiates haunted the most forlorn and forgotten corners of the Steppe. Wherever I stopped the car, they materialised from the bush like genies, ostrich feathers bobbing on their heads as they danced and begged with outstretched hands. On the main safari routes, they beguiled tourists by the dozen to leave the beaten track and empty their pockets. Then for several years, they had vanished from the scene. My arrival had caught the changeover from one age-set period to another. The abundance of circumcisions was due to the fact that there would be a ban on circumcisions for an unknown period of years, so boys pressurised their parents to let them be circumcised before the deadline.

Each *olaji* is given a unique name. Everybody knows to which one they belong, in the same way in which we know our date of birth. It is unimaginable for a male Maasai to grow up outside an *olaji*. It is like being nameless, or stateless. These generation groupings transcend clan distinctions, economic status and geographical location, including national borders. It means that upon circumcision, a Maasai boy, whether living in Tanzania or Kenya or elsewhere, gains an additional identity, a new bond of loyalty. From that moment on he does not primarily identify himself with his family, or as an individual, but rather with his *olaji*.

When a Maasai moves through the different categories from being a child to being a senior elder, he does not leave one age-set and enter another. His *olaji* moves with him in a staggered transition process. After circumcision, they become *morani* for a period of twelve to fifteen years, followed by the ceremony of *Eunoto*, which marks transition to the next stage of junior elder. The final promotion is to senior eldership. Each stage carries its specific roles and responsibilities, but the fundamental tenet of *olaji* is respect for those in the age-sets above one, culminating with the senior elders who are highly revered for their wisdom and experience.

The Maasai are quite democratic in their organisation. There is no tribal chief or leader who exerts overall political authority, although there are two overall *loiboni* who are not chiefs in the usual sense of the word, and have no political function. Local level disputes and decisions are the responsibility of all the elders. They will meet together in an open assembly or *baraza* to reach a settlement or decision through a process of debate and consensus. Where punishment is deemed necessary, this generally takes the form of fines which are paid in cattle.

Other matters will be dealt with by the *olaigwenani*, who are the leaders of each age-set. Every *olaji* in a locality elects one of their members to be their leader and representative. This person is chosen on merit and is somebody who has won the respect of his local age-set, a man whom they believe will make a strong and responsible leader for them. The selection takes place at an assembly attended by as many members of the age-set as possible. The *olaigwenani* holds that position for life, and is responsible for order and discipline within his age-set, and seeing that they conform to Maasai traditions and rules.

"*Olaji* are very important," Baba Kicheche told me. "They guide us to respect each other. The younger generation should respect their elders. But the elders respect the *morani* for their strength and bravery. If we keep this hierarchy of respect and responsibilities, then everybody has a role and contribution to make. With our *olaji* system, even though modernity comes to the Steppe, our core values won't be affected."

The importance which they attach to age-sets was brought home to me during a beading workshop with Mama Masai. An animated conversation had broken out between Oloserian and the women. They were laughing and jabbering in Maa language at a speeding-ticket rate. Curious to know the topic which was causing such excitement, I asked for a translation.

"We're talking about *olaji*," Esta explained, her face beaming with happiness. "I've just discovered that Oloserian and I both belong to the same one – *ilandisi*."

This discovery clearly delighted her. It was of no consequence that he was male and she female, that Oloserian came from Monduli district and Esta from Simanjiro, or that they were from different clans. There was an instant bond, even though women are not assigned to age-sets but adopt that of their husband upon marriage. Yet in this case, Esta was not claiming the age-set of her husband, for he was a generation older than Oloserian, but appeared to be identifying with the date of her own circumcision.

It was curious, and their interest in *olaji* struck me as a little wistful. The truth is that women are not truly part of this fundamental system of being Maasai. They are not consulted, nor do they participate in any major decisions or governance issues. Within their gender, there are no designated leadership positions, and hence women get no opportunities to develop skills of leadership. The Maasai system is democratic only in so far as the organisation of men is concerned.

After circumcision, boys go through a period of recovery at the end of which a small ceremony marks their emergence as full-blown *morani*.

They are then allowed to grow their hair long and adorn themselves with jewellery. From then on they belong to the named peer-group of that generation of initiates.

As *morani*, it is their responsibility to maintain the herds in good health by leading them to the best pastures at the appropriate time. Thus even today, the *morani* who remain in the Steppe live a semi-nomadic life with the herds, sleeping rough, living on cow's milk, constantly on the move.

For *morani*, there are various taboos as well as responsibilities that they must respect. For example, they should never drink milk or eat meat without another *moran* being present, and they should never consume the two together. They are not allowed to marry, although they can have girlfriends. It is only when a man has gone through the ceremony of *eunoto* to become a junior elder, that he may take a bride, settle down and have children. Thus men do not marry until they are around thirty years of age. Women, on the other hand, marry as soon as they reach puberty and are circumcised. In the past, girls were married as young as thirteen years of age; nowadays they are likely to be at least fifteen, and the age is slowly creeping upward.

Which is how I finally spotted the solution to my maths problem! Wives are always at least one generation younger than their husbands.

Maasai communities living their traditional lifestyle in remote places like the Steppe, without access to health care or contraception, experience high birth and death rates. Their population pyramid has a broad base and a narrow top. Approximately fifty per cent of Maasai are under fifteen years in age. There are many more one-year-olds than five-year-olds; more five-year-olds than fifteen-year-olds; more adolescent girls available for marriage than men in their thirties looking for a wife. The delay in the marriageable age for men ensures that they can take their pick from the peer group of girls just reaching puberty, and by the time the men are forty or fifty years old, they can dip into the next generation as well.

Why this tradition developed I never learnt, but I can see a number of practical benefits. In the past, the *morani* risked death – being mauled by lions, or killed by warring tribes on their cattle raids. It lowers the risk that a woman will be widowed while young and her children orphaned while still small. The system means that by the time a man gets married, he has sown his wild oats and put his roving instinct behind him. He has the wisdom of age, and is ready to settle down into married life. It ensures that children grow up having a father who has wisdom and experience, a stable role model who is physically present in the home.

It is possible that the system may grind to a halt at some future date. If modern health care becomes accessible and affordable, this could bring startling changes to birth and death rates that would throw the polygamous marriage system out of kilter. But even before that day arrives, perhaps progress in the education of girls may bring about more rapid changes, if girls choose to delay marriage in order to pursue secondary or tertiary education, or begin to show a preference for monogamy.

*Moran*hood is a time of great pride, of bravery and physical prowess, of fun and adventure; the *morani* are men in the prime of life, at the peak of physical fitness, and naturally with the sexual desire which goes with this.

The men whom I knew recalled this period with fondness and nostalgia.

"My happiest years were when I was a *moran*," recalled Kaika. "As a *moran* you are respected by everybody. I was so strong. I felt I could do anything. I was proud to be one of the warriors."

In his autobiography,[2] *The Worlds of a Maasai Warrior,* Tepilit Ole Saitoti writes:

> When a society respects the individual and displays confidence in him the way the Maasai do their warriors, the individual can grow to his fullest potential. Whenever there was a task requiring physical strength or bravery, the Maasai would call upon their warriors. They hardly ever fall short of what is demanded of them

and so are characterized by pride, confidence, and an extreme sense of freedom ...

As long as I live I will never forget the day my head was shaved and I emerged a man, a Maasai warrior. I felt a sense of control over my destiny so great that no words can accurately describe it. I now stood with confidence, pride, and happiness of being, for all around me I was desired and loved by beautiful, sensuous Maasai maidens.[3]

The sexual freedom granted to Maasai *morani* is deplored by some and applauded by others. I heard mixed reports. One woman told me that girls loathed it, while others recalled their passion for certain *morani* when they were young and unmarried.

"I was overjoyed on my wedding day. I was laughing, not crying. You see, he was my *moran* – we were already lovers!" recalled Mboi's eighty-year-old mother.

Giving an important role to young men in their teens and twenties – a role which recognises their manhood, strength and bravery; a role which nobody else can perform with the same degree of panache – is one of the most astute of Maasai traditions, one which has helped to sustain the health of their society. Youth do not rebel against their parents or society; they are not repressed – instead, they are honoured. At the same time, their behaviour is regulated by certain obligations and norms.

But for Bereta, the oldest member of Mama Masai, mention of *moran*hood stirred up painful memories. "When I was young, the *morani* used to dance. They had special drums, very big, and when other people heard the Maasai drums and music they became very frightened. The *morani* used to fight each other with their spears. Sometimes they would fight to the death, beat and stab each other until one of them died. We stayed inside, but we used to watch them through the cracks. I hated it utterly. The memory still torments me."

In the past, *moran*hood was a time of risk and danger. It is still their duty to defend their herds and their family against all harm.

Circumcised boys still go through a period of orientation and training to prepare them. "We are taught that when a *moran* hears someone crying 'help!' he must be the first to race to their aid," explained Nyange. In the past, this cry would mean an attack by a wild animal and speed was of the essence.

Kaika's cousin, Moses, had a wooden leg. Grey-haired and soft-spoken, Moses recounted how in his youth, when lions troubled their herds, he used to go on a lion hunt with other *morani* in the area. One time, he had been the one to carry back the lion's tail on the tip of his spear. "That's the trophy for the one who throws the first spear. When the first spear lands, the lion attacks that person and he is defenceless, because his spear is in the lion's side. It's dangerous. You have to act quickly."

For some years, I surmised that a lion had cost Moses his left leg, but when I finally inquired, he recounted another story from his *moran* days.

"I lost it in a battle – over there near Hedaru." He waved his hand to the distant blue ridge of mountains. "There was a drought in this area and no grazing left, that's why we took our cattle to the foot of the Paré Mountains where the grass was green and fresh. But the Pare people attacked us. We were too few to overcome them, and someone called the police. They came with guns and shot us. That's how I lost my leg. It was long ago, when I was a *moran*. We no longer fight; we live in peace. We are all the same now. Nowadays it is we, the Maasai, who are taking up cultivation, and it is they who are grazing their cows over here – on our land in the Steppe!" He chuckled ironically. "Our *morani* no longer know how to hunt lion. They've grown soft in Dar es Salaam. A few years ago when we were troubled by lions we had to use poison bait," he added, with a hint of regret and nostalgia.

Having completed their ordeal in the early morning, the circumcised boys were absent from the rest of the day's proceedings. In the privacy of their hut, they were fed cow's blood and milk to replenish their blood loss, and a litre of cow fat to guard against infection.

Groups of elders sat under the shade-tree wrapped in tartanesque *orlokaraha* shawls, looking like a lost clan of slightly bizarre Macdonalds. Smoke poured from the hut where women were preparing the feast. The *morani* had vanished into the bush to slaughter and barbecue a cow, to gorge themselves on meat and herbal stimulants in preparation for their dance. Once more, Mboi broke protocol and took me to meet them.

We found scores of young men in their checkered crimson wraps draped around the trees. Maasai warriors have an extraordinary gift for posing, a natural grace rather like cats. When they are not standing on one leg and leaning on their sticks in the middle of the plains, they are leaning against the twisted trunks of spreading acacias, entwining their long limbs with those of the tree. They might have been preparing for a fashion parade. Some were applying red ochre earth mixed with fat to their skin; others were braiding their hair into hundreds of fine braids. On their backs these were looped through an ornament of horn or copper, and on their foreheads the locks were woven into a tassled fringe. Everyone of them sported thick casts of beads and dangling sequin chains on their ankles and wrists.

There was laughter and a few cries of alarm when I arrived, but Mboi smoothed their concerns aside. One of the rules of warriorhood is that a *moran* should never eat meat alone, and never eat meat in the presence of women. So once or twice a year the men gather in the bush for *orpul* – meat-feasts. *Orpul* means 'nourishment', in the sense of nourishing both physical and mental faculties. Meat is eaten with soup containing *Acacia nilotica*, a bitter-tasting stimulant which aids digestion, enabling them to consume the large quantities of meat, fat and milk in their diet.

Back in the *manyatta,* an exuberant Maasai celebration was in full swing. Sinyati beckoned me to participate in her circle. Fierce competition had broken out among the groups of women. The best singer led with a line or two of a song, which the others took up and repeated as refrains. They seemed to compose the lines on the spot. As one group faltered for new words or new verses, another pitched in from a different corner of the *manyatta*. The intensity increased; they formed circles and chains, swaying their bodies and moving their feet in a slow stately dance, until finally they started jumping up and down, higher and higher, their *esosi* necklaces rising up and down their necks like pistons. I hummed along with my group and made a few jumps in the air. Even the older women took part, leaping like gazelles. I did my part, but I had neither the lift nor the grace which they had. Worried that my costume was slipping undone, I soon retired to the shade of a hut to enjoy watching the spectacle.

No sooner had I sat down than Mboi presented me with a plate of immensely tough hunks of barbequed beef. He mounted guard over me and the plate so that I couldn't secretly dispose of this kind gift. I noticed he was wearing a brand-new *orlokaraha,* and sporting what looked like a gold watch.

He laughed with delight when I complimented him on it, and held out his wrist so I could see it more clearly. The hands were missing.

"After the boys are circumcised, what then?" I asked, pushing the plate of indigestible meat towards him.

Mboi took a large chunk and drove his teeth into it with obvious relish. "After four days or so – when they've recovered – they can leave the hut. For the next six months they wear only black. They're given a large beaded belt, and should wear only leather on their feet."

"And they paint their faces with white paint?"

"That's to scare people!" laughed Mboi. "They hope people will give them more money. But it also protects them from bad people."

"What sort of bad people?"

"People who have 'bad' eyes – women, for example."

"*Women?*"

"Yes, indeed. Women cause a lot of mischief with their eyes."

I let it pass and he continued. "The inhabitants of the places they visit should slaughter a goat to give the initiates. It's important that they grow tall and strong, you see. So they must eat lots of meat, drink lots of blood and milk and fat. They're allowed to wander from *engang* to *engang* begging for money and food. When they first arrive at the entrance of a new *engang*, they perform a dance to attract attention."

"That's when they wear those headdresses? With ostrich feathers and the like?"

"Ostrich or eagle – even guinea fowl. Whatever they can find that looks good. They dance and people give them food, or sometimes coins."

"So they basically have a lot of fun for six months, touring around and being given food and money?"

"No, no! They undergo instruction," he corrected me, helping himself to more chunks of meat. "They are taught the skills they'll need to survive and to protect the cattle. How to make a bow and arrow, how to aim and shoot, how to throw a spear, how to make a small dart and shoot it into the jugular vein of a cow to extract the blood; how to castrate a bull or treat a sick cow, where to gather medicinal herbs and how to prepare them, where and when good pasture can be found, which trees indicate that water is in the ground; how to study the skies, understand the weather, read the stars so that they know in which direction to walk the herds to find fresh grass after rainfall. The boys learn that a good *moran* must have respect for all, be ready to help with any problem. After six months they're ready to become full warriors. Another ceremony is held where they are given their knife and spear. Then they can wear the red robes and grow their hair long."

"I've heard that they have to kill a lion as well? To show their bravery?"

"Not any more. In the past, we did that, but only if a lion was troubling our cattle. There are very few lions here. They don't usually trouble us."

The plate was empty. Mboi had eaten the bulk of it without noticing that I had refrained.

It is tradition for the *morani* to live together in a specially constructed *engang* called a *manyatta*. The British tried to abolish the *manyatta* system. They perceived them as military-style training camps where boys were trained to fight. Since cattle raiding had been outlawed, they saw no need for the continuation of the *manyatta*. This campaign failed – like most which concerned the Maasai – and the British came to appreciate that the *manyatta* was more like an indigenous school than a military camp. By 1938, the Annual Report for one of the Maasai districts noted that *manyattas* could provide 'a useful training ground'. Although not explicitly stated, they had in mind a new breed of Maasai who would have more sympathy with colonial ways and greater respect for the administration.

By this time the British had developed a grudging admiration for the Maasai. Many of the values which the young Maasai acquired during their formative *moran* period, such as respect for elders, responsibility, initiative, honesty, honour and bravery, were quite similar to those inculcated at British public schools of the time. Kathryn Tidrick, a social historian and specialist in British colonial history, believes that there was much about the Maasai social system which evoked feelings of affinity in the colonial officers who had largely attended public schools: 'Administrators who remembered the way their own adolescent energies and rivalries had been worked off in school sports tried unsuccessfully, but with remarkable persistence, to introduce football into the manyattas, believing that they were providing the Masai with an attractive alternative to stock raiding'.[4]

Alas, the Maasai would not play ball! 'Their administrators had supposed too readily that the pleasure derived from kicking a ball across a stretch of grass was interchangeable with the real danger and excitement of a raid.'[5]

One enthusiastic district officer sought to more radically remodel the *manyatta* system. He drew up a detailed curriculum which could be offered. The day would begin with gymnastic exercises before breakfast. The *morani* would then work for two or three hours on something related to animal husbandry, bush clearing, or fencing. In the afternoon, they would have a choice of a lecture or football practice. Filmstrips could be shown once a week. Wrestling, boxing and toxophily would be offered and, later on, elementary reading and writing.[6]

To our ears it smacks of paternalism. Not surprisingly, attempts to introduce such a curriculum ended once more in failure. 'If the Maasai had an educational system of their own which was functioning well according to their own criteria there was no reason for them to view with favour the introduction into it, by people whose hegemony they accepted but did not welcome, of alien elements.' To the frustration of the British, the Maasai remained aloof, continued to locate their *manyattas* in accessible places, and successfully evaded the administration's efforts "to turn their manyattas into miniature Wellingtons and Haileyburys".[7]

Nonetheless, there was much about the Maasai which was appealing. Their openness, honesty and lack of servility meant that British officials commonly developed a respect and even an affection for them as time went by.

'All Europeans who deal with the Maasai inevitably, after a short period, appreciate that the Maasai have certain characteristics which we, the British, deeply applaud,' wrote a British district officer in Kenya in 1955.[8] His counterpart in Tanganyika witnessed a terrible drought in Maasailand in the early 1960s, and wrote in his annual report: 'They are a people who ask for little but who are enormously and genuinely grateful for any help. They live a hard life uncomplainingly.'[9]

In this respect I can say that they have not changed.

As the shadows lengthened, older women served us meat pilao. Even the younger women took a break from their singing and dancing. We ate as if famine would begin tomorrow.

The sun began its majestic departure. And, on cue, the *morani* made their spectacular entrance. A long, sinuous chain of warriors, gleaming with cowfat, ochre and sequins, shouting and stamping their feet and spears in unison. Spreading around the centre of the enclosure in a circle, they began their famous leaping, whooping dance: "*U-hoo! U-hoo! U-hoo!*" A thick dust of dried cow manure rose into the air from their stamping feet, clogging the shutter of my camera.

20

·●○)○●●●○)●●○(○)●●●○)●●●○(○)○●●●●●○○)●●●●●○-

Mobile Maasai

In a subtle yet radical way, the Steppe was changing. Invisible waves moved across its vast spaces, reshaping its geography as surely as wind and rain had eroded it. New features sprouted overnight, old features which had seemed valueless assumed instant importance. They were not marked on any map, but in the Steppe we began referring to them as significant landmarks, as if they were signposted and listed. The Vodacom anthill, the Mobitel thorn tree, the Celtel hilltop.

Mobile phones had arrived and Tanzania was hit with mobile phone fever.

As communication towers pushed northwards and westwards along trunk roads, and began to penetrate the interior in the early noughties, beer sales plummeted. Economic analysts were mystified, but after ruling out every other possible cause they came to the conclusion that the population had switched their disposable income from boozing to talk-talking. Suddenly, it seemed, everyone had a phone clamped to their ear, the alacrity of this adoption encouraged by the dire state of the fixed-line phone service.

In Dar es Salaam, the war of the mobile companies began. A huge billboard was erected at Salender Bridge traffic lights, advertising the strength of the Vodacom network with an image of a male lion roaring and the words 'The lion rules the Serengeti, Vodacom rules the rest!' Shortly afterwards, Celtel erected an even larger billboard immediately in front of the Vodacom one. Theirs featured a Maasai warrior with his spear and a mobile phone to his ear with the caption 'Lion's nightmare'! Indeed, the nomadic Maasai took to the mobile phone like birds to the air. Tourists snapping a photo of a traditional tribesman were disconcerted to find a mobile phone hanging from his beaded belt, wrecking the composition of the 'unsophisticated tribal'.

For a country still struggling to supply its people with basic services and infrastructure, mobile phones had one huge advantage over conventional phones at that time – the storage and transmission of text messages. Texting was affordable to most. It opened up the possibility that I could communicate with the Mama Masai groups without getting in my car and driving for eight hours. The distance between Dar es Salaam and the Steppe became a matter of a few seconds and shillings.

Improved communications opened up better business prospects for Mama Masai. In the beginning, the link was a tenuous one. Phone companies concentrated their network of signal towers in populated areas. Much of the Steppe lay in a dead zone. But the mobile phone could live up to its name and be mobile; it could travel to a spot where there was a signal. Initially, only a few Maasai men could afford a mobile phone. They journeyed fairly regularly to cattle markets or to Arusha to buy grain and other supplies, and when they passed close enough to a network tower their mobile phones picked up text messages. It was not quite the instantaneous communication that we associate with mobiles, but it was a revolution for the Steppe.

After the Project closed down, I relied on Charles, the truck driver, to carry messages for me. Then Baba Kicheche acquired a phone and so did Kaika. My method was to send everyone an SMS in plenty of time, and hope that within a few weeks somebody's mobile phone would pass within reach of a tower. This method had a number of weaknesses, like a game of Chinese whispers. It was fine to send word 'I am coming', but details of dates, times, or any specific instructions would suffer a small distortion multiplied by the number of people the message had to be transferred through. A text message has another flaw – it assumes the person at the other end is literate. Errors could creep in via the translation, for I texted in Swahili not in Maa. Of course, there were also technical issues, such as the lack of electricity, which made it impossible to recharge batteries.

Slowly, phone companies multiplied and extended their coverage. Radio-waves began to penetrate the Steppe. It became possible to pick up a signal when the weather was clear and there was a direct line of vision to one of the towers on the main road. The towers were, however, invisible with the haze of distance, so it was a matter of finding these spots by trial and error. In the early days, I spent hours tramping up and down small hills, trying to identify them.

Loiborsoit lay in a radio-wave dead spot. In the early morning, if the weather cooperated, the skies were clear and certain stars and planets were in conjunction, the locals assured me it was possible to pick up a signal at the training centre. Under their direction I clawed my way up the window ledges, scrambled on top of the water tank, waved my phone in the air, but to no avail.

So it was that when I stayed at Loiborsoit I often found myself jumping into the car and driving fifteen kilometres to an anthill. It was an imposing ant-tower, worthy of a plaque such as those marking archaeological ruins. Rising several metres high out of a barren mudpan, it conveniently marked the spot where a Vodacom signal could be picked up. This anthill became well known and well loved. It was fairly reliable at getting the signal. We talked about it in the way we referred to old friends. It became a reference point. "Turn left after the Vodacom anthill and you'll find their *engang* on the right." Everybody understood what we were talking about.

Those with Celtel could try walking up a particular hill, while for Mobitel, there was a certain thorn tree. To find this tree it was necessary to visit a nearby *engang* and pick up a child who could lead one there. Maasai children became conversant with the nearest signal spots and the networks they corresponded to, even though most of them had never held a mobile phone in their hands. During my trip with Happiness, I learnt that Rehema's husband had acquired a phone. On our return journey, we passed by Rehema's *engang* so that I could note its number for future reference. Rehema was at home, but she couldn't recall the number. We waited while she ran to find her husband, who was visiting a nearby *engang*.

She came back breathless. "The number's *lakhi tano*." Five hundred thousand.

I wrote down a number 5 and waited for the remainder of the number.

"What are the other numbers? What comes after the five?" I asked. "Five hundred thousand and what?"

Rehema looked blank.

"Mobile phone numbers have six figures," added Happiness.

"There should be some hundreds," I suggested.

Rehema tried again. "Five hundred thousand and ... and ... I don't know. I don't understand numbers. I'll go and ask again."

"Ask him to write it down this time," suggested Happiness.

Ten minutes later, Rehema came running back waving a piece of paper. On it were a five and five zeroes. *Lakhi tano*. Five hundred thousand. Just as Rehema had said.

I apologised for not believing her.

"*Lakhi tano*! How did you manage to get a number like that?" exclaimed Happiness, consumed with envy that this auspicious number had been allocated to a person who had only a nominal concept of numbers and no appreciation of her number's exceptional value.

I wrote down a five followed by five zeroes, and made a mental note of their pressing need for further numeracy classes.

Being mobile is nothing new for the Maasai. They have always been on the move, ranging the Steppe with the pattern of rainfall, following the migration cycle of the wildebeest in the Serengeti. Their recent transition to permanent settlements was largely the result of deliberate government policy under Nyerere.

During the first *ujamaa* (resettlement) campaign, the Maasai were left alone, but the second campaign launched in 1975 targeted them and was known as Operation Imparnati, meaning 'permanent habitation'. The aim was to facilitate socio-economic development through the provision of schools, health care and water supply. It had far-reaching repercussions, both on Maasai culture and on the natural environment.

By the late 1990s, practically all Maasai had adopted a permanent base – although its permanence was shaky, as my encounters had shown. There was an unforeseen environmental impact: the grazing resources around a permanent settlement could not support their herds throughout the year, particularly with rainfall patterns becoming less predictable. The Maasai's solution is for some of their herds to remain mobile, herded by their *morani* who continue to follow the ancestral grazing routes, sleeping rough at nights, surviving on milk and blood from the cattle. In the permanent settlements, elders, women and children subsist on a limited number of milking cows and goats which they keep nearby. The declaration of further game parks, hunting reserves and commercial farms on former grazing lands has further curtailed the mobility of the Maasai, leaving them with very few cards to play when drought strikes.

In some areas (although not in the Maasai Steppe), Operation Imparnati was coupled with a renewed effort to lure the Maasai from subsistence pastoralism to a cash economy, this time through the provision of milk-collection centres. As with colonial interventions, these transformed milk from a subsistence product managed by women – one which they traditionally would share with those in need – into a cash product controlled by men.

'It is no longer easy for the "have nots" to obtain milk from the "haves" freely since the surplus produced is sent to the market ... [and this has] individualized livestock contrary to the pastoral mode of production in which ownership was inclusive,' comments one study in 1982 on the impact of Operation Imparnati.[1] An unfortunate outcome for a socialist state policy.

"In the past, we used to shift continuously," said Baba Kicheche, sketching a map in the sand. "Now we've realised that if we continue this lifestyle, someone will seize our land. We must stay put in order to claim title to it. There are many changes. Education has helped us to understand that we can have leaders from other tribes, we can work together. The problem is land. President Mwinyi was the one who took our land away; he thought we weren't using it.[2] We live in the hope to win some of our ancestral lands back. There are lawyers and human rights organisations fighting our case on the Loliondo issue."

The latter referred to a hunting concession granted by Mwinyi's government to a safari company linked with the United Arab Emirates, which subsequently led to the eviction of Maasai from the area. 'Tourism is a curse,' reported one Maasai activitist.[3]

Tourism is non-existent in the Steppe, but elsewhere it is on the rise. The Maasai find themselves hailed as both its icon and its villain, wedged literally as well as metaphorically between a rock and a hard place. Politicians castigate them for their conservative ways, their antiquated dress, their reluctance to abandon subsistence pastoralism, while tourism, a major money-earner for the economy, seeks to preserve the Maasai in their traditional culture. One moment their faces beam from the pages of a safari brochure, the next they are accused of holding on to a lifestyle that is incompatible with nature conservation.

Crippled by the loss of so much of their traditional grazing lands, the southerly migration of the Maasai is still proceeding. During my eight years in the country, I observed Maasai becoming more numerous on the coastal strip south of Dar es Salaam, moving closer and closer to the Mozambique border, and becoming more prevalent in the south-west towards Lake Nyasa. I read press reports of skirmishes between Maasai and cultivators in Morogoro, a region which straddles the main trunk route west, and small groups of them are reported to have crossed the border and settled in Zambia. It was curious to observe history in the making.

A century ago, the British labelled the Maasai as a warlike tribe with an expansionist agenda. When the Maasai moved south in the past, though conflicts did occur, they generally moved into uninhabited areas – land that was too dry and infertile for cultivation, or into highlands like Ngorongoro, which were too cold for the tropical crops of the Bantu cultivators.

If their migration is placed in the wider context of the region it takes on a different light. Permanent settlement of any kind appears to be a relatively recent phenomenon in Tanzania. Some anthropologists argue that it is less than one thousand years, and possibly only five hundred years, since portions of the interior were settled with permanent colonies of people. In other words, as the Maasai were moving southwards, the Bantu-group cultivators were still migrating eastwards into virgin land.

The fact that Tanzania is almost the last place on earth where vast herds of wild animals still follow ancient migration patterns, lends support to this theory. If human settlers were late arrivals, it would help explain how the animals and their habitats have survived longer here than anywhere else. Before this time, there were nomadic hunter-gatherer people speaking a click language, similar to the San people in southern Africa.

On a hilltop in Kondoa, overlooking the western edge of the Maasai Steppe, rock paintings dating back 1,500 years provide a rare glimpse into the past. They trace the passage of hunter-gatherer people and the wild animals which they hunted. They also record the transition from hunting to the keeping of domestic animals, and to cultivation, which over time led to permanent settlements. Only a few hunter-gatherer tribes remain today. Most succumbed to the clearing of forests by the Bantu cultivators who had been pushing their way eastwards and southwards across the continent of Africa. This rapid expansion was aided by the arrival of a new species of tree, brought in the cargo of Indonesian sailors around 300 CE. The cultivation of bananas quickly spread across East Africa. Around Lake Victoria, where the climate was particularly suitable, bananas became the main staple in the local diet.

Viewed in the light of these transitions, the Maasai form one of many instalments in the ebb and flow of peoples into and out of East

Africa. There have been immigrants from beyond Africa – Indonesians, Portuguese, Arabs and Indians, followed by white colonials, the Germans, the British, Boers from South Africa, Greeks from Smyrna, and other European settlers. More recently, there has been a wave of migrant domestic workers from Malawi as well as inundations of refugees from Sudan, Somalia, Rwanda, Burundi, Congo, Mozambique, Zimbabwe and South Africa. At the time of my first visit to the Maasai Steppe in 1999, Tanzania was host to almost one million registered refugees in addition to unnumbered illegals. The size of the refugee camps on its western borders made them the largest settlements in that quarter of the country.

If the relatively short period of human settlement is correct, it is surely ironic, given the presence of those early hominid footprints crossing the hot ash and lava in northern Tanzania over three million years ago. The Tanzania Department of Tourism proudly presents the country as the 'cradle of mankind', and Olduvai Gorge is a common stop on the tourist route between Ngorongoro Crater and Serengeti. It was here that Mary Leakey first unearthed a 1.8 million-year-old skull of *Australopithecus boisei,* and where she later discovered the footprints of a family of hominids in volcanic ash strata dating back 3.6 million years – at that time, the oldest evidence of ancestors who walked upright.

Today, the Maasai stride over the same volcanic strata, and regard the volatile Rift Valley volcano of Ol Donyo Lengai as the sacred mountain of God. But for how much longer will this be the case?

The order from the Far East had rejuvenated the Mama Masai groups. They showed a renewed zeal for beadwork, and waited expectantly for me to find them further customers.

Mobile phones might have made their debut, but the women remained frustratingly immobile. Despite our orientation trips to Dar es Salaam and Arusha, and their induction to the joys of bus travel, they clung to their *engangs*. Reluctantly, I came to accept that travel to

189

distant marketplaces at their own expense was not one of their gender rights – as yet.

I could not spend my life hauling beads and beaded products to and fro by car. My husband was patient and understanding, but there were limits. Maasai beadwork had invaded our house and threatened to make my family refugees. From its HQ in the spare room it had muscled into other parts of the house; cupboards formerly occupied by clothing had been commandeered by a menagerie of beaded animals; the dresser for the dinner service displayed only beaded ring-plates of *esosi* design. The latest victim of raids by Maasai beadwork was our dining table.

"When do you plan for us to use the table again?" my husband asked with a quizzical look, balancing his supper tray on his lap.

"What's your problem? The children seem happy eating on the floor."

He shook his head in a despairing way and counter-attacked. "If you were to count up all the hours you spend, the cost of your trips there, and paid yourself the going rate, the project would be rejected as poor value for money." He was absolutely right. I could rely on him to deliver a dose of reality with an understanding smile. But it was too late. These women were not cold statistics on a page. They were individuals whom I knew and cared about.

I decided the time had come to pay a visit to Frida, to see if she could help me solve the immobility problem of the Maasai women.

The waters covering the House of God were unruffled as I drove across the dam and looked northwards. A flock of pink-backed pelicans and hottentot teal floated in waters so peaceful that a crescent of snow was reflected in them. For how much longer, I wondered. Kilimanjaro was being stripped of her bridal veil. On flights to London from Dar es Salaam, the peak lay on the flight path, and the pilots commonly gave passengers a close-up view, even on occasion performing a 360-degree tour around its crater. It was from these overhead views that one could really see the extent of the shrinking snow cap. I had climbed the peak in the early seventies and could remember wading for hours through thigh-deep snow. In the space of three decades, the snow cap had visibly shrunk, in line with retreating glaciers in the Alps and receding ice sheets of the Arctic and Antarctic. If one needed evidence of climate change, it was here in Africa, as elsewhere.

For the Maasai, the disappearing snow-cap of Kili is a ticking time-bomb. The temperature increase which is causing snow to melt at an altitude of 19,000 feet (5,895 metres) is causing increasing droughts and barrenness on the plains below. Greater heat means that less rain falls, or that more of it is lost in evaporation. As rain diminishes so do the grasslands. The Ruvu River that most of the Mama Masai members relied on for their water supply, is fed by the meltwater of the Kili snowcap. Less snow means less meltwater, and lower and less predictable flow in the Ruvu.

It was imperative that the Maasai develop new sources of income before disaster struck. Mama Masai had to be successful. But the way forward for Mama Masai remained as hazy as the Steppe in drought.

Frida was working as a livestock officer and living in government quarters above the lake at Nyumba ya Mungu. At her home, she plied me with food and cold drinks while her five daughters seized the opportunity to practise their English. After supper, we settled down to talk business and brainstorm the options for Mama Masai. Since Tumaini had dropped out of the picture due to ill-health, Frida had been offering to be the conduit, begging me to give her a loan which would enable her to buy beads and their finished products, making a small profit on the side.

I had delayed while I turned over the pros and cons. For anyone stepping into that role, the opportunity to cheat the women was there. With their low levels of literacy and numeracy, Mama Masai were like the ducks on the lake – sitting targets. There was also the risk that the business would make losses rather than profit. The fact that Frida had become more of a friend than a work colleague actually complicated the decision.

But we decided to give it a go. Frida would act both as 'development-facilitator' and as 'business-agent', an unusual but not incongruous combination. She would supply the groups with beads, assist them to improve the quality of their production, transport their products to market, and in return earn commission on their sales. The system depended greatly on the sturdiness of Frida's *piki-piki,* and the advent of mobile phones. Now I could phone an order through to Frida. It simply remained for me to find such customers, preferably a few regulars who would buy in bulk. Mama Masai members were happy with the arrangement. It was disappointing that they did not feel sufficiently empowered to manage the task themselves, but this compromise might pave the way for them to do so in future.

After concluding our business agreement, Frida and I drove north to visit some new Mama Masai groups which had sprung up at Magadini.

Along the lake's edge, women in bright *kanga* cloth mingled with Maasai as they fetched water, wading to the cleaner, deeper water past egrets and marabou storks that patrolled the shallows. Offshore, fishermen paddled in small dugout canoes, and on the beach, a chain of men and women hauled in nets. Naked children splashed in the shallows. A line of girls in blue school dresses carried buckets of water on their heads.

We made slow progress as I kept stopping the car to look through my binoculars. The lake presented a rich cornucopia of bird life. A host of waders blotted the shoreline; in deeper water, flocks of whistling duck, Egyptian geese, terns and skimmers; jacana crept stealthily through the reed beds while weavers repaired their dangling nests; in grassy clearings, glossy ibis, pratincole, snipe and plovers searched for food. Near the shoreline, trees were so laden with herons and storks, and cormorants drying their wings, that there was no perching space for more.

It was such a different world to where the other Mama Masai groups lived.

But this paradise, too, was threatened by global warming.

21

Highway in the sky

In the slowness of the mid-afternoon, when time seemed to impale itself on the barbs of the thornbrush, I sat with Mboi's mother and two of his wives – Kikama and Sinyati.

"When Mboi was a child, we used to live Kiteto way, near Makame," his mother recounted. "Life was not bad there. Grazing was good and we had plenty of cattle."

"Why did you move?"

"Because the government started opening schools. Mboi's father feared they would force our boys into school. Back then we didn't trust education, you see. So we left. When we arrived here we felt safe, because it was hidden and there were no schools as yet."

"You mean, Mboi didn't go to school?"

"Back then we were foolish – we didn't know any better. We thought we were doing the best thing. We didn't understand education."

"And now you feel differently?"

"*Yes*! Education is good. We need it."

"Loiborsoit's a long way from Makame. Why did you move so far?"

"We needed water. We came for the river."

"How long did the journey take?"

"From one full moon to the next. I don't remember the days exactly. We had to move slowly because of the herds. I was pregnant

193

and the journey was hard. Even after we arrived here life was not easy. I lost that baby. He died soon after birth. I had another son, but he also died. In fact, I lost all my sons except Mboi ..." Her eyes were rheumy. It was impossible to tell if they were more moist than usual as she journeyed back into the past.

"A few years later my husband died. Up there, on the escarpment. Mboi was a young *moran* at the time. Not much older than this one," she said, pointing to her grandson who was playing nearby with a homemade truck. It was made from wire with bits of plastic and wood, and wheels cut out from old flip-flops, and he steered it with a long stick.

"Ah – to be a child again – we had no worries back then!" sighed Kikama, Mboi's oldest wife. "Wasn't it the happiest time of life? It seemed like nothing bad could ever happen."

"It was a lot of fun," agreed Sinyati. "I used to run around wearing nothing at all! Such a wonderful free feeling! Do you remember how we used to pee in the sand and model mud toys when we were herding the animals?"

"It seemed that the worst that could happen was to find sand in your food. My food always had sand in it!" continued Kikama. "My only bad memory is the way I used to treat my grandmother. I used to tease her because she was blind. I'm ashamed when I remember. I was young then. I didn't understand."

"My worst memory is falling into the fire," said Sinyati. "I was jumping on the bed and I lost my balance and fell into the hot coals. It was agony. Mother put some grease and herbs on the burn, but it didn't stop the pain."

Kikama chuckled. "After my circumcision, I decorated myself with coils of copper wire on my legs and arms. I thought I looked beautiful and felt so happy and proud. But one day while gathering firewood my coils caught on a thorn tree. I twisted and struggled, but I was trapped. It was hours until somebody rescued me. See, here – the scars. By the time my wounds had healed my marriage had taken place."

"Was that a happy occasion?"

"Women have no choice in the matter," Kikama replied with unusual vehemence. "I had to go with Mboi because my parents had already eaten the dowry cows which his father had given them. *You see?* They sold me just like goods in a shop! I cried for two whole days and nights. Then I thought, 'this isn't going to change anything'. I told myself it was better to try to love my husband and try to like his parents."

"The day Mboi took me away was the worst day of my life!" chimed in Sinyati. "I'd only seen him once before – *and I didn't like him at all!* But he paid my parents four cows. This place Loiborsoit seemed like a wilderness compared to where I grew up. I didn't know Kikama. I didn't know anyone here. I cried so hard. I remember my mother-in-law coming to me and saying, 'Wipe your tears away. This place is just the same as the home you know. Everything will be alright'."

Mboi's mother laughed. "All my son's brides cried when they first came. They were young. I used to have to go and comfort them. That was my role as their mother-in-law."

"Mboi also tried to comfort me," remembered Sinyati. "He begged me not to be sad because of him. Then he gave me some cows and that made me feel better, and after three months I found I had fallen in love with him. I love him still. He only beats us when we deserve it; when we neglect the animals. One day I pretended to be so sick that I couldn't take the animals out, but actually I was feeling lazy and jealous. Mboi had just married his third wife and he was very much in love with her. When he realised that I was faking it, he gave me a beating. See my scars! If I ever get lost in Dar es Salaam he'll be able to identify me by these marks!"

Our conversation came to an abrupt end. Cattle bells sounded in the distance.

"*The herds!*" cried Kikama.

Both wives took off at a sprint.

After the Project's termination and the bats' invasion of the training centre, I spent most of my visits in somebody's *engang,* and over the years, from 2004 onwards, friendships deepened considerably. Mboi's homestead was the closest to the training centre at Loiborsoit. Although bats could still be seen flitting in the twilight, the training centre had been renovated after bats' invasion – the holes in the ceiling were patched over and the bat smell had receded. Once more, I slept at the centre but ate my meals with Sinyati and Mboi. Often Jacopo was there too, with his wife Elisabet who was a close friend of Sinyati.

"What time shall I come?" I would inquire, when they invited me for tea or a meal.

"Come at milking time," Mboi would always say.

It was a magical hour. With the sun ballooning red just above the horizon, the melodic jangle of cow bells announced the return of the herds. As they entered the enclosure, Sinyati would emerge from her hut, her dark skin shining with body oil and beautifully adorned with beads, clutching a beaded calabash for the milking. From a hut on the opposite side of the *engang,* Kikama would appear with her calabashes. Compared to the soft plumpness of Sinyati, Kikama was wan and bony, dressed in shabby clothes with hardly any decoration. There was no doubt as to who the husband's favourite was.

When Mboi discovered that I had never milked a cow, he insisted that I learn. He shouted some commands to Sinyati. She cornered a reddish jungle-striped cow and brought it over. It eyed me suspiciously. It could sense instantly that here was an utter novice, one who did not have the smell of Africa in her body. It bucked, and its hooves narrowly missed my knees. Mboi and Sinyati assured me this was the most docile cow they owned.

"Start with milking into a mug; it's easier than aiming into the neck of a calabash." Sinyati released a chuckle, as if anticipating the entertainment that lay in store. She gave a demonstration. Milk gushed out. Then it was my turn.

The moment that I squatted down in her place, the cow tried to make a run for it. Mboi roared with laughter. He caught the cow by its horns and brought her back and Sinyati grabbed her tail. I squatted down by the udders, wedged the enamel mug between my knees and reached for a teat. Missed. Missed again. Not only did the cow keep moving, but there was competition for the udder. A velvety liquid nose kept blocking my access. This small calf had immensely more job experience than I. It pulled and sucked at one or other of the teats while I tried to grab an unoccupied one. But once I learnt the technique of pulling and squeezing in a smooth downward movement, it was very satisfying to hear the squirt of milk as it hit the mug. I was concentrating so hard I didn't realise that Sinyati and Mboi had moved away to tend to other cows. Without warning, my cow lowered her head and kicked. My hard-won milk spilled into the dung-heap.

As a token of our growing friendship, Mboi gave me a gift.

"It's not too big. It will easily fit in your car," he assured me. The gift spread its hind legs and poured out a pile of droppings.

At that time, I was trying to down-size our menagerie. We already had two goats as well as dogs, cats, tortoises and a broken cage of lovebirds who flew around our garden during daylight hours. It was chiefly the friction between the goats and the dogs that was getting me down. They were well matched in strength, so sometimes one had the upper hand and sometimes the other. I was tiring of their conflicts and had already decided that the goats must depart.

I thanked Mboi profusely and explained why I couldn't take his gift home with me.

"Do you want to eat it?" he asked. The goat fixed me with a penetrating stare.

"Keep it for me. Perhaps next time."

After milking was done, Sinyati retired to her *enkaji* to prepare the evening meal. Sometimes I sat with her in the outer chamber. It was a simple scene. Hanging from the rafters was a pair of plastic saddlebags for the donkeys, two protective udder guards for goats and a rolled-up leather hide. On a 'scout-camp' stick-rack were three tin mugs, two tin plates and one spoon; scattered on the floor were a couple of plastic buckets with lids, useful for storage and seating, one or two small plastic bowls, a broken plastic jerrycan for water, a low stool carved from a single piece of wood, one or two bottle-gourds, a thermos and a kerosene lamp. The fireplace, where Sinyati cooked the evening food in a cooking pot resting on three stones, glowed in the centre of the room.

If the smoke from the cooking fire was too thick, I would sit outside with Mboi and Jacopo, watching the children play. Sometimes I brought balls, balloons or bubble mix for the children. Although they quickly burst on the thorns, they were sport while they lasted.

The sun always slithered very quickly behind the scarp-face, and a curtain-call blush spread through the sky, silhouetting the thorn trees. At these times, we sometimes talked, and sometimes were silent, content to contemplate the bush settling in for the night. Silences were never awkward; there was a feeling of calm, of continuity, of things repeating a pattern that had existed for as long as Maasai had lived in the Steppe. With this came a sense of security. What our forefathers had done, we do; what had worked for those in the past, would work for us too. Life was circular, not linear.

After nightfall, we would remain sitting outside if it was hot. Sometimes I lay down on a leather hide in the middle of the *engang* and gazed at the mesmerising display of stars.

Dominating the display, lay the Milky Way arching high above Mboi's *engang* like a flyover slicing the sky into two halves. According to legend, *Engai* created it by pouring milk into the sky and it turned into stars. Jacopo called it 'the highway crossing the sky' or the 'White Cloud' and explained how Maasai use it to fix their bearings. At certain months of the year the Southern Cross appeared low in the sky in the early evening, while at other months I could spot the Plough and Pole Star in the northern skies. These were among the few that I could recognise and name.

But the Maasai were cognisants. While I lay on my back, Jacopo guided me around the heavens. Like every Maasai who has passed time as a *moran*, wandering the savannah with the herds and sleeping under the stars, he could name every constellation. He explained how they use them as a map to guide direction or to tell the time of night, the time of the year, the season when to plant crops, when to bring the cattle down to the river or send them up to the hills, when the rains were coming and when they were ending.

He showed me how to tell the hour by noting the position of a certain star in relation to the ridge that ran behind Mboi's *boma*. Venus they call the Big Star. The Pleiades or Seven Sisters they call 'The Meeting'. It is a happy constellation, he told me, as he recounted the legend of how the three had invited the four to visit, and how they have been talking ever since. The three stars of Orion's Belt represent their herds, the brightest one being 'cow', which is the elder of 'sheep' and 'goat'. But another story says that the three stars are a convoy of father, elder and warrior on their way to ask for the hand of someone's daughter, and the single tiny star nearby is a goat taken to the future father-in-law as a gift.

"Their appearance tells us that the dry season will end soon and people should prepare for rain. We should bring the cattle down to the plains. There's another star we seldom see nowadays. It appears after the rains. If we see it, that's a good omen. It means our cattle will be healthy. Then there's *Kilekin*, which appears in the morning around four a.m. It tells us the time, that soon we can let our cattle out to graze. And a star called *Ormukala olor labha* is the brother-in-law of the moon and is always sighted nearby. It's a big bright star that helps the moon shine brighter."

I loved the night vista so much that I bought a star map of the southern skies and began consulting a lunar calendar so as to time my visits to avoid the full moon. On one occasion, there was a spectacular display of shooting stars and Jacopo explained that these are a good omen. When you see one, you must pray immediately to *Engai* to give you money, for your wish will be granted. And when you see the new moon, you must pray for health and strength.

Then he shared another legend:

Long ago, in the beginning of time, the sun fell in love with the milky beauty of the moon, and they were married. After they had been married a short while, they had a quarrel. The sun scratched the moon's face and plucked out one of her eyes. The moon struck the sun and battered his face.

The sun was so ashamed of his battered face that he became dazzlingly bright so that people cannot see his scars. But the moon was not embarrassed; she doesn't mind if people see her scars and notice that her mouth is drooping and one eye is missing.

Since that time the two always travel in the same direction, the sun leading, and the moon following. After travelling for many days, the moon grows weary from her unending journey and is carried by the sun for three days. On these nights people cannot see the moon. On the fourth night donkeys bray to tell the moon they need her light, and on the fifth night the moon recovers and reappears.

When people see the moon reappear, men must say, "Moon – give me strength; give me long life." Women must throw milk towards the moon and say, "Moon – deliver my child safely."

Sitting under the stars, I loved to hear their stories of long ago.

"We were constantly on the move from place to place," recalled Mboi's mother. "I didn't like it. Sometimes we had not even finished building our *enkaji* when we had to tear them down again and move on! My friends were here one day and gone the next. I might not see them again for another year or more. It made me sad. And strange neighbours would arrive whom we had never seen before."

Anna Moses had been one of the first girls to attend school. "I had to board. From time to time my parents would pass by and give me some pocket money or a small gift. When school closed for the holidays, I never knew where I'd find my family. Sometimes I walked to the spot where home had been, only to find it had gone. The problem was worse in the rainy season when they'd travel to wherever grass had sprouted. If I couldn't find my home, I'd walk back to the school, and one of the teachers would ask around to see if anyone knew where my family had gone. If they'd gone far, I spent the holiday at school. I knew my family would return sooner or later."

"I'm surprised your parents even sent a daughter to school."

"They didn't want to! My father refused for a long time. He feared I would be given in marriage to another tribe. But the missionaries pleaded with him – it was a church school under white people at Ruvu Remiti. The day I started school my mother cried and cried!"

"And how did you feel?"

"I was shaking. They came to collect us in a big lorry. Slowly, I became used to school and enjoyed my studies. After two years, they sent me to a bigger school at Naberera. It was so cold there, up in the hills. After I completed sixth grade, I wanted to go on to secondary school, but my father made me get married."

"Schooling was the orders of the *mzungu* government. They told our parents that one child from every family must go to school," interjected Moses, Anna's husband. "If they refused, they could be sent to jail."

"So you didn't like the *mzungu*?"

"As a child I was terrified of them! During the time of their government we feared them greatly. When they visited the Maasai Steppe, they always had guards with them. And the guards carried guns. We only had spears. We were afraid they'd shoot us. Women would flee if they saw a white person."

"And now?"

"We're happy. Everyone wants their children to go to school."

"And what about *mzungu* people?"

"We like them very much – even you!"

"*Really*?! But how can you, after all that's happened?"

"We've realised you are people just like us."

"I heard the British took a lot of land from the Maasai ..."

"Yes, they took land. And they took tax. But they started schools, and that was good."

Thanks to his schooling in the days of the British, Moses could speak English, unlike the younger generation who were taught in

Swahili. I was amazed that after only seven years of schooling more than fifty years ago, Moses could still hold a conversation in this foreign language.

Sainoi recalled seeing many *wazungu* in the 1940s. "We used to cry out, '*Mzungu* have come!' and ask each other, 'Why are these people so very white?' They would try to talk to us, but we couldn't understand their speech. We knew nothing in the past, but I think we had a good relationship with the *wazungu*."

"Tell me more about your youth," I begged Moses. "How were things different back then?"

"There were more trees, more grass and more wild animals. We used to see lion while herding the animals up on the ridge, and even down here on the plains. One day, when I was still quite young, I remember coming upon a lion eating a kill. He was a large male. I was terrified. His eyes were fixed on me and he stretched his claws as a warning. I was sure he was going to charge. I was alone, with no spear as I wasn't yet a *moran*. There was no-one nearby to help me, and nowhere to run to."

"What happened?"

"I yelled as loudly as I could, jumped up and down, waved my arms above my head."

"Go on – what happened next?" Moses was a typical Maasai; he did not readily boast of his exploits.

"The lion retreated!"

In Ngage, Baba Kicheche recounted that lion had ceased to trouble them since a hunting safari company set up a tented camp by the river. "Their hunters finished them off for us! We're grateful."

His family guarded memories from the time they had migrated south from Kenya. He explained that there were two routes that the Kisongo Maasai used to enter Tanganyika: one to the west of Mount Meru, and one to the east.

"My grandfather's family entered with others by the eastern route, over the saddle between Meru and Kilimanjaro. It was densely populated. We ignored the cultivators, but we fought anyone who kept cows. When we arrived in the Steppe, we fought the Wakwavi. They were herders, dressed like us, even spoke the same language. My grandfather took part in a battle by the Ruvu at Gunge – where it narrows into a small gorge. I remember him describing how the river flowed red. Many Wakwavi jumped into the river trying to flee – they didn't realise it was so deep and they couldn't swim. Some drowned and some were slain by the Maasai. The survivors fled south to Morogoro."

"Are they the Parakuyo?"

"Yes. After the battle, Grandfather found a man hiding near our well. He didn't know him and he thought he was Mkwavi – there was something different about him, but he couldn't be sure. He didn't say anything, but he watched him carefully for nearly a month until he was sure the man was indeed an Mkwavi. Then he killed him."

"Why did we kill the Wakwavi? We killed them simply because they kept cattle – they were our competition. Now we realise how wrong we were – we killed our own people! It's taken us generations to achieve reconciliation with them. We did it through encouraging our children to intermarry. Now we have a good relationship. Nyerere was good for our country because he created understanding and cooperation between the different tribes. We're all one people. We work together. We speak one language. It's good."

I found their memories of Maasai life fascinating, but stranger still was the story of Mama John. She lived a stone's throw from Mboi's *engang* and was the leader of a satellite Mama Masai group. On first meeting, it was obvious she was not Maasai, for she had a full head of hair, wore a *kanga* wrap, and her facial features were very different. But she spoke Maa language fluently and could bead like a true Maasai. For years, I assumed she was from a neighbouring tribe across the river, until one day her extraordinary story slipped out.

"I'm not Tanzanian – my parents came from Zambia. I've no idea which tribe, or even where I was born. I've no memories of Zambia! My father was a civil servant in the colonial government. In 1959, he was sent here to be administrator for this division. My earliest memories are of this place. Both my parents learnt Maa and I grew up speaking it. We lived with a Maasai woman near Pangalala. My brother went to school, but my father refused to send me. He feared if I went to school I'd be taken by the *wazungu.*

"Quite suddenly, both my parents died. We were alone, my brother and I, without a home or family. I was still quite young. Life became very hard."

"Didn't any relatives come from Zambia to collect you?"

"No-one came. We were dependent on the Maasai. They were good to us. The woman we lived with gave us food. A Maasai man paid the fees so my brother could continue in school. Later, my brother got a job and we could support ourselves."

With the Maasai Mama John has remained, a Zambian stranded in the Steppe, a forgotten casualty of colonialism. There is not a hint of self-pity in the way she tells her story, but for me it has a poignancy when I think of her father – educated, professional, English-speaking – and the dreams the couple must have had for their children. Life has been hard on their daughter. She and her husband own almost nothing. Their home is a hovel. She looks old beyond her years, riddled with arthritis.

Very rarely, I found myself with spare time during the daylight hours and then I liked to go to the river for birdwatching. Birds were abundant everywhere. The trees inside the Maasai *engangs* were hung with the messy dangling nests of sparrow weavers; tiny turquoise cordon-bleu hopped in the sand beneath and steely blue-green starlings flashed iridescent feathers as they flew off. Hornbills and golden bush-shrikes lived in the thornbush, and orange-bellied parrots in the hollowed trunks of baobab trees. As I drove along the tracks, doves and barbets rose from the sand and guinea fowl scurried for cover. Across brown plains I might spot a secretary bird striding after prey, tall as a person, or the long neck of a Kori bustard. On one occasion, I was treated to the unforgettable sight of a Kori bustard – the world's heaviest flying bird – taking to the air.

Baboons and vervet monkeys were common near the river; when the grass was green, herds of impala and zebra grazed the plains. In the dry bush dik-dik and hares were common. Dik-dik were so small and the hares so big that from a distance I sometimes mistook the two. Occasionally, I saw gerenuk, and on the ridge top, eland and kudu. Every morning at Loiborsoit I inspected the tracks outside the training centre and tried to identify who had passed by in the night. One time only, I spotted big cat prints – either lion or leopard.

One day Mboi took me and some friends on a bushwalk. In every dry gully he identified the tracks that were visible. Every bush and tree he could name, and expound its medicinal or other properties, and whether they used it to treat humans or animals, to tan leather, for firewood, as a building material, to make arrows ... Every type of grass or plant he could identify and say whether it was good for milk production, or for fattening the cattle, or improving their health, or warding off disease.

The Maasai are renowned as traditional healers and their botanical knowledge of medicinal plants is phenomenal. It is said that it was the Ndorobo, a hunter-gatherer people still found in Tanzania, who taught the Maasai their herbal healing skills. This knowledge is not limited to designated traditional healers, but is acquired by both women and men. From their savannah back garden they gather leaves, bark, fruits, seeds, nuts and roots which they use to treat diseases and conditions ranging from common colds, wounds, eye infections, sores and skin diseases, to snakebite, malaria, brucellosis, respiratory infections, stomach problems, urinary conditions and arthritis, to name but a selection.

There were so many names, such encyclopaedic knowledge, that I was overwhelmed and the only specimen I learnt to recognise was the toothbrush tree, since a prime example grew at the entrance to Namunyak's *engang*. When Sinyati learnt that I liked the taste, she always prepared my tea with an extract of *olkiloriti (Acacia nilotica)*. It had a distinctive bitter taste, different to that of regular tea. Many types of acacia are used by *morani* – as stimulants to reduce fear, hunger, thirst and fatigue. Despite their high intake of red meat and animal fat, Maasai rarely suffer from heart disease, so undoubtedly the herbal treatments work.

Most of their treatments have a scientific basis to them. A good example is their reason for removing their two lower canine teeth. As I had learned early in my conversations with Mama Masai women, this is done in case they contract tetanus, so they can be fed milk through a straw. Given their poor access to immunisation, and their proximity to thorns and animal dung, tetanus must have been a common risk in the past.

Occasionally, I came across more bizarre health beliefs. I once gave a lift to a woman who was suffering from a high fever and had a swollen gland in her neck. She told me that a year earlier she had swallowed a fly and it was still alive. She could feel it buzzing inside her swollen gland.

Every trip to the Steppe was an adventure for me. I usually travelled alone and needed to be prepared for all eventualities. The day before, I always spent the day preparing for the trip. I would buy five- or ten-litre containers of drinking water, several kilos of potatoes, carrots and onions, and some tea and sugar as gifts, together with apples and snacks. Before loading these items along with my sleeping bag and carrier bags of beads, reels of wire and other materials, the most important task was to check that the spare tyre was in good condition, that the tool kit and jack were in their places. On this particular occasion, the car was sent to the garage to fix a starter problem.

The most dangerous part of the drive was the main road from Dar es Salaam to Arusha. It was a good road and there was little traffic. Buses travelled at speed on poorly inflated and worn-out tyres. On corners, centrifugal force sent them careering into oncoming traffic.

Once I had left the main road, I could relax. In the Steppe, it was impossible to speed and there was virtually no other traffic. Should the car have a puncture or a breakdown, I knew that I could rely on the Maasai to help me, though I might have to wait some hours until someone appeared. Punctures were an ever-present risk. Thorns grew the size of daggers. Changing the tyre was not the problem. Rather, it was the worry that should there be a second puncture there was no spare tyre. Along the Ruvu route there was no place for a repair job and to get it fixed involved a day's detour.

Besides the punctures and the one occasion when the wheel fell off, there was also the trip when the shock absorbers broke. On that occasion, I was returning from Esta's *engang* and had given a lift to one of her relatives – a wrinkled Maasai *koko*. She had elected to sit on the back seat. In the middle of a flat straight stretch of road, we hit a hidden rut at speed. From then on *Koko* started bouncing up and down, and became increasingly vocal. Each time we hit a bump she cried, "A*aaarooh! Orararaaa!*" Approaching Orkasmet, the plateau road becomes rocky and rough. Through the rear-view mirror I caught glimpses of *Koko* like a yo-yo, flying up to the roof, hitting her head, and crash-landing on the seat with her earrings in a tangle. I slowed down, but the problem grew worse. We crawled into the town. To my amazement, I found a mechanic who was able to do a temporary fix the next day. This was the good thing about the bush. Things broke down, but people were wonderfully ingenious at fixing them with very few resources.

A minor inconvenience was the recurrent mystery of the missing radio antenna. It was always present on the car when I left Dar es Salaam, and invariably missing when I returned. I never saw the culprit. It seemed a pointless piece of vandalism, completely out of character with the Maasai. They never stole or broke anything else of mine, never damaged the car in any other way. But invariably the antenna disappeared. I never solved this mystery to my satisfaction. There didn't seem to be any purposeful use for a length of broken antenna until it occurred to me that the diameter of the hollow metal tube more or less matched the size of the ring-shaped scars imprinted on the cheeks of every Maasai to protect their eyes against disease. The scars were created by pressing a ring of heated metal against the cheek. Could this be the motivation for the theft? Were my broken antennas recycled as branding instruments?

Our car experienced the Steppe in many different weathers: dust storms, torrential downpours and scorching heat. When rain fell, the vast flat pans in the Ruvu valley turned into lakes of mud burying any hope of seeing where the road was. Entering one of these mud-lakes, the car tyres soon lost traction. The wipers were designed for rain, not a fountain of mud. The car would perform skids, spins and pirouettes. It was best to remember to lock the four-wheel drive hub on the wheels before plunging into these sloughs so that one didn't have to slide about in the middle of the slurry to do so.

But there was no bad weather, and nobody to blame but myself, the day I made the journey from Loiborsoit to Orkasmet with Mboi and Sinyati.

We were sitting in their *engang* one evening when I casually let drop that Frida and I planned to drive to Orkasmet the next day. We hoped to talk the District Education Office into running further literacy classes for the women. Sinyati and Mboi immediately announced they would accompany us. They urgently needed to go to Orkasmet. Did I have spare seats?

The issue of spare seats and passengers required careful management. Normally, I kept my departure and destination a secret until the last possible moment. Despite this tactic and a pre-dawn departure, I might still encounter would-be passengers who appeared to have spent the night sleeping upright against the car.

My rule was: priority to sick people or the elderly, then to Mama Masai members and their children, then other women, and finally men.

"My wife needs to go to the hospital in Orkasmet," said Mboi, "and I must accompany her."

"Okay," I said, "But absolutely no more. No others. You understand?"

"Of course," said Sinyati and Mboi. "Nobody except William."

"Why William? Is he sick?" William was a nephew who herded Mboi's cattle in his school holidays.

"No, but you have a spare seat in your car. He has to go back to school."

"I don't want too much weight in the car. I plan to take the ridge route to Orkasmet."

"It's impassable," said Mboi. "The road was destroyed last rainy season."

"But I heard a jeep came that way not long ago."

The ridge route to the district headquarters climbed directly up the escarpment not far from Mboi's *boma*. It saved considerable back-tracking if one was going on to Orkasmet. I had travelled the route a couple of times with Oloserian, and although the road was steep and rough, it presented no problems to a four-wheel drive vehicle.

A long discussion ensued on whether to take this route or not. Other people were consulted, and the general consensus was that the road was in bad shape, but a vehicle had passed through within recent weeks.

That was sufficient for me. Early the next morning we set off. Mboi settled himself in the front passenger seat and Sinyati, Frida and William in the back. Sinyati didn't offer any details of the reason for her medical trip. As she looked in good health and was talking with her usual gusto, I guessed it could be connected with her desire to have more children. She had 'only three', and naturally wanted more. Her youngest was already eight years old so I figured she might be experiencing fertility problems which herbal potions had failed to fix. Had they not seized the chance of a lift with me, they would face a full day's walk to Ruvu Remiti, an overnight stay there, followed by a three-hour bus ride to Orkasmet the next day.

At the outset, we found the ridge route in fine shape and I was reassured. A good decision had been made. But as the gradient began to climb, the thorn trees pressed closer and closer until we were trapped in their vice-like grip. The squeaks and squeals as our car squeezed past the thorns set my teeth on edge. I couldn't see how much damage they were doing to the paintwork, but feared my husband would not be pleased. Since turning around was impossible, I had no choice but to press onwards and upwards.

When I was well past the point of no return, the gradient shifted into low gear. The track vanished. In its place was a rocky gully. We pressed onwards and upwards, my regrets mounting with the slope. Sometimes the car was able to straddle the gully and other times it had to lean at uncomfortable angles, half in and half out. On the dashboard there was a gauge that measured the angle of left-right slope. Out of the corner of my eye I could see it flickering towards the red-light maximum, when overturn occurs.

As conditions became worse and worse, Mboi's laughter became less frequent. Even Sinyati fell silent. When I thought the situation was as bad as it could ever be, I suddenly remembered the starter problem. I broke out in sweat and a lump of dread settled in the pit of my stomach.

Although our car had been to the garage to fix the starter problem, and it was working normally when I left Dar, when I had stopped to refuel before entering the Steppe, it had failed again. Subsequently, it had required a push-start each time. This was no big inconvenience since there were usually plenty of people willing to help. But in choosing the hill route, I had foolishly forgotten the starter problem. I castigated myself for being an utter idiot. If the car stalled while we were crawling up this ravine, there was no way we could push-start it.

"Look at my wife," said Mboi. I glanced in the mirror and saw Sinyati's face, her hands gripping the seat in front, her eyes staring in horror. She was struck dumb – a state unknown for her. Mboi allowed himself a chuckle. Inside, I was feeling like Sinyati. The car was clambering up and over boulders. The ravine had narrowed and deepened and I had a wheel on either side. The frontier of thornbush prevented any diversion to the side, but anyway I couldn't now get my wheels off the ravine without plummeting into its depths.

I was certain that this time I was going to have to pay my respects and hold a funeral for the car in the ravine. My husband would be devastated. I tried to think up plausible excuses and how I could lay the blame elsewhere.

The car was already in four-wheel drive 'low', when the angle became so steep that the wheels skidded and we started slipping backwards down the slope. On one side the wheel was lodged against a steep outcrop of rock; on the other side the chasm had widened and half the wheel hung over air. I slammed on the brake with my left foot and kept my right revving the engine. My passengers exited the car as fast as they could.

There was no way back; no place to turn. Did the car have the power to surmount this obstacle? Was its wheelbase wide enough? If it fell into the ravine, we were not enough people to haul the car out. Not to mention the starter problem. I could only keep my foot on the accelerator and pray. I tightened my seatbelt.

"Be ready to jump out of the way in case the car rolls or skids. Ready? *Push*!"

The four of them threw their weight against the rear end. Like a lion pursued by Maasai, the car roared its way up the rock face ... another ... and another ... I was glad I couldn't see how few centimetres of ground were under the wheels; the gully expanded and contracted in a nerve-wracking way. As the car crested each outcrop, I had no idea what lay ahead as the windscreen pointed at the sky.

To my great, unending relief the car and I arrived intact at the top of the escarpment, and my world returned to normality. The track reappeared among the trees. I parked and waited for those on foot while my racing heartbeat slowed its pace.

Does my memory exaggerate? I don't know. I can only say that the trip is imprinted on Mboi's memory as well as my own. Whenever we meet, he takes pleasure in teasing me: "Do you remember the time we drove to Orkasmet?!" He grins broadly and play-acts me wrenching the steering wheel around. "My wife – she was like this!" and he swaps roles and acts out Sinyati's part, gripping the seat with horror-struck eyes.

22

●○○●●○○●○○●○●●○○●●○○●○●●●●●●○○●●●●○

Ashi Engai!

Life in the Steppe was a constant endurance test. The elements were unmoderated; either the sun blazed an unadulterated dose of ultraviolet, or the skies exploded and sluiced rain like waterfalls, or the wind hurled the contents of the Steppe into our faces like a child throwing a tantrum at the paucity of playthings in its backyard. The dryness left a constant catch in my throat and soreness in my eyes. The heat could set my head pulsing.

I cannot count the number of times my clothing became caught up on thorns, or my flip-flops became so pierced with them that I felt like a *sadhu* walking on nails. No wonder the Maasai wore sandals cut from old tyres. Every living thing was scaly or designed to hurt and repel. Even the grass where it grew had tips pointed into vicious barbs. Every seed and fruit was spiny. At the end of each day I had to unpick a bed of seeds from the hem of my clothes.

The luxuries of life were the silence, the space, the timelessness, the birds and insect song, the cowbells and cattle lowing, the laughter of children, the stars, a mug of sweet milky tea, a full stomach, a joke shared, the visit of a friend, a bucket of water, a shady tree, the singing of young girls, an embrace, a birth, a sense of belonging …

Three weeks was about my physical and mental limit at any one time, yet the Maasai lived there day after day, year after year, unblinking, uncomplaining, even enjoying their spartan life.

I could hardly believe it when Frida told me that the leather-tanning cooperative had finally been reconstituted and was producing leather again. It was five years since the first training workshop. I immediately wanted to resurrect production of the small leather bags and proposed a refresher training course.

The only time I was free to conduct the training was over the new year. Frida did not think this would be a problem for the participants – and nor did I. In a society where people do not refer to diaries and calendars, where they judge the seasons and the time by the movement of the stars, I could not imagine that an arbitrary date concocted by the Romans and Pope Gregory would have any meaning. But when I inquired if it was convenient for them to attend the training on New Year's Day, the women replied that they wanted the day free for their celebrations.

I was taken aback. "You celebrate New Year's Day? Why? What does it mean for you?"

It was the women's turn to look surprised. "Surely you know why? For the same reason that everyone celebrates the new year."

"And what's that?" I asked, thinking about it for the first time in my life. "It's merely a date. On New Year's Eve we party and have a good time. How about you?"

"It's the most important day of the year for us. We celebrate that we've survived. We thank *Engai* that we've lived to see another year."

Reflecting on this exchange over the next few days, I came to realise that where life is comfortable and secure, we have largely lost the sense of gratitude for collective survival. Individual birthdays celebrate the passing of the years, but even then we rarely reflect on the fortune of still being alive. Life is taken for granted. Only in the United States do they have the celebration of Thanksgiving – a hangover from a less secure past.

'These worst of heathen, these truculent savages who conquer or die, death having no terrors for them,'[1] wrote Ludwig Krapf from the mission field. Thomson records that 'their conception of the Deity seems to be marvelously vague' but 'their prayers to him were incessant'.[2] In *Out of Africa,* Karen Von Blixen writes that 'the Masai have no religion whatever, nor the slightest interest in anything above this earth'.[3]

The truth is the Maasai are a people of strong faith. They believe in one God whose name is *Engai*. There are no idols or icons or images of *Engai*, no shrines, in the sense that people of various religious persuasions know them. Theirs is essentially a religion of the inner self. Although there are mountains and groves which carry special spiritual significance, there are no man-made places of worship, no written scriptures and no priesthood. For *Engai* is a God without encumbrances, free to travel with the Maasai on their nomadic pathways.

Near to the soda lake of Natron, rising from the Rift Valley plains where none but the Maasai live, is an active volcano named Ol Doinyo Lengai. Uniquely, the lava thrown up by Ol Doinyo is low in silica and rich in carbonates and sodium, and it is this carbonate-rich ash which maintains the fertility of the vast grasslands of the Serengeti. Geologists say it marks a dome where the earth's crust is being stretched and thinned in response to movements of the continental plates; unlike other active volcanoes, Ol Doinyo's lava emerges from a pool of magma not far below the surface.

Its name means 'Mountain of God' in Maa language and it is a sacred place for the Maasai. "We go there to pray for rain when there's a prolonged drought, or to pray for a baby if one is suffering from infertility," I was told.

"You believe that *Engai* lives on that mountain?"

"*Engai* is there. But *Engai* is here, *Engai* is everywhere. We can pray to *Engai* right here in our *engang*!"

"How often do you pray?"

"All the time, every day – when we get up in the morning and when the night falls."

"And what do you pray for?"

"We ask *Engai* to bless the day, to protect us from harm. We pray for good health, for food, for our children. Especially for our children, if one of them is sick."

Engai is one God with two aspects: Black Narok and Red Nanyoki. Ninety-nine per cent of the time it is Black Narok whom they worship and to whom they address their prayers. Black Narok is kind and good. Not black as in many people's concept of blackness, symbolic of sin or evil, but black like the skins of her followers, black like the colour of the clouds which bring rain. Black Narok is the God of every-day life. While Red Nanyoki commands courage, anger and vengeance. Red like the clouds of dust in drought, like the clouds which flash with lightning but bring no rain; red like blood. Most of the time, Black Narok keeps the power of Red Nanyoki at bay. It was to Red Nanyoki that warriors used to pray for courage before departing on a lion hunt or a cattle raid.

To me, the most fascinating aspect is that *Engai* is female, *eng* or *en* being the feminine prefix in the Maa language. Thus *Engai* is part of the feminine world of the women *(engitok)*, the homestead *(engang)*, the hut *(enkaji)*, the child *(engerai)*, the cow *(engiteng)*, food *(endaa)*, water *(engare)* and earth *(enkop)*. Familiar forms of address for *Engai* such as "She of the growing grasses" or "My mother with the wet clothes"[4] indicate how the Maasai see God as their symbolic mother, the one who gives birth and who nurtures them, and these offer a touching illustration of the tenderness of the relationship they enjoy.

It is not surprising to learn that *Engai* has a special regard for women. The Maasai recognise that women are more naturally at home in the spiritual domain than men. According to Nyange and others I spoke with, women are more fervent in their prayers, and men believe that *Engai* is more likely to answer the prayer of a woman than the prayer of a man. When a drought becomes prolonged, it is to women that the elders and the *loiboni* turn, beseeching them to pray, to sing their psalms of supplication, to plead with Black Narok to send the storm clouds that will chase away the red haze of Nanyoki.

"Maasai women are and have always been more spiritual than men; it is their nature. Women are just more compassionate – if some-one is hurt or hit, women aren't violent, men are," explained a Maasai man, interviewed by the anthropologist Dorothy Hodgson.[5]

"You men just don't want it. For me, there is usually not a day when I don't come out and pray to *Engai*. Even when I'm sleeping, I pray to *Engai*. But you men pray to *Engai* only if you have a problem," a middle-aged Maasai woman says to a young *moran*.[6]

Some claim that *Engai* is not exclusively female but both male and female. It is tempting to interpret Black Narok as the feminine aspect and Red Narok as the masculine, but nowhere have I heard or read this. *Engai* also means 'rain', and 'sky'. The association is understandable for a people whose livelihood is so dependent on rain.

Rather at odds with this belief system are the people referred to as *loiboni*. They are hard to classify. They are not priests, or witch-doctors or sorcerers, as some earlier accounts claimed; nor are they tribal chiefs or political leaders, as the British assumed when negotiating their land seizures. 'Prophet' is a term sometimes used, but they are not moral spiritual leaders. Minor *loiboni* function at local level. Maasai might consult them if they have a problem or an important decision to make. The *loiboni* throw small stones or other objects from a horn or calabash and interpret these to predict the future or explain the past. They use an array of herbal medicines to heal or protect people from illness and sorcery. "They have the power to see things far away," is how the Maasai explained it to me. Diviner-healers is the best term that I can offer.

Loiboni are almost exclusively male, and the role is hereditary. The story goes that one day a Maasai herder on the Ngong Hills found a young boy and took him home. The child, named Kidongoi, showed extraordinary powers, able to work miracles and predict the future. He was adopted by the Laiser clan of Maasai, and over time his supernatural powers were passed on to his progeny, and a sub-clan called Inkidongi was established. These are the *loiboni*.

I never heard women refer to the *loiboni*. Their existence and role seem to sit uneasily alongside the women's direct and fervent prayer-line to *Engai*. In fact, scholars suspect that the concept of *loiboni* is an import from Bantu tribes. They first appeared about two hundred years ago – just the time when the Maasai began their move southwards through Kenya and encountered Bantu tribes such as the Kikuyu, with their animistic beliefs, for the first time. Evidence suggests that Kidongoi was not Maasai, but possibly of Kikuyu origin.

Curiously, among the neck ornaments of the Maasai women I would not uncommonly see a beaded cross. Indeed, they frequently gave me these as gifts – for many of them were also churchgoers.

Our beadwork discussions were commonly prefaced with the acclamation *"Ashi Engai!"* (Thanks be to God). Our training workshops were punctuated with detailed prayers – at the start of the day, at the tea break and the meal time, and again in the evening, asking for *Engai*'s blessing on every activity and its aspects.

Who were they praying to? Naturally, they also refer to the God of the Bible as *Engai*.

When I considered how much change they have resisted, how strong their culture is and how robustly they have clung to their traditions, I was very surprised that the Maasai had ever arrived at accepting a foreign religion.

Baba Kicheche seemed to treat the matter lightly when I discussed it with him. "Religion is not something to fight against. We Maasai are not against change. If something is useful to us, we can adopt it. Of course, there are our key tenets which we will never change," he vowed. "For example, *olaji*. But there are other things where we can change if we see that these things are good. Nowadays, we boil our milk before drinking it because we understand how disease is spread. And then there are some things where it is up to each individual to decide for themselves, providing there is nothing counter to our core tenets. Like whether to go to church or not."

"Do you go to church?"

"No. But I encourage women to go. It's beneficial. They might learn to read by listening to the Bible and singing hymns."

Nyange was more critical. "The missionaries came and preached the Jesus news. They told us 'Don't consult the *loiboni*! Don't wear your beads! It's okay to eat meat with women!' But some Christian doctrines

217

are so implausible – how can educated people believe in them? Even our own traditions are waning. We used to ask *Engai* to bless us with rain. Nowadays, you'll meet educated Maasai who no longer believe."

"And what about you – what do you believe?"

"I believe in *Engai*, the same God as the Christians, but we communicate in different ways. My life, the person I am, is due to *Engai*. I arrived at this conclusion through my intellect. My intellect is given to me by God. I try to help people. That is what *Engai* tells me to do. We have this life to prepare ourselves for death.

"And after death?"

"Our bodies die but our souls remain alive," he answered.

The history of the interface between missions, missionaries and the Maasai, is a complex one and it is risky to generalise. Nonetheless, I suggest that one reason for the eventual conversion of many Maasai is that the two religions are not so fundamentally different.

There are quite a number of parallel concepts with Christianity, and the resemblance to Judaism is perhaps even more striking. Indeed, as mentioned earlier, Merker even posits that the Maasai are one of the lost tribes of the children of Israel.[7] While this seems far-fetched, it would be surprising if the Maasai had not rubbed shoulders with people of other beliefs as they made their way up the Nile – with Coptic Christians and Jews of Ethiopia, or with Muslims as Islam spread south through Sudan.

With their monotheistic belief, they are much closer to Christian and Jewish theology than the diffuse animistic beliefs of Bantu tribes in the past. Prayer is more important than ritual. God is good and merciful; Black Narok cares for her people; she loves them, she listens to them. Sometimes in Tanzania, Islam or Christianity appear like a thin veneer, grating against the indigenous belief systems which lie beneath. I never sensed this was the case with the Maasai.

Similarities with Christianity and Judaism include belief in one God; faith based on a personal relationship with this God, like the Children of Israel; belief that God cares for each of them, as individuals, as

families, and as a people; the concept of a loving, caring God, even
a forgiving God (in the sense that if a Maasai sins and then makes
amends to those he has wronged by giving a gift of cattle, the matter
is closed); that God is not limited to a specific place, but can be prayed
to anywhere, at any time; the lack of graven images. In addition, there
are various myths which although different, carry echoes of Judaic and
Muslim myths of creation, the fall of man, the special relation with a
chosen people.

The major differences are the gender of God; the lack of a priesthood or institutional hierarchy; the lack of a building or even a shrine
dedicated for worship; the lack of written scriptures or doctrine; no
clear beliefs about life after death; and no belief in the need for a medi-
ator or saviour such as Jesus, as in the case of Christianity.

But on the whole, the similarities are stronger than the differences.
Here, for example, is a traditional prayer-song of Maasai women
which has been paraphrased; it could easily slide unnoticed into the
Book of Psalms:

My God, to thee alone I pray
That offspring may to me be given
Thee only I invoke each day,
O morning star in highest heaven.
God of the thunder and the rain,
Give ear unto my suppliant strain.
Lord of the powers of the air,
To thee I raise my daily prayer.

My God to thee alone I pray,
Whose savour is as passing sweet
As only choicest herbs display,
Thy blessing daily I entreat.
Thou hearest when I pray to thee,
And listenest in thy clemency.
Lord of the powers of the air,
To thee I raise my daily prayer.[8]

219

In her book, *The Church of Women*,[9] Hodgson discusses how, although the missionaries specifically targeted Maasai men in their evangelisation and education efforts, the churches ended up filled almost exclusively with women. The vast majority of men remained unresponsive to the missionaries' teaching, fearing that it might impinge on their *moran* traditions or stop them practising polygamy. Not so the women. They heard the missionaries' message and responded. Hodgson sees this movement as related to the subservient role which women had been pushed into following the loss of their barter trade.

The churches provided leadership opportunities for women – roles which were normally denied to them – and a place where Maasai women were able "to create an alternative female community beyond the control of men." Even where men were placed in the visible formal roles of leadership within the church, women were the invisible but more respected leaders. They were interested not so much in the formal hierarchies and obligations of church bureaucracy, but rather in coming together to learn, to pray to *Engai*, and to talk to one another.

If objections were raised by their husbands, then the women succumbed to an attack of *orpeko* – an evil spirit which manifested itself in physical symptoms. It spread like an epidemic – and the only permanent cure was to be baptised. One Maasai elder explained:

> There is a sickness that has spread into this area recently that was not here before ... this *orpeko*. It hasn't entered men, but women. But when you take a woman to the *oloiboni* he says, "She is cursed." ... When we put women in there (the church) they were healed; really it helped them. Why else would so many have joined?[10]

According to Hodgson, the symptoms of *orpeko* expressed in embodied terms women's consternation over their economic disenfranchisement, political marginalisation, and increased workloads and isolation. By resorting to claims of spirit possession, Maasai women were able to overcome any reluctance on the part of men to allow them to join the church.

For women, the church became a social space as well as a place of worship, providing them with the opportunity to meet together on a regular basis. Hodgson describes the visible joy of Maasai women at one Easter service she attended. After the service, they continued to celebrate, touring from one homestead to another in a large group, sharing tea, food and alcohol, laughing, talking, dancing and singing hymns until nightfall, while the men kept their distance.

Hodgson is referring largely to Catholic missions and churches, but the Church of Women would be an apt description for the Maasai Lutheran congregations which I encountered, and her book echoes many of my own impressions and experiences with the Maasai. But I believe the Maasai women were attracted to church not only because of the space and freedom which it gave them from men, but also because the message resonated with them; it fitted with their close personal relationship with *Engai*, and their unique position as mediators between *Engai* and men.

But this still leaves the question: to whom are the women praying in church?

Hodgson uses the past tense to describe the traditional beliefs and practices of the Maasai in acknowledgement of the changes which have taken place in Maasai culture over the past few decades. I have kept the present tense because I do not believe that their traditional religion has disappeared. In saying this, I realise that change in the Steppe lags behind places with easier access. I feel fortunate to have seen and connected with what may be the tail end of many Maasai traditions.

As far as I can see, the faith of those Maasai who call themselves Christians is sincere and heartfelt. I saw no sign of any foreign intervention; I never encountered any missionaries in the Steppe. Christianity no longer appears as something imposed from the outside but has become fairly thoroughly indigenised.

But I have the sense that they have not converted and abandoned *Engai*, but that *Engai* has moved with them; *Engai* has adopted more permanent accommodation, just like the Maasai.

In splicing the two belief systems together, they do not appear troubled by any conflict in theology. Although the central theological difference between the Christian and Maasai faiths is the belief in Jesus and his message, Hodgson notes that Jesus was rarely mentioned in the many conversations and interviews which she held with them regarding their beliefs. I found the same. One elderly grandmother explained to Hodgson that she started going to church 'because it was about praying to *Engai* and I like to pray to *Engai* since I pray all the time'.[11]

Maasai who are practising Christians still partake in all the traditional Maasai ceremonies; they still practise polygamy; they still pray for rain. And when they do this, or say grace, or shout the greeting *"Ashi Engai!"*, it is impossible to know whether they are addressing *Engai* as Black Narok, or *Engai* as Jehovah, or to fathom out whether there is any fundamental difference between the two.

And ultimately, does it matter? These are merely labels, and language is a poor signifier for the emotions and deep-seated beliefs which drive religious expression. The women I knew were not interested in dialectics. For them, *Engai* was a constant presence, as much a reality as the wind which rustled the Steppe. As I compare their lives with my own, the main difference is not between religions, but between those who take survival and the material world for granted, and those who do not.

Where death is a constant presence, faith has greater intensity.

It happened that New Year's Day fell on a Sunday and, instead of holding the workshop, I attended church with members of Mama Masai.

When the missionaries came to Tanganyika, they divided the country geographically among the main denominations, so as to avoid competition. Since the early German settlers had arrived first and preferred the climate of the highlands, the north-eastern portion of the country around Mount Kilimanjaro was largely Lutheran territory. And so in the Steppe, if any Maasai were practising Christians, it was generally a Lutheran church that they attended.

Luther and the reformers would have approved of the simplicity of their church buildings. The one near Ngage consisted of some rough benches in rows under some trees – the kind which scouts might make in camp. One bench, slightly larger than the others, was the altar table. Two sticks lashed together formed a cross. There were no walls, but the roof was a trellis of branches to provide some shade. William, the semi-itinerant pastor, was leading the service. The singing was unrestrained, led by a choir. The congregation was largely women, and the service was lively, with a horde of children and babies present. William's approach was refreshingly participatory, his sermon more like a quiz, to which the congregation joyfully chorused the answers.

Near Kaika's *engang* at Engorini, they had built a more solid church; it had a thatched roof and wattle and daub walls which incorporated a window space shaped as a cross above the altar. Inside, were the same scout-camp benches. The service was led by Anna Moses and her husband recited the Bible lesson.

After the service, the choir proceeded out of the church, followed by the congregation. Still singing, they formed a circle under some nearby shade trees. Led by Mariamu, one of Kaika's wives, the choir launched into a traditional melody. As they sang, Mariamu called out two people's names at random. The two selected stepped into the circle and danced towards each other, Maasai-style, arms pinned to their sides and legs together, ramrod straight, looking each other in the eye. For several minutes they performed their traditional dance, laughing and leaping higher and higher. "*Ashi Engai!*" they shouted out as they became airborne the final time and retreated out of the circle. Mariamu called out two more names at random, and in this way, pair by pair, the congregants connected with each other in song and dance, and were dismissed.

Thank God the Maasai have found a way to liven up the piety of the reformers.

23

When vultures gathered

For the first time since the caravans of Arab merchants ceased their travels after the railways were built, beads were being traded along the Ruvu-Pangani valley.

Frida was a regular traveller along the route. On the way south her *piki-piki* carried in beads, cowrie shells and reels of fishing wire, and on the way north she carried out Mama Masai's beaded products. Every few months she took the bus to Dar es Salaam, delivered their products, and returned with more orders and raw materials.

Although there were still unresolved issues, the arrangement was working better than I had anticipated. Frida's energy and commitment made a tremendous difference. The women were becoming notice-ably more competent. There were by now nearly two hundred women in over twenty groups. It was hard to keep track of them all, since groups tended to grow and splinter. The challenge still remained to find reliable commercial outlets, willing to pay fair prices, in Dar es Salaam. Our family would be leaving Tanzania in June 2006 when my husband's job was due to end. I was very much aware that less than a year remained in which to put Mama Masai on a sustainable footing. Tumaini had fallen sick and stopped buying, and various other avenues had proved to be dead ends. With my departure looming, I changed tack and gathered together some like-minded volunteers who would continue to help Mama Masai after I had gone. We named ourselves Fair Trade Friends. We did some fundraising and with this capital we were able to buy and hold a quantity of stock until we found a market for it, which provided Mama Masai with a more regular income. As the year progressed, it seemed that even if the goals were not fully achieved, Mama Masai was heading in the right direction.

The long rains of March to May failed that year. Not a single drop fell in the *engangs* or grazing pastures of Mama Masai members. It was the second year in a row that rainfall had been slight, and waterholes and wells were already depleted. Then the short rains failed to appear in November. The Maasai continued to pray for their late arrival in December or early January.

Driving from Remiti to Loiborsoit just after Christmas, I noticed that embryonic sand dunes had formed where previously I remembered small bushes and grass. They had appeared from nowhere, in less than three months. The wind must have lifted the sand from elsewhere and tossed it around. It was disquieting to see the rate at which desertification could happen.

During the leather products workshop held over New Year's Day of 2006, the women were unusually quiet. Their chatter, when it occurred, lacked its natural exuberance. All of them were deeply concerned for their herds. Their survival depended upon rain falling in the next few weeks.

At Mama Kicheche's *engang*, we were sitting under a tree discussing their group activities when a cow collapsed nearby. It had no flesh on its bones, only skin hanging like wet washing on a post. "Pull it up! Yank its tail!" Mama Kicheche shouted to her children who were playing nearby. They hauled on its tail but the cow remained prostrate. Mama Kicheche ran over to help. She pulled its horns while the children hauled on its tail. The cow rose totteringly to her hooves and continued her apathetic search for fodder.

"Why did you do that? That cow seems sick. Isn't it better that it rests?" I inquired.

"When a cow is sick and lies down like that, it never gets up again. It will surely die. If you can keep it on its feet, it will have a fighting chance."

It was as hot as it ever gets in the Steppe. Sweat dried instantaneously on our skin. Too many goats squeezed into the patch of shade under my car to count the precise number. The cows had ceased giving milk so we drank black tea. Sinyati took me across the Ruvu River in a dug-out canoe and we went skinny-dipping in an irrigation channel while Mboi mounted guard at a distance. She assured me it was crocodile free. I have had many swims in hot places, but that swim under a burning afternoon sky ranks as one of the most pleasurable. For half an hour we forgot our woes and revelled in the cool water.

When Frida paid out some sales money, Sinyati immediately passed every shilling on to the group members. Every family was desperate to buy supplies. Early the next morning, Sinyati and Mboi travelled across the Ruvu to Same District to see what they could buy in the way of fodder. It was nearly dark when they returned with loads of browning maize stalks on their backs. Drought demanded strategic thinking. Certain cows were selected for feeding, and others were neglected. Experience had taught the Maasai that the only way to save some was to starve others.

At Engorini, Kaika's cattle were unrecognisable. They had been skinny some months earlier, but now their skeletal frames could barely summon up the energy to reach the river for their daily drink. Kaika was grim but cool. Drought was not an unfamiliar occurrence. They would ride it out, he said. Some cattle would die. But most of his herd were already several days' distant, walking steadily southwards in the hope of finding sustenance.

Sainoi's *engang* at Engurashi, which normally teemed with animals, was surrounded by carcasses of cattle. They looked like pieces of brittle leather, shrunken and shrivelled, but with recognisable heads and hooves. The Maasai's main mechanism for drought is to migrate with their herds. But this safety net is no longer working as it once did, and not only because their drought refuge areas have become protected game parks. Nyange explained the reasons to me:

"It is not as simple as it sounds. First, there's the decision: to send the herds away or to wait it out. Timing's crucial. It's expensive to send cattle hundreds of kilometres. If you make the decision too soon you waste money because maybe the drought is about to end. But if you wait too long the cattle may die on the trail because they're too weak to walk. Some families will consult a *loibon*. He throws a gourd of stones and makes the prediction based on how they fall. But we also decide on the basis of past experience."

He went through the logistics of sending large numbers of cattle hundreds of kilometres. "You don't know where there is green grass. First you must send emissaries to find out. This takes time. They go here, they go there, checking where's best. Then they report back. Suppose they say that there is pasture over there, 150 kilometres away. It may still not be feasible to send your herds there. Cattle walk slowly. It can take up to a month to reach the new grazing area. While they're walking they must eat something; they must drink water, or they'll die. The itinerary has to be planned very carefully. That's why we know where every waterhole is located. Every day is planned in detail. The place where we'll rest, the place where the herd can briefly graze, the place where we'll find water, the place where there's some shade for the middle of the day. If it's very hot we walk the cattle at night and rest during the day."

Each area and each clan has designated dry-season grazing which they reserve for times of drought. The system used to work well in the past, but modern-day changes are leading to its breakdown. Game parks and arable farming have claimed many of these dry-season grazing areas. Where they still exist, access to them may be blocked by cultivators. For Nyange's family, their traditional reserve area was towards Mombasa, adjacent to the Mkomazi Game Reserve, a trek of 150 kilometres or more. To reach it they had to cross through the intensively cultivated area of the South Paré Mountains. I could imagine the challenges of taking a herd of several hundred half-starved cattle on pathways bordering cultivated fields without their snatching some mouthfuls. This is how most of the conflicts between Maasai and other tribes arise.

"Families don't have the manpower to send their herds away like they used to," continued Nyange. "It takes several *morani* and they will be gone several months. It's a big expense. Nowadays, so many of our *morani* are missing. This year, it's a big challenge for all of us. Where are our young men? They're off in the city working as night guards! Even if we call them home to help, they don't have the skills any more, they've forgotten the ways of the bush."

Elections took place and a new president was sworn in as the drought intensified. In his inauguration speech to Parliament, President Kikwete laid out the key points of his agriculture agenda: "We must abandon altogether nomadic pastoralism which makes the whole country pastureland ... The cattle are bony, and the pastoralists are sacks of skeletons. We cannot move forward with this type of pastoralism in the twenty-first century."[1] In a speech made a few months later, he said, "It is better for a few pastoralists to be angry, but protect the lives of the next generation."[2]

The Maasai, at that moment, were skeletal indeed. But this statement seemed to blame them for the drought and for holding back the rest of the country. Nomadic pastoralism is not a cause of, but a coping mechanism for drought. It was clearly a populist statement designed to go down well with the majority population who were farmers. Hidden by the question of agriculture policy was the irritating fact that the Maasai did not conform with the image of a modern, forward-looking country that the government wished to project. Yet this image was curiously at odds with the fact that Kikwete's party – Chama cha Mapinduzi (CCM) – has been continuously in power since Tanganyika gained independence from the British in 1961.[3] Forty-five years without a change of party did not set a good example of dynamism; it suggested the government and the electorate had a serious allergy to change.

But the pastoralist Maasai were easy scapegoats – for drought, for traditions, for embarrassing the country by looking like 'sacks of skeletons'.

The year finished as dry as it had started, and the new year brought no relief. The short rains never materialised. Sunrise and sunset blossomed into ever greater spectacles, but as the dust haze mounted in the night sky, the stars faded from the show.

Every third day, the cattle descended from the plateau to the river, but on each trip there were more and more who failed to make it. Every vertebra, every bone, poked through their skin. The Maasai slashed the big trees that grew by the river. I thought a tornado had powered through the area. Every tree with a hint of leaves was broken in two so that its upper branches fell to browsing level for the herds.

It was an environmental disaster.

Everything became brittle. Twigs and branches snapped with ease. Every leaf shrivelled and dropped. As the desiccation intensified, the mudpans by the river developed a network of cracks which penetrated deeper and deeper. When I walked there, the salt-encrusted mud crunched as though I was walking on potato crisps. Wind lifted its ultralight flakes and deposited them on people's clothing and in their eyes. Dust devils played tag as they scampered past, growing taller and stronger as they bumped into each other. Lips cracked. Eyes turned the colour of sunset as trachoma spread.

At Nyumba ya Mungu, the lake retreated until it was a quarter of its former area, and out of its waters rose a forest of ghost trees drowned long ago. Month by month, the fishermen at Nyumba ya Mungu walked further and further out across the dried-up shoreline to reach their boats. The water level was far too low to feed the turbines beneath the dam. In Dar es Salaam, we urban dwellers cursed the drought, but only because the electricity cuts lasted from dawn to dusk each day.

The Ruvu River still held pools of water. Wild animals began invading the area. Lion were seen nearby. Guided by an ancient memory, elephant also appeared. Elephant were unknown in this part of Siman-jiro; there were Maasai who had lived here all their lives and never seen an elephant. Fetching water became hazardous; several people were killed by an elephant when they unknowingly entered the area where it was hiding.

Every day the Maasai searched the horizon, hoping to see rain clouds. Delegations of elders and prayer-teams of women gathered on Ol Doinyo Lengai and beseeched *Engai* to send rain.

Cattle prices plummeted and the price of maize doubled. The cows had long ago ceased producing milk. The government and aid agencies distributed sacks of food aid, but the deliveries were irregular and insufficient. The women of Mama Masai reduced their food consumption to one meal a day, then to alternate days, and finally to three meals a week.

Kaika led his wives and children with their few remaining cows and goats across the river to a place where the situation was slightly less dire. "We didn't bother building shelters. We laid our hides on the ground and slept in the open until the rains returned," said Raheli. "Many cattle died. There was much sickness. Anna's baby was very young. I feared it wouldn't survive."

The new year proceeded as dry as the old one had ended. The cattle could stand no more. During January, February and March 2006, they dropped like flies – in their hundreds, and then in their thousands. Carcasses of dead animals piled up outside every *engang*. Hot winds and thermals carried the stench of rotting flesh to every desolate spot in the Steppe. Hundreds of vultures appeared in the cloudless skies. Descending in circles, they gorged themselves until they were too heavy to fly away.

Storm clouds began to brew during March and finally, by the end of the month, the first drops of the long rains fell. On schedule that year.

But too late to save the cattle of the Maasai.

The Steppe looked magnificent after the rains; greener than I ever remembered it being. The sand dunes had vanished. Lush grass grew by the river. *Ungrazed* green grass – priceless a few months earlier, now utterly valueless. It flourished only to mock.

Sinyati, Kikama and Elisabet managed to summon a smile to their faces as they greeted me. But I was shocked. Sinyati had become as skinny as co-wife Kikama, while Elisabet was skeletal.

"Look at us, I'm nude!" lamented Sinyati, pointing to her empty ear lobes, her neck and shoulders bare of beads. All her ornaments were gone. "We sold everything to buy food. Look at my arms!" She smiled ruefully, clutching wrinkled folds of loose skin.

Milking time was no longer the magical hour it had been. Their *engangs* were silent. No cattle bells were heard. No hoofprints marked the pathways, no fresh dung filled the inner corral. No milking into bottle-gourds by women. Mboi sat disconsolate in the empty enclosure with his head in his hands. He could not look me in the eye.

I was horrified to see how close they had come to starvation. The men made a sorrier sight than the women. They roamed their empty *engangs*, visibly depressed. Unemployed, income-less. As though a limb of their bodies had been wrenched away. *Engai* had entrusted them with her cattle, and they had failed. The pride and joy of their lives had been destroyed.

A few of Mboi's cows had survived. His goats had done better, and he kindly pointed out that 'my goat' was one of the lucky ones. Kaika's situation was better. He had had the resources to send most of his herds south to Handeni. He told me that it was the worst drought in living memory. "We say 'even in a bad drought the goats and *morani* will survive'. But this drought was so bad even goats were dying. *Ashi Engai!* My family survived!" Every man I spoke with emphasised the fact that nobody had died. At least they could be proud of this.

The drought might be over, but the real trial was just beginning. The District Livestock Office estimated that eighty per cent of the cattle in this part of the Steppe had died. Herds that had migrated further afield had a better survival rate. With their cattle decimated, there were no milking cows and larders were empty. Few cows remained to sell or exchange for maize. Government and humanitarian agencies were reported to be distributing tons of maize. But to the empty bellies and hungry mouths of the population, the distribution was erratic and insufficient. Famine remained an ever-present threat.

One source of income, however, had not died.

As the drought tightened its grip, Mama Masai's production of beadwork had doubled and then trebled. In the twelve months following the drought, it continued to increase exponentially. The women beaded day and night.

Frida's marketing trips to Dar es Salaam became more and more frequent. She staggered under the weight of Mama Masai products. She bought a bigger bag to carry them, and finally a large suitcase with roller wheels. Fair Trade Friends had been set up in the nick of time. With their capital, they bought every product of marketable quality.

"We've never worked so hard as we worked in the twelve months following the drought," recalled Sinyati. "We've never earned so much money as we earned that year. At that time, a Mama Masai group could earn half a million shillings on a single shipment! Without the beadwork income we wouldn't have survived. Men sought us out from far away. They'd somehow heard about Mama Masai. They pleaded and begged us: "Lend me five thousand shillings so I can buy my family some food. We've nothing to eat. We've heard that you Mama Masai have some money. *Please* – give us a small loan and we can buy maize."

Sinyati and Kikama both gave birth in the aftermath of the drought, having been babyless for many years – a curious and unexplained repercussion of near-starvation. "I feared I would lose the baby," Sinyati confided. "There was nothing to eat while I was pregnant; nothing to drink except black tea. I was eaten by anxiety."

But as I had feared, the drought carried a vicious sting in its tail.

Some months after the rains had fallen, epidemics of malaria and meningitis swept through the area. People rarely die of starvation itself; they die of infections which their malnourished bodies are too weak to fight. In the north, three or four members of Mama Masai died, and several others lost children or close relatives. In the south, the worst tragedy hit the family of Jacopo, the nightguard at the Loiborsoit training centre who had so faithfully and solicitously cared for my needs over the years. Four of his family died, including his beloved wife Elisabet. Sinyati was grief-stricken at losing her best friend, and so was I. Elisabet, with her young children in tow, and her calm demeanor and beautiful smile, was one of the fixtures of my visits to Loiborsoit. Jacopo was inconsolable.

Witnessing Jacopo's vacant *engang*, I felt confused, my emotions in a spin. As a community of pastoralists, they had suffered a mortal blow. The devastation was terrible to witness; the pulsing heartbeat of their life had been destroyed. Nonetheless, Mama Masai had helped to fill the void. The groups had fulfilled the purpose for which they were established: a safety net to carry them through times of drought.

Ashi Engai! We survived! was the refrain on everyone's lips, despite their losses.

24

Recollections

When we think no-one is looking, we slip out of the *engang*. I have told Kaika's wives that I want to talk privately, which is impossible inside the enclosure. Frida is with me, along with Raheli, Anna and Magilena; the other wives are absent or have work to do. We have hardly had time to settle under a shady acacia when children begin to appear in ones and twos. Magilena and Raheli shoo them away with a stream of Masai threats.

I notice that Anna has tears in her eyes:

Anna

My eyes are wet because today my older sister paid me a visit. It must be twenty-five years since I last saw her. I didn't recognise her until my mother said, "Look, here's your sister." Really, I had forgotten her face and only remembered her name. She looks very different now – much fatter, and she used to be so thin.

We were circumcised together on the same day. I remember the day clearly; it was so painful. I was in agony for three days. Immediately after that my sister got married, and so did I, and our lives took us in different directions.

I'd never met my husband before he married me, but I'd heard about him because he knew my family. When I was born he was still young –

a moran – *but he begged my mother to be allowed to marry me when I was bigger. I was about seven years old when my mother told me I was to be Kaika's wife.*

I was happy because he had a good reputation. He was strong and admired by other men. As soon as I reached puberty I was circumcised, and as soon as I was circumcised he married me. My parents received eight cows from him. I felt proud that I was worth eight cows. I don't see the custom of dowry cows in a bad light at all.

There was no big fuss for the wedding. My parents slaughtered a sheep and made me eat the fat of it. The night after the ceremony, I went with my husband and his relatives. Nobody from my family escorted me, except the cows which my father gave me. When I arrived here, I found there were four other wives.

I like being one of many wives. We visit each other, tell stories, live like one family. It's a big help because we can leave our babies or animals with the others when we need to. Sometimes we cook and eat together, but normally we eat and sleep separately in our own huts. I didn't have my own hut at first but lived with my mother-in-law. Jealousy isn't something I know, but some wives are jealous. It's stupid to feel jealous – a husband won't love a jealous wife and he may even send her back, so there's no point in being jealous.

My husband treats us well. Occasionally, he has to beat us. For example, if we don't look after the animals properly, if we don't realise that an animal is sick and we let it out to graze when it should be kept in a pen, or if a cow goes missing. It's normal. But if a husband should beat a wife too hard, or too frequently, she'll complain to her parents and they'll intervene and beg him to treat their daughter with more respect.

I consider myself married for life. There's no such thing as divorce. If we should chance to become pregnant by another man – such things can happen, you know, and it's not too serious if it happens just once – your husband should forgive you. But if it happens a second time, it's wise to confess your error before he finds out. Beg a cow from your friends or your parents; first give the cow to your husband – it will put him in a good mood – and then make your confession. Mistakes like this can happen, but it's not wise, because your husband will stop loving you.

I was young when I was married. Even now some girls are married as young as I was, but times are changing. In the past, there was the custom for a man to provide sexual hospitality to male guests by offering one of his wives for the night. That's stopped now. We know it spreads disease. Nowadays, we've even stopped female circumcision. The government doesn't approve of it. They've had a campaign here to stop the practice. I've been lucky because I've never suffered any complications from being circumcised, but some women suffer a lot. We still hold the circumcision ceremony and the girl receives her circumcision cows, but there's no knife.

Nowadays, girls go to school. They don't marry immediately after circumcision but delay until they've completed primary or even secondary school. Women don't like to have so many children these days. Some of us use contraception – the pill, or injections or patches. I did for a while, but they made me feel sick.

I feel lucky. I've always been happy. My fondest memory is the time I visited Dar es Salaam and stayed in Koko's home. I remember her dogs. Of course there've been hard times too. I lost some pregnancies, and after the birth of my seventh child, I was very sick. That was the time of the great drought when we all went hungry, even the children. But I'm grateful I've never had any big problems in my life. Each day

I ask Engai *to care for us, to provide our food, to watch over our animals, and help my children study well in school.*

Magilena

When I was young, I loved school. My father sent all his daughters to school. I studied hard and I passed my primary school exam. I wanted to go to secondary school, but my father refused. He'd already made arrangements for my marriage, without telling me.

When I learnt I was to marry an old man, I wept. I was fourteen at the time and dreamed of marrying a young man!

I only realised Kaika was to be my husband the day of our marriage, although I had some premonitions. One day at school I was in a line-up of girls waiting to be punished. Two girls ahead of me were made to do press-ups while the teacher caned them. It was horrible, you could see their breasts and up their skirts. A Maasai man appeared – I didn't know who he was at the time – and he told the teacher to stop. He said it wasn't right to punish girls in this way. I didn't want to be caned, and while they were talking, my friend and I ran away. That's when she told me 'that Maasai man is Kaika, and he's going to be your husband'. I didn't know whether to believe her or not. I went home and asked my parents if it was true. They said, "Don't worry – you're not going to be married."

It wasn't true. They tricked me! I cried all the way to his engang, *and Kaika kept begging me to stop. I cried not only because my husband was old, but because I'd lost my home and the chance to continue my education.*

When we arrived at his engang, *I discovered he already had five wives. I was stunned! But the other wives were very kind at first. In the beginning, I lived with Raheli; later, I built my own* enkaji. *I get along better with some wives than with others. Quarrels happen. The common things we quarrel over are the behaviour of our children, or whether Kaika favours one of us more than another.*

My education has helped me to progress. It gave me the opportunity to attend training courses on business, to become a literacy teacher for adults. Now I've started my own onion farm on the other side of the river. I decided not to share with my husband but to invest my own money.

It's thirteen years since I was married and I've had six children. My two oldest boys are already morani! *The happiest day of my life was when I finally gave birth to a baby girl – after five sons. I won't circumcise her – they'd send me to prison! And no-one will force her to get married. My dream is for her to study. I'm saving up my money so I can send her to a private school.*

Raheli

I don't know my age. I can't even remember how many years I've been married. I'm a local girl; I grew up at Engurashi. Yes, my father was the man who had twelve wives. He sent three of his sons to school. How I wished to be one of them and go to school!

When I was young, I never thought about the future. I was very happy. I was beautiful. We had so much fun. When my father informed me that he'd concluded a marriage arrangement for me with Kaika, I was deliriously happy. Because secretly, I was already in love with Kaika!

At that time, we were already seeing each other. He was a fine young man, from a good engang, *and he knew how to speak. He doesn't say a lot, but he says it well. We used to dance and tell each other stories and laugh together. He would come to me and say, "Tomorrow there'll be a ceremony at such-and-such village – let's go there so we can dance together." That's what we did. And naturally we made love to each other. I would never have slept with him if I'd thought he wouldn't become my husband.*

I was very young and I was Kaika's first wife. He gave my father one cow for me at the time of my marriage – he wasn't a wealthy man back then. But later, after I had borne him many children, my father came and took three more cows. He didn't want to take too many as he liked Kaika.

I didn't mind when Kaika married again. He always told me what he was planning to do, and I'd say, "It's fine – bring another wife." I was happy for him to have many wives, but now I feel that six is enough. And the other five agree. So we try to make a happy environment for Kaika so that he's content and won't go seeking a seventh wife.

Actually, Kaika didn't plan to marry Magilena. He was looking to marry a fifth wife and he and his father went searching separately. Kaika returned with Anna as his wife, but at the same time his father had negotiated a marriage arrangement with Magilena's parents. As his father had already accepted the dowry cows from Magilena's family, Kaika was obliged to marry Magilena as well.

But he loves Magilena, and she makes him happy. So we tell him: "Go with her" and we tell her: "Take care of him and please him" so that he doesn't look for number seven. Magilena's sons are still small, and it's good for Kaika to sleep in her enkaji so he can protect them if anything should happen.

Our husband tries to be fair and is careful to allocate an equal number of cows and goats to each of us. I know that other husbands are not so fair. So we appreciate this aspect of Kaika. He always tries to buy things equally for us. It's true when we misbehave he beats us, for example, if we go to another engang without his permission. One time, he beat me because a cow had delivered in the night and I was not awake to attend to her.

I've had seven children altogether. Two of them died when small. My firstborn didn't attend school because schooling wasn't the custom back then. He's living in Sudan where he sells herbal medicine. All the rest of my children got some education. One of my daughters even completed lower secondary before she got married.

I'll never forget living through the great drought. It was the worst experience of my life. Nowadays, the income from our cows isn't enough, so we buy food with our Mama Masai income, along with cloth, utensils and things like that.

Since my child-bearing years are done, I feel happiest when I sell some beadwork and get some money of my own to spend. I put some of it aside as savings until I have enough to ask Charles to bring me a can of diesel in his truck. I pour the diesel into bottles and sell it to men who own a piki-piki. *Charles passes by every Thursday and he only charges me the transport money. I'd saved nearly fifty thousand shillings when my youngest child fell ill and I spent all my savings on his treatment.*

The sun is sinking low. As we prepare to return home, Frida makes a confession: "At the beginning, I didn't like helping Mama Masai with their beadwork. I loathed beads! Do you remember?" There is a grin on her face.

"Yes, I remember," I reply, "but I never understood why you thought it such a bad idea."

Frida pauses to control a chuckle. "Because where I come from, in the Paré Mountains, we Mparé women wear beads only for intercourse!"

"How do you mean – as decoration?"

"No, no! As part of the act. We wear bands of them around our waist and hips. The man gets arousal by rubbing against them." Frida provides a demonstration, and we collapse with laughter.

This is not the case for the Maasai, Kaika's wives assure me, and Frida hastens to add that she no longer condemns beadwork and has even grown to like it. We lapse into silence while I reflect on how ignorant I have been of things beneath the surface. Of all the reasons on which a development initiative might have foundered, this one surely would have won the prize.

The sun touches the ground. Still giggling like foolish girls, we head towards the *engang* where a multitude of hungry-eyed children await our return.

Epilogue

A book entitled *The Last of the Masai* first appeared in 1901, and the extinction of the Maasai has been a recurring thread in the literature ever since. [1]

In 1905, Hollis wrote: 'It has often been proved in other parts of the globe that the native, on the advent of the white man, alters his habits or ceases to exist, and it is hoped that the Masai will choose the first of these alternatives.'[2] Change or be damned, in other words.

But the Maasai were still the same in the 1950s when Father Donovan started work in the Maasai Steppe, for he writes: 'There is no future tense in the Masai language. Tomorrow will be like today. The Masai are utter conservatives, afraid of change of any kind. They are practically the only tribe in Tanzania that has been exposed to every kind of change, and has successfully resisted it'.[3]

The Maasai were still around for the dawning of the new millennium, still distinctively Maasai, against all the odds, the prejudice and the hype. Even so, as I travel around the Maasai Steppe in the second decade of the twenty-first century, and see evidence of the tremendous changes and pressures that are encroaching, I too wonder whether they can adapt and keep their heads above the current flood, or whether I really am witnessing the final fling of the Maasai tartan.

Although I left Tanzania in 2006, I continue to visit Mama Masai annually. Since these visits are spaced further apart, I have been better able to notice and register the changes that are occurring. Mobile phones are not the only modern phenomenon to invade their bush: almost every trip I note something new. They are assailed on all fronts:

education, climate change, land attrition, HIV and AIDS, the migration of *morani* to the cities, tourism and 'Maasai iconism' as well as the spread of religious and other dogma. Even people like me, trying to promote women's rights, are part of the onslaught. Some changes are good and the Maasai appreciate them; some are mixed, and some are destructive. Some are the result of deliberate campaigns, of government policy, of economic competition, and some are physical change – climate, land degradation – but even in these, human agency is visible. Some changes make me feel hopeful, and other changes, fearful for their future.

Sitting in an *engang* under an open sky with the cattle lowing and goats bleating, it is easy to feel that time is suspended, the outside world a distant mirage. But Baba Kicheche had spoken these words: "We want our children to participate in the world."

"In the past, we had to rely upon outsiders to bring new ideas to us," he expanded. "Now we have Maasai who are agricultural officers, and members of parliament. In the past, we lived in low-roofed *enkaji* without ventilation. We changed because we understood how disease is transmitted. We want our children to benefit from knowledge, education, health dispensaries, water and sanitation. But we don't change just for the sake of change. We'll never mimic other people's fashions."

Baba Kicheche and Nyange are useful informants for me because they reflect upon the issues and are able to articulate how the Maasai regard the threats and opportunities of the new world order. But as they are well-educated, their views may not represent the Maasai mainstream. Neither has chosen to take more than one wife, which in itself speaks of the changes that education foments.

"What does the future hold for the Maasai people?" Nyange repeated the question I had posed. "For me, it is to stand upright, neither to move forwards nor backwards. There are men who get an education but who still return to the Steppe. Education is useful to us. I hope I'm a good example. I hope others see me and are encouraged to send their children to school. And in ten years' time I hope these children with their education will remain connected to us."

Baba Kicheche's dream has been fulfilled and a lower secondary school opened at Ngage. It has led to a dramatic increase in enrolment, primary as well as secondary, girls as well as boys. Out of this emerged a new challenge: girls who complete school are refusing to be married to old men. If they have not achieved the marks or funding to continue their education, they prefer to stay at home with their parents, or to marry men of their own choosing.

When I originally inquired, all the women were adamant that polygamy was good; they liked it. But on the last occasion, one or two expressed the opinion that they might like to be the only wife of their husband. That practice has not yet changed in any significant way, but other traditions have.

One of the changes which dismays me more than others is the loss of their beads. Some women no longer wear them. This change is largely restricted to the area around Loiborsoit and Ngage. At first, I assumed it was a legacy from the drought, but later I learnt that it was a teaching emanating from the church.

"We don't forbid them to wear ornaments, but we teach them that it's not important whether you wear them or not. If they're not helping you, then it's better to leave them off," Anna Moses explained to me. "Many women felt that the beads were heavy and uncomfortable on their necks and ears – some get painful scarring around their lobes from the weight – and so they decided to remove them. It was their choice. It's like we used to wear wire on our legs and arms, and then they taught us that this was bad, it would scar and cripple us, so we stopped that practice."

Although her words suggested that it is their own decision whether to wear traditional ornaments or not, I suspect that outside influences are at work. In recent years, Anna has attended church seminars elsewhere, and I notice that non-Maasai clergy are now preaching at the Ngage church. And their arrival is connected to all the other changes which are happening – to the fact that there are better roads (though still unpaved) from Ngage to Orkasmet and to Nyumba ya Mungu, better mobile phone networks, electricity in certain places, and that irrigation and onion farming have expanded near Ngage, bringing more shops and consumer items to the settlement. Consequently, it is not such a hardship for outsiders and their world view to enter the Steppe. Elsewhere, women continue to wear their beads, and within the disapproving churches, some like *Koko* Sainoi defiantly still wear their full beaded regalia. "I don't care what they teach about beads. I go to church to pray," she told me.

The Maasai are aware that education is a two-edged sword; it may destroy them, but they cannot afford to avoid it. "I'm not sure whether to feel optimistic or pessimistic," pondered Nyange. "The next generation will be very mixed up. Most of my children are studying – my goal is to find a way to send them all to university. Because in this century, there are changes which will bring opportunities – but only to those who are educated. In the future, we'll have a big problem with land, so my children will need their education to cope. If they're successful in their studies, I suspect they won't want to live here at Engurashi as I am living. They'll stay in the towns, far away from the animals. Perhaps they'll buy me some cows to stay here with me, and when they need animals for a ceremony they can visit me and take one." He smiled gently, and his smile contained all the perplexity of the Maasai at the paradoxes with which they are having to deal.

The Mama Masai groups still exist and total around 250 women as members. Some groups have collapsed, others are struggling, and to my chagrin, many of the original thorny problems regarding beads, mobility and marketing still remain. But groups with strong leadership have seized other opportunities and are thriving. They have managed to diversify into poultry raising and onion farming, and the figures they write in their account books continue to rise. Nowadays, I'm more likely to see a mobile phone around their necks than an *esosi* necklace. Frida still acts as agent for the beadwork and pays some groups by mobile phone banking. Invariably, men find a way to get their bite of the income: "My husband used to buy maize for the family; now he makes us buy with our own money," they say.

245

Sometimes I am amazed by the distance they have travelled. At Magadini, their local school needed new classrooms; a building fund was set up and the committee announced that every man must contribute a certain sum. The Mama Masai women were indignant that they were not counted. They went to the Committee and objected: "Don't you realise that we women have our own independent income? We want to pay *our* contribution. We're mothers. These are our children. We want them to get the best education possible. We want our say in the future of the school."

Such stories are infectious. Encouraged by the example from Magadini, Mama Masai members in Loiborsoit intervened to save their health dispensary. For several years it had been closed due to lack of staff. "We came to realise that unless we took action the situation might never change," said Mama John, "so we talked with the elders, and we told them our children are constantly sick and we really need the dispensary to be open. Then we invited the ward councillor to a meeting and requested him to talk to the government. Now the dispensary is staffed and open again!"

Nobody had taught them about lobbying and advocacy or urged them to do it. It was something that emerged in a spontaneous manner. One should never underestimate the power that women feel when they earn even a little bit of money by their own efforts.

"We've rolled the stepping stone ahead," Anna said with justifiable pride. "Some of us bought ourselves a goat or built a new house. Women can be elected leaders now. We own something of value and that's given us the power to lead like men."

"Women have more power than they had before," agreed Nyange. "Yes, it makes us men feel a little uneasy, but I believe women should study, work, fight, and do all the things that men do."

It is not only the quantity of changes, but the pace of change. In the Steppe, it accelerated following the drought of 2006. There was a second drought in 2009 and the pace speeded up further. In the past twelve months I believe I have seen greater changes in Loiborsoit than in the previous twelve years – especially in the physical environment. Whereas the Maasai *engangs* used to be hidden, suddenly they are visible everywhere. There are fewer thorns in my shoes and clothes. Because the thorn bushes are almost gone. The reason bleats.

Mboi now keeps many more goats than cows. He lost nearly his whole cattle herd in the drought of 2006. After painstakingly rebuilding his stock, he again lost numbers in the droughts of the past few years. "The cattle are dying; there's nothing for them to eat. But sheep and goats can survive. I've developed a taste for goat's milk – now I like it better than cow's. Sheep don't give milk but they're good for meat and fat. *Engai* gave me these animals," he notes with satisfaction.

The ramifications of climate change are many and curious. "I won't marry another wife, because of global warming," Moses informed me. "Life's more difficult. Last year, some of my cows died from the drought and the rains are few this year."

"Our cattle are diminishing with each drought," confirmed Baba Kicheche. "Our *morani* no longer herd; they're running beauty salons in Sudan and Ethiopia. Their skills are in demand because they're skilled at braiding and beautifying their own hair. When the guards at the border see the red *orlokaraha* of a Maasai, they wave him through without a passport. Language is no barrier. *Engai* has given us a special gift: we learn other languages very fast. Even when we don't speak a language, we can somehow understand what other people are saying and thinking because we have a natural intuition for human psychology."

Many have questioned whether the Maasai can remain Maasai without their cattle. If they forsake pastoralism, does that lead to the demise of the Maasai way of life?

"Our animals will decrease but we will remain the same," was Nyange's response.

"Nowdays, we're also farming; we're growing onions by the river; there's not such a big difference between us and other tribes, but we'll still be Maasai. When I look to the future, I see that we will advance," said Moses.

"We're proud of being Maasai because of our culture," explained Baba Kicheche. "The *morani* still return home to get married. Age-sets will continue. Although many things have changed, we try to hold onto the most important customs – for example, we'll never pass by another Maasai person without greeting him."

I was reminded of an early experience in Dar es Salaam when he said this. One Sunday, my husband and I had attended a service in a huge Lutheran church in Msasani. There were over a thousand people in the church. Ours were the only white faces. In the front row sat four Maasai *morani* with braided hair and scarlet *orlokaraha* shawls. At the end of the service, they were the only ones who approached us, shook our hands, and spoke words of welcome.

Despite the changes, I find the Maasai of the Steppe unchanged in their warmth, openness, honesty and courage in the face of uncertainty and adversity.

John Galaty, an anthropologist who has carried out research on the Maasai, explains that tradition and change are not alternatives but are two forces simultaneously at work; cultural codes are what help people to synthesise the two.[4] I find this perspective helpful. The fact that the Maasai have survived into the twenty-first century, established permanent settlements, embraced education and cultivation, yet remain distinctively Maasai, shows the tremendous resilience of their culture and offers hope for the future.

I feel fortunate and honoured to have known them at this time. It is a rare gift, to have had a glimpse into their traditional life, and at the same time to have travelled with them through the changing scenery – sometimes bleak and sometimes beautiful – of drought and social change.

The times are turbulent for the Maasai of the Steppe. I see them on a giant roller-coaster ride. Stomachs churning, fingers clinging to the familiar, but eyes fixed on the future. I hope that when the ride ends, they will step out with the best of their values and traditions still intact. We have so much to learn from them.

Fourteen years after my first visit, I lie on my back in Mboi's *engang* listening to the ringing of cowbells, watching the darkness deepen and the stars splash across the sky. Singing fills the cool night air. I gaze at the Milky Way slicing through the sky.

Mama Masai set out on a journey. It has not been an easy journey and it is not over yet. On many occasions, they fell into a gully or lost their way, or had to backtrack. Many of the problems and challenges of transforming their love of beads into a sustainable business still remain. Who knows where their destination lies – for the Maasai as a people as well as for Mama Masai.

Before the drought struck, Mama Masai's existence was in the balance. They had not truly grasped the possibilities; had not fully committed themselves to the venture; had not been ready to take risks. Then they were plunged into the inferno of the drought. That year, they seemed to take a quantum leap forward. A new confidence and resolve appeared.

Would this have happened without the drought? I don't think so.

Though the pregnancy was long and tiring, filled with complications and setbacks, though the labour pains were agonising, out of the suffering and harshness of the drought, Mama Masai gave birth to themselves. It was not an ending, but a new beginning.

Like true nomads, their journey continues.

Joy Stephens, 2013

Glossary

Swahili

badai	later
bado	not yet
bao	'board' game played throughout Africa
boma	homestead enclosure
bongo flava	Tanzanian rap music
burka	complete cover-up gown worn by Muslim women
dhow	boat with lateen-rigged sails
hamna shida	no problem
hayupo	s/he is not here
kanga	wrap worn around the waist by women
kanzu	long, loose gown worn by Muslim men
kofiya	embroidered cap worn by Muslim men
lakhi	one hundred thousand
madafu	coconut milk
mama	mother
mashua	open fishing boat
mbwa	dog
mishkaki	beef kebabs marinated with chillies and lime juice, traditional to coastal East Africa
mkali	fierce
mzungu (pl. *wazungu*)	white-skinned person (literally 'one who wanders in circles')
ngalawa	small wooden sailboat with outriggers, used for fishing
piki-piki	motorcycle
polé (kwa safari)	sorry (for the journey)
tano	five

ugali	thick porridge, usually made from maize, widely eaten in Tanzania
ujamaa	villagisation

Maa

Ashi Engai	Thanks be to God
endaa	food
Engai	God
engang	homestead enclosure
engare	water
engerai	child
engiteng	cow
engitok	woman
enkaji	hut/house
enkop	earth
esosi	beaded neck-bands
etejo	she says
iko/ipa	fine
illkarash	thin, colourful wrap, often red
koko	grandmother
layoni	young, uncircumcised boys
loibon/loiboni/oloiboni	traditional diviner-healer
manyatta	special homestead enclosure where traditionally, *morani* live
moran/morani	young Maasai men/warriors
olaigwenani	leader of an *olaji/olporror* peer-group
olaji	age-set (generation peer-group); each *olaji* has two sub-divisions known as *olporror*
orlokaraha	thick scarlet shawl, commonly worn by men
orpeko	spirit possession
seri	goodbye
sidai	good
sopai?	how are you? (to man)
takwenya?	how are you? (to woman)
yeyo	mother

Bibliography

Author's note

1. See www.mamamasai.com.
2. In January 2006 TCRS became independent from LWF and started operating as a Tanzanian NGO.

Chapter 1

1. Krapf J.L. 1860. *Travels, Researches and Missionary Labours During Eighteen Years' Residence in Eastern Africa*, p. 292. Frank Cass and Company Ltd, Abingdon, U.K.
2. Smith, A. 1962. *Throw Out Two Hands*. Allen & Unwin, London.

Chapter 2

1. As it was then known. Tanganyika was renamed Tanzania in 1964 when it was united to form one country with Zanzibar.
2. I Chronicles 9:10.
3. Merker, M. 1904. *Die Masai: Ethnographische Monographie eines ostafrikanischen Semitenvolkes*, Chapter 1. Reimer, Berlin.
4. Quoted by V. Kimesera, 2004, in a paper titled 'Brief Background and History of the People of "Maa"', presented at the Maasai Cultural Festival held at the Village Museum, National Museum of Tanzania, 7–8 November 1998 and later published as Chapter 3 in *The History and Some Traditions of the Maasai*, National Museum of Tanzania, 2004, p. 25.

Chapter 8

1. Baumann, O. 1894. *Durch Massailand zur Nilquelle* ('Through Massailand to the Source of the Nile'), p. 32. Reimer, Berlin.

2. Lugard, F.J.D. 1893, quoted on the website of the Pribright Institute/Preventing and Controlling Viral Diseases: Disease Facts – Rinderpest. Accessed 3 January 2014, www.iah.ac.uk/disease/rinderpest.aspx.

3. El-Sawalhy, A. 2011.*The Eradication of Rinderpest from Africa: A Great Milestone*. African Union-Interafrican Bureau for Animal Resources, Nairobi.

4. Kjekshush, H. 1977. *Ecology Control and Economic Development in East African History*. University of California Press, Berkeley, CA.

5. Thomson, J. 1885 (2nd edition 1887). *Through Masai Land: A Journey of Exploration among the Snowclad Volcanic Mountains and Strange Tribes of Eastern Equatorial Africa*, p. xi. Sampson Low, Marston, Searle & Rivington, London.

6. Thomson, *Through Masai Land*, pp. 236–237.

7. Sir Donald Stewart, Acting Commissioner, British East Africa, F.O. 2/842, Stewart to Lansdowne, 16 August 1904 and F.O. 2/841, Lansdowne to Stewart, 2 August 1904. Quoted in G.D. Adhi, 2009, 'Fixation with the Past or Vision for the Future: Challenges of Land Tenure Reform in Kenya with Special Focus on Land Rights of the Maasai and Borana Pastoralists', p. 99. Master's thesis, Murdoch University, Perth, Australia.

8. East African Protectorate, Correspondence Relating to the Maasai, Cmd No. 20360, received 28 March 1910. House of Commons Parliament Papers 1911, Volume LII 1, pp. 730–731. Quoted in Adhi, 'Fixation with the Past or Vision for the Future', p. 101.

9. Spoken by Lewis Harcourt, Secretary of State for the Colonies in the House of Commons, 20 July 1911, *Hansard* Vol 28, col. 1350. Quoted in Adhi, 'Fixation with the Past or Vision for the Future', p. 99.

10. Sir Charles Eliot in a Memorandum dated 07 September 1903 on Native Rights in the Naivasha Province. Quoted in G.R. Sandford, 1919, *An Administrative and Political History of the Masai Reserve*. Printed by Waterlow & Sons Ltd, London. Republished as an Amazon e-book. Quotation from Loc. 619–620.

11. Tidrick, K. 1980. 'The Masai and Their Masters: A Psychological Study of District Administration', p. 24. *African Studies Review* 23(1), pp. 15–32.
12. Latham, G. and Latham, M. 1994. *Kilimanjaro Tales*, p. 190. The Radcliffe Press, London.
13. Allan, T. 2006. *Ndutu Memories*. Accessed 9 July 2016, www.ntz. info/gen/b00950.html.
14. Hinde, S. and Hinde, H. 1901. *The Last of the Masai*, p. 120. Heinemann, London.

Additional sources

Crosby, L.P. 1989. The Maasai, Persistent or Perishing Pastoralists? Accessed 15 July 2016, https://scholarworks.alaska.edu/ under Theses/ Dissertations.

Fischer, G.A. 1884. In Proceedings of the Royal Geographical Society and Monthly Record of Geography Volume 6, No. 2, p.83.

Grandin, B.E. 1991. 'The Maasai: Socio-Historical Context and Group Ranches'. In S. Bekure, P.N. de Leeuw, B.E. Grandin, and P.J.H. Neate, *Maasai herding: An Analysis of the Livestock Production System of Maasai Pastoralists in eastern Kajiado District, Kenya.* FAO Corporate Document Repository. Accessed 3 July 2016, http:// www.fao.org/wairdocs/ilri/x5552e/x5552e05.htm#chapter%203:%20 the%20maasai:%20socio%20historical%20context%20and%20 group%20ranches.

Hughes, L. 2006. 'Malice in Maasailand: The Historical Roots of Current Political Struggles'. Paper presented at the international symposium, 'Les Frontières de la Question Foncière', Montpellier, 17–19 May 2006. Accessed 15 July 2016, https://www.mpl.ird.fr/ colloque_foncier/Communications/PDF/Hughes.pdf.

Lynn, S. 2010. *The Pastoral to Agro-Pastoral Transition in Tanzania: Human Adaptation in an Ecosystem Context.* Accessed 9 July 2016, http://economics-of-cc-in-tanzania.org/images/Stacy_Lynn_Pastoralism_ TZ_Draft_2010_08-09_draft_2_v2.pdf.

Chapter 9

1. *Masai Annual Report 1921–1922*, p. 9. Quoted by L. Hughes, 2006, 'Beautiful Beasts and Brave Warriors: The Longevity of a Maasai Stereotype', in L. Romanucci-Ross, G.A. de Vos, and T. Tsuda (eds), *Ethnic Identity: Problems and Prospects for the Twenty-First Century*, p. 286. AltaMira Press, Lanham, MD.

Chapter 13

1. Ndorobo: people of disputed origin who dress like Maasai, speak the same language, but are hunter-gatherers and artisans, rather than herders.
2. Sheldon, M.F. 2008. *Sultan to Sultan: Adventures of a Woman among the Masai and Other Tribes of East Africa*, p. 332. Trotamundas Press Ltd, Coventry, UK. First published 1892, Arena Press, Boston, MA.
3. Sheldon, *Sultan to Sultan*, p. 14.
4. Anderson, M. 2006. *Women and the Politics of Travel 1870–1914*, p. 21. Associated University Presses, Cranbury, NJ.
5. Sheldon, M.F. 1894. 'An African Expedition'. In M.K.O. Eagle (ed). *The Congress of Women: Chicago USA 1893*, p. 131. Monarch Book Company, Chicago, IL.
6. Sheldon, 'An African Expedition', p. 131.
7. Sheldon, 'An African Expedition', p. 131.
8. Sheldon, *Sultan to Sultan*, p. 84.
9. Sheldon, 'An African Expedition', p. 131.
10. Sheldon, *Sultan to Sultan*, p. 237.
11. Sheldon, 'An African Expedition', p. 131.
12. Sheldon, 'An African Expedition', p. 131.
13. Polygamy is a broad term. Strictly speaking, the Maasai practise polygyny – having multiple wives.

Chapter 14

1. Sheldon, M.F. 1894. 'An African Expedition'. In M.K.O. Eagle (ed). *The Congress of Women: Chicago USA 1893*, p. 131. Monarch Book Company, Chicago, IL.
2. Thomson, J. 1885 (2nd edition 1887). *Through Masai Land: A Journey of Exploration among the Snowclad Volcanic Mountains and Strange Tribes of Eastern Equatorial Africa*, p. 93. Sampson Low, Marston, Searle & Rivington, London.
3. Merker, M. 1904. *Die Masai: Ethnographische Monographie eines ostafrikanischen Semitenvolkes*. Reimer, Berlin. Quoted in translation in C. Masterjohn, *A Land of Milk and Honey, Bananas from Afar*, posted 13 September 2011. Accessed 14 July 2016, http://bit.ly/29wKQfC.
4. Baxter (DO/MaD) to PC/NP, 7 August 1931, TNA 69/47/MS. Quoted in D. Hodgson, 1999. 'Pastoralism, Patriarchy and History: Changing Gender Relations among Maasai in Tanganyika 1890–1940'. *Journal of African History* 40, pp. 41–65.
5. Quoted in D.L. Hodgson, 2001, *Once Intrepid Warriors: Gender, Ethnicity, and the Cultural Politics in Maasai Development*, p. 84. Indiana University Press, Bloomington, IL.
6. At 2014 exchange rates.
7. Hodgson, D.L. 1999. 'Pastoralism, Patriarchy and History: Changing Gender Relations among Maasai in Tanganyika 1890–1940'. *Journal of African History* 40, pp. 41–65.

Chapter 15

1. Sheldon, M.F. 2008. *Sultan to Sultan: Adventures of a Woman among the Masai and Other Tribes of East Africa*, p. 325. Trotamundas Press Ltd, Coventry, UK. First published 1892, Arena Press, Boston, MA.
2. Thomson, J. 1885 (2nd edition 1887). *Through Masai Land: A Journey of Exploration among the Snowclad Volcanic Mountains and Strange Tribes of Eastern Equatorial Africa*, p. 251. Sampson Low, Marston, Searle & Rivington, London.

3. Sheldon, *Sultan to Sultan*, p. 306.
4. Thomson, *Through Masai Land*, p. 250.
5. Thomson, *Through Masai Land*, p. 56.
6. Thomson, *Through Masai Land*, p. 57.
7. Sheldon, *Sultan to Sultan*, p. 371.
8. Sheldon, *Sultan to Sultan*, p. 288.
9. See Chami, F. 'Roman Beads from the Rufiji Delta, Tanzania'. *Current Anthropology* 40, pp. 237–241.

Additional sources

Blauer, E. 2008. *The Glory of African Beadwork*. Accessed 6 February 2008, www.worldandi.com/specialreport/afrobead/.

Graeber, D. 1996. 'Beads and Money: Notes Towards a Theory of Wealth and Power'. *American Ethnologist* 23 (1), pp. 2–24.

Chapter 16

1. Krapf, J.L. 1860. *Travels, Researches and Missionary Labours During Eighteen Years' Residence in Eastern Africa*, p. 292. Frank Cass and Company Ltd, Abingdon, U.K.
2. Thomson, J. 1885 (2nd edition 1887). *Through Masai Land: A Journey of Exploration among the Snowclad Volcanic Mountains and Strange Tribes of Eastern Equatorial Africa*. Sampson Low, Marston, Searle & Rivington, London.
3. Thomson, *Through Masai Land*, p. 4.
4. Thomson, *Through Masai Land*, p. 74.
5. Thomson, *Through Masai Land*, p. 89.
6. Thomson, *Through Masai Land*, p. 89.
7. Thomson, *Through Masai Land*, p. 90.
8. Thomson, *Through Masai Land*, p. 93.
9. Thomson, *Through Masai Land*, p. 167.
10. Thomson, *Through Masai Land*, p. 94.
11. Thomson, *Through Masai Land*, p. 195.
12. Thomson, *Through Masai Land*, p. 195.
13. Thomson, *Through Masai Land*, p. 155.

14. Thomson, *Through Masai Land*, p. 206.

15. Last, J.T. 1883. 'A Visit to the Masai People Living beyond the Borders of Nguru Country'. *Proceedings of the Royal Geographical Society*, Vol 5, new series. Quoted by L. Hughes, 2006, 'Beautiful Beasts and Brave Warriors: The Longevity of a Maasai Stereotype', in L. Romanucci-Ross, G.A. de Vos, and T. Tsuda (eds), *Ethnic Identity: Problems and Prospects for the Twenty-First Century*, p. 280. AltaMira Press, Lanham, MD.

16. Hughes, 'Beautiful Beasts', in Romanucci-Ross, De Vos, and Tsuda, *Ethnic Identity*, p. 284.

17. Sheldon, M.F. 2008. *Sultan to Sultan: Adventures of a Woman among the Masai and Other Tribes of East Africa*, pp. 130–133. Trotamundas Press Ltd, Coventry, UK. First published 1892, Arena Press, Boston, MA.

18. Sheldon, *Sultan to Sultan*, p. 321.

19. Sheldon, *Sultan to Sultan*, p. 319.

20. Sheldon, *Sultan to Sultan*, p. 323.

21. Sheldon, *Sultan to Sultan*, p. 332.

22. Hughes, 'Beautiful Beasts', in Romanucci-Ross, De Vos, and Tsuda, *Ethnic Identity*, p. 281.

23. Saitoti, T.O. 1986. *The Worlds of a Maasai Warrior: An Autobiography*, p. 106. University of California Press, Berkeley, CA.

24. Eliot, C. 1903. Memorandum on Native Rights in the Naivasha Province. Published in *Africa* 8 (1904), London HMSO, September 2. Quoted in Hughes, 'Beautiful Beasts', in Romanucci-Ross, De Vos, and Tsuda, *Ethnic Identity*, p. 285.

25. Eliot, C. 1905. *The East African Protectorate*, p.143. Quoted in Hughes, 'Beautiful Beasts', in Romanucci-Ross, De Vos, and Tsuda, *Ethnic Identity*, p. 285.

26. Eliot, C. Foreign Office Memorandum 2/835 to Lord Lansdowne, Secretary of State for Foreign Affairs, 19 April, 1904. Quoted in G.D. Adhi, 2009, 'Fixation with the Past or Vision for the Future: Challenges of Land Tenure Reform in Kenya with Special Focus

on Land Rights of the Maasai and Borana Pastoralists', p. 89. Master's thesis, Murdoch University, Perth, Australia.

27. Sandford, G.R. 1919. *An Administrative and Political History of the Masai Reserve.* Printed by Waterlow & Sons Ltd, London. Republished as an Amazon e-book. Quotation from Loc. 719.

28. Hughes, L. 2006. *Moving the Maasai: A Colonial Misadventure.* St Anthony's Series. Palgrave Macmillan, Basingstoke, UK.

29. *Masai Annual Report 1921–1922*, p. 9. Quoted in Hughes, 'Beautiful Beasts', in Romanucci-Ross, De Vos, and Tsuda, *Ethnic Identity*, p. 286.

30. Tidrick, K. 1980. 'The Masai and Their Masters: A Psychological Study of District Administration', p. 21. *African Studies Review* 23(1), pp. 15–32.

31. Dinesen, I. 1937. *Out of Africa.* Putnam, London. Republished as an Amazon e-book. Quotation from Loc. 1750.

32. V. Kimesera, 2004, in a paper titled 'Brief Background and History of the People of "Maa"', presented at the Maasai Cultural Festival held at the Village Museum, National Museum of Tanzania, 7–8 November 1998 and later published as Chapter 3 in *The History and Some Traditions of the Maasai*, National Museum of Tanzania, 2004, p. 26.

Chapter 19

1. Also referred to as *olporror*. A new age division (*olporror*) is formed every seven years. Approximately two of these merge to form an age-set (*olaji*).

2. Saitoti, T.O. 1986. *The Worlds of a Maasai Warrior: An Autobiography*, p. 71. University of California Press, Berkeley, CA.

3. Saitoti was born in 1949 so the period he is referring to would be in the 1960s.

4. Tidrick, K. 1980. 'The Masai and Their Masters: A Psychological Study of District Administration', p. 19. *African Studies Review* 23(1), pp. 15–32.

5. Tidrick, 'The Masai and their Masters', p. 19.

6. Tidrick, 'The Masai and their Masters', p. 20.
7. Tidrick, 'The Masai and their Masters', pp. 16–17.
8. Tidrick, 'The Masai and their Masters', p. 17.
9. Tidrick, 'The Masai and their Masters', p. 21.

Chapter 20

1. Ndagala, D.K. 1982. 'Operation Imparnati: The Sedenterisation of the Pastoral Maasai in Tanzania', p. 36. *Nomadic Peoples* 10, pp. 28–39.
2. President Ali Hassan Mwinyi took over from Nyerere as President of Tanzania, ruling from 1985 to 1995. Under pressure from international donors and finance institutions, Mwinyi's government began to liberalise the economy.
3. Renton, A. 'Tourism is a curse to us'. *The Observer*, 6 September 2009.

Chapter 22

1. Krapf, J.L. 1860. *Travels, Researches and Missionary Labours During Eighteen Years' Residence in Eastern Africa*, pp. 359–360. Frank Cass and Company Ltd, Abingdon, U.K.
2. Thomson, J. 1885 (2nd edition 1887). *Through Masai Land: A Journey of Exploration among the Snowclad Volcanic Mountains and Strange Tribes of Eastern Equatorial Africa*, p. 260. Sampson Low, Marston, Searle & Rivington, London.
3. Dinesen, I. 1937. *Out of Africa*. Putnam, London. Republished as an Amazon e-book. Quotation from Loc. 1920.
4. This is a reference to the burst waters of the womb in childbirth.
5. Hodgson, D.L. 2005. *The Church of Women: Gendered Encounters between Maasai and Missionaries*, p. 212. Indiana University Press, Bloomington, IL.
6. Hodgson, *The Church of Women*, p. 211.
7. Merker, M. 1904. *Die Masai: Ethnographische Monographie eines ostafrikanischen Semitenvolkes*. Reimer, Berlin. Referred to by Sir Charles Eliot in the Introduction to A.C. Hollis, 1905, *The Masai: Their Language and Folklore*, Clarendon Press, Oxford.

8. Hollis, A.C. 1905. *The Masai: Their Language and Folklore*. Clarendon Press, Oxford.
9. Hodgson, *The Church of Women*, p. 212.
10. Hodgson, *The Church of Women*, p. 217.
11. Hodgson, *The Church of Women*, p. 169.

Chapter 23

1. Hansard, 30 December 2005, Parliament of the United Republic of Tanzania.
2. From a speech made by Kikwete, 22 February 2006, quoted in *The Guardian* (Tanzania), 2 March 2006.
3. CCM, or Party of the Revolution, was previously known as the Tanzania African National Union (TANU). CCM was formed in 1977 after a merger of TANU with the Afro-Shirazi Party of Zanzibar.

Epilogue

1. Hinde, S.L. and Hinde, H. 1901. *The Last of the Masai*. Heinemann, London.
2. Hollis, A.C. 1905. *The Masai: Their Language and Folklore*, p. v. Clarendon Press, Oxford.
3. Donovan, V. 1978. *Christianity Rediscovered*. Orbis Books, New York. Republished as an Amazon e-book. Quotation from Loc. 616.
4. Galaty, J. 1981. 'Land and Livestock among Kenyan Maasai'. *Journal of Asian and African Studies* 16(1–2), pp. 68–88.

Index